Statistical Methods for
Software Quality

Using Metrics to Control Process
and Product Quality

JOIN US ON THE INTERNET VIA WWW, GOPHER,
FTP OR EMAIL:

WWW:	http://www.thomson.com
GOPHER:	gopher.thomson.com
FTP:	ftp.thomson.com
EMAIL:	findit@kiosk.thomson.com

A service of I (T) P

Contents

To an industry that believes in its art
but who would like to produce
masterpieces at every stroke of the brush

Process Maturity
when the running-to-keep-up stops because
the wise company discovers the benefit
of operating with processes that are repeatable, in control
and just ahead of the competition

This book is about getting control of the immature process
in order to direct it, control it and then
to continually maximise the benefits available

Acknowledgements

The authors wish to express their sincere thanks and to acknowledge the contributions made by colleagues during the production of this book. Our first thanks must go to our wives and friends who have cheered and helped us along this lonely road.

We thank the contributors of the examples both for the data provided and the opportunity to discuss frankly the quality and maturity issues. In particular our thanks to:

Digital Equipment Corporation, Reading, UK for the metrics from their software developments and the discussions on software quality issues.

Information Processing Limited, Bath, UK for the CANTATA test tool outputs and the discussions of the meaning of this data.

Aspentech for the use of metrics in the examples resulting from their testing activities.

Thanks also to Martin Neil, now of South Bank University, London who provided examples of data from his PhD thesis, assisting our understanding of the the relationships between software metrics.

We wish to acknowledge and thank Norman Fenton of City University, London, for his hard work throughout the production of this book. He has provided comments and dedicated reviewing which are reflected in the quality of book that you now have before you. He has also provided the foreword for the book.

Several companies have contributed to the diagrams by allowing us to use their software. Our thanks go to:

Adept Scientific and North West Analytical for the use of Quality Analyst to produce many of the charts.

ASI Quality Systems for assistance with the production of the QFD example, Oscar Software for discussions about the use of QFD methods.

Our thanks also go to particular people who have assisted and supported us by discussing the subject of statistical methods. In particular we are grateful to our colleagues at the British Computer Society Specialist Interest Group in Software Testing (SIGIST), those who support the Sub-group on Statistical Methods, the Software Quality Group of the British Computer Society, and the members of courses that we both run on statistical methods. We also thank friends and colleagues at the University of North London and Glamorgan University, and Eric Sargeant at Racal. All have supported us with discussions and comments on some of the techniques that are included in the book.

There are many colleagues who have contributed to our knowledge and experience over the years by discussing quality and statistical methods and supporting us while we practiced our skills within their organisations. We know that they have benefited from the experience. Books such as this show that we have also gained much from putting theory into practice and we are grateful for these experiences.

Thanks to QCC, Tom Gilb and Dorothy Graham, Darrel Ince and Network Consultants who have each provided support in the development and delivery of training courses for statistical methods.

Please accept our apologies for any omissions. Our warmest thanks to you all.

Adrian Burr & Mal Owen

Preface

What is Statistical Process Control?

Much has been discussed regarding metrics for software process improvement but statistical techniques provide metrics that:

- are repeatable
- relate to the performance of the development process
- can be compared across companies producing similar products
- provide confidence in the product being delivered.

The techniques are based on sound and proven principles developed over many years in manufacturing industry. They have more recently been applied to all aspects of managing business in industries ranging from hospitals to banks and building societies, hotels to holiday companies.

SPC for software

In the software industry we have become used to the idea that the process was not repeatable – we are always producing something new and unique. But SPC is entirely comparable with the design and development of new products, and even more so since the advent of re-usable code.

What SPC delivers

The techniques described in this book can provide you with a leading edge over your competitors by improving profitability and reducing software defects. They are designed to help you to reduce the amount of work required to produce your product, while ensuring that the product is of consistently higher and ever improving quality.

What is quality?

The quality target for software development is 'zero defects', but having no defects is not realistic to many since the cost of removal of the last defect is prohibitive. This is satisfactory providing that the quality of the product is defined at the outset as having a defect level that will be acceptable. The difficulty then is estimating how many defects are left. The answer to this is to measure the conformance of the product to its specification and only release those items with fewer than a fixed number and type of defects. That defines the quality of acceptance. The software may be sold with a few known defects or 'features'.

Features and bugs

In software terms a few extra undocumented 'features', as some suppliers call them, are quite acceptable. The difference between the features and bugs is that features are not unknown. The definition of a 'bug' can change to 'a defect that causes a surprising or unexpected output'. Undocumented features are definitely not bugs!

However the development process is about delivering the product:

- on time
- at cost
- with performance to specification.

Project tracking

So methods of tracking the time and costs are required as well as the measurement of conformance. The process that develops software is often a manual activity with only the broadest guidelines controlling how it is carried out. This is important so that the ingenuity of developers is not stifled. But this is in conflict with good process control techniques. A method of measuring the normal variance of the process is required so that an early detection system can be built into the process to prevent over indulgence and over complication from affecting the two most often forgotten (by the developer) parameters – time and cost.

Foreword

Statistical process control has for some time been used with good effect in various manufacturing industries. Central to this approach is the role of measurement. In the last few years there has been widespread awareness of the important role of measurement in software engineering. This has led to a proliferation of papers and books on 'software metrics'. However, little of this software metrics material has made explicit the potential for applying statistical process control to software development. What makes this book by Burr and Owen so important is that it is the first comprehensive account of how to exploit this crucial link. Thus, this book describes a range of quantitative methods to help software developers and managers.

More than anything else this book provides the statistical background needed to both collect and analyse metrics data. Other books on software metrics cover this, at best superficially, assuming that such knowledge is obtained elsewhere. In fact it now seems to be the case that many software engineers and managers, who would gain most out of using software metrics, do NOT have much background in statistics, and nor do they have easy access to the necessary background material. Thus, my hunch is that many do not use the existing software metrics books because they do not provide a truly self-contained account of how metrics are used pragmatically. Hence, this book offers them potentially a 'one-stop' solution to this problem, by covering the background statistical techniques.

It is widely accepted that there is a problem with poor software quality and productivity, but still relatively few people bother to quantify the situation, and fewer still understand the potential improvements provided by statistical measurement. As the serious ramifications of NOT performing proper measurement have dawned on the software industry, the status of software metrics as a key subject in its own right has been elevated. I believe that the publication of this book can provide a new major boost for the subject.

Norman Fenton

Part I
Statistical Process Control, the Development Cycle and Metrics

This book contains subject matter that will help the reader learn many of the techniques available for measuring process and product conformance and for tracking project time and costs. The techniques include:
- variables and attributes charting
- SPC for test reduction
- SPC for process improvement
- the benefits of using statistical metrics, as opposed to selective and limited coverage metrics
- methods for selecting appropriate tools for analysing the metrics

obtainable from almost any software development activity
- which tools are approriate to different parts of the development cycle
- how to develop a model for identifying the cost benefits of using the methods within their company or project.

Our aim is to provide a handbook to assist you in your search for the most profitable and rewarding development methods that will match your company or software development or maintenance situation. The mathematics has been kept to a minimum so that the key indicators provide immediate information for corrective action. However, a little understanding of the background may be necessary so a bibliography of some of the statistical methods is provided for your further reading.

In the first part some essential background to the processes of quality, statistical methods and software development cycles are provided. Chapter 1 provides background to the **software development process** particularly in the context of **quality initiatives and different development cycles**. Chapter 2 shows metrics in the development cycle, and how they are used. Finally Chapter 3 looks at how to properly **design a measurement system**.

1 Statistical Methods and Software Development

1.1 Introduction

Software development has been dogged by large and spectacular project failures which do nothing to improve the confidence of customers of the industry or the confidence of managers or their IT departments or development teams.

This is true of all sectors of the software industry, from the most humble software package to the sophisticated control systems for aerospace and nuclear industries, or the maintenance of large existing systems in the financial and insurance sectors. All need procedures for improving the development process on two fronts:

- to increase confidence between the customer and the supplier
- to reduce both the development and the product costs.

This represents a change in maturity for the industry. This will be evident when a development can be requested with absolute confidence that it can be produced on time, within budget, with predicted defectiveness level and known reliability. This is the target of any organisation that aims to be known for the quality of its customer service.

To achieve this many companies have taken steps to measure the products and processes by introducing metrics as part of their quality system and as a way of controlling the development process. This is based on the principle that, if a metric can be correlated against either the number of defects found in the product, or the ability of the product to reliably reproduce output, then the measured variable can be used to control the process. This strategy has been developed by several prominent researchers over the 1980s, with attempts to correlate the metrics associated with the development process with the product error rates (1,2). This correlation research has not led to spectacular success and this book will provide some answers as to why this is true. Other developments have concentrated on changing the methods themselves in order to obtain greater process maturity. Techniques such as rapid application development and prototyping (3) and the development of the V model (4) to a W model (5) have all been attempts at improving the process.

The first book on statistical methods for software development appeared in 1980 and was written by Chin Kuei Cho (6). Cho likened the software product to a factory repeatedly churning out near identical products, the differences in the repeated process causing differences in the product output characteristics. The latest understanding of the repeatability of software products recognises that this is due to some untested condition or state within the product. It is not due to a varying control factor such as found in most factory situations. However we can sympathise with the view that an external influence (in this case an untested state or condition) is the cause of the failure. These techniques, which have more recently been addressed in reliability and test selection modelling, do not address process improvement methods that can be used to prevent future failures. This must be the purpose of any action to reduce costs and process errors which will in turn provide the desired improvements to process maturity and control.

Further developments have concentrated on the idea of using risk as a control factor, and applying appropriate management to controlling and minimising future risks. This has been the subject of a European research project, RISKMAN (7), as well as of authors from within IBM (8).

Each of these works helps to build up a picture of how our understanding of the software development process is improving, but one important factor is missing. W. Edwards Deming has said (9):

If I had reduce my message for management to just a few word, I'd say it all had to do with reducing variation.

Variance, as described by Deming and Shewhart, is the measure of this variation in the process. If all other things remain constant the small changes that occur in any process, whether the process be a machine or a human activity, will cause the output to change. This output variability for the software development process usually results in development errors and subsequent code defects, and possibly functional differences from the stated requirements.

This book, then, provides the technical details of how software development can be controlled using the principles of variance management. It builds on the works of Deming and other quality gurus (10-12). It equally builds on the works of many researchers in software engineering who have designed models for the development process (13,14), correlated process and product metrics (1,2,15) as well as developed risk management practice (16) and methods of measuring reliability (17). Research has also continued in other industries with statistical project management used by the construction industry (18) and error mapping used in archeology (19), both principles that are equally valuable to the software industry. Lastly, measurement used in software development relies on the works of researchers (20,21) and practitioners, such as McCabe (22) and Halstead (23), who have established metrics that have been used as the basis of software development and test tools (24,25).

It is appropriate at this point to look at some background of where statistical process control comes from and recent developments in applying statistical ideas to the workplace.

█ 1.2 Quality Management

The principles of quality management have taken many years to formulate, but now we have an international standard, ISO 9000 (26), that sets out a minimum set of requirements for assuring quality. This standard was initially developed for the manufacturing industry and was not easily interpreted for project based industries such as software development. A new version called TickIT was initiated in the UK in the early 1990s (27). This was a guideline document on how to interpret the UK Quality Management standard (BS 5750) for the software industry. It has been incorporated as guidelines as ISO 9000-3 (28) which does the same for international standards.

Recognising that ISO 9000 is a minimum requirement for a quality system, total quality management (TQM) was developed in the 1980s to provide a framework for continuing development of quality. Quality management is the term for providing a product that meets the market requirements at the same time as making a profit for the company. TQM, then, targets every part of the organisation to minimise costs and errors and maximise efficiency and effectiveness. The models for quality management can be found in many of the award schemes for total quality, such as the Baldrige Award (29) and the European Quality Award (30).

Once a basic quality control level has been achieved by satisfying quality standards, most companies aim to achieve 'world class' status by developing company processes. This activity aims to take a process which is inherently not 'in control'- that is, it cannot consistently reproduce the desired output from a stable set of inputs — to a state where it is both in control and capable of consistent production. The measure of the capability of a process to repeatably reproduce the output is called its control status. The capability is measured by comparing the desired output from the process with the achieved consistency.

This control status is also used to measure the effectiveness of the development process in order to determine the maturity of the capability of the process. A number of capability maturity models have been developed which are discussed in detail in Chapter 8. These include:

- the Software Engineering Institute's (SEI) five level model (31) which has been specifically developed for the software industry
- the Bootstrap maturity profile model (32)
- a more generic six level model called the Lattice methodology (33), which may be used for any type of process and was developed in the UK.

While none of these models specifically mention the use of Statistical Control techniques in their earliest versions, they are all used to assess the level of maturity based on collected data. Both the SEI and Lattice models use the Deming philosophy of process improvement which requires the use statistical control methods be used in the higher levels of maturity.

As we will see later in this book, statistical methods can be used at the outset of quality improvement to remove variation from a process. They should be implemented at the earliest stages of embarking on a process improvement project.

In order to achieve any benefit from process improvement or maturity, or even the initial control of quality, the costs of using the techniques and the aims for a world class status project are required. Some of the benefits obtainable from analysing quality costs are considered, and the chapter ends with a discussion on the relationship between software development and the customers of the product. The topics in this introduction provide a theme for each of the subsequent chapters.

▨ 1.3 Statistical Methods in the Workplace

Of all the techniques that have been provided for us by statisticians, the control chart is arguably the most powerful. It can be applied wherever readings are available in sequence as shown in Fig. 1.1, and has far-reaching implications for management. We will see in Chapters 5 and 6 how it provides a highly effective means of communicating, and when given the opportunity, can significantly increase effective decision-making. It can be linked with the ability of a computer to handle large amounts of data yet is simple in its pictorial representation of process performance. A control chart is the key component of statistical process control (SPC) which owes its origins to the work of an American statistician — Walter Shewhart (34).

▨ 1.3.1 Some historical background

The principles of charting process performance, the basis of SPC as we now know it, are not new. Walter Shewhart was one of a team of scientists and engineers working at the Bell Telephone Laboratories in the USA in the 1920s. He began to analyse manufacturing processes by taking small repeated samples at regular intervals and used the information to develop a control chart. Shewhart's work was published in 1931 (34). The book has become a landmark in the development of quality improvement as a major strategic element of corporate planning.

The group of specialists working with Shewhart included W. Edwards Deming. Deming cooperated with Shewhart in the early developments of the control chart and both were prime movers in providing courses in variation in the USA during the war years. Whilst these courses emphasised the need to understand statistical methods in analysing processes, they also made reference to the management understanding that would be necessary to support the use of the techniques. The management philosophy

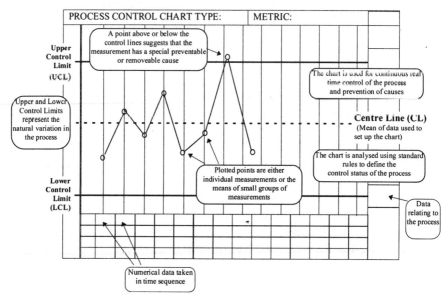

Fig. 1.1 A control chart with principal features.

later became known as Deming's '14 points for management'.

The war effort generated a need for training courses in statistical methods. After the war the need was less apparent. With no competition, America's products found a ready market and the need for statistical methods to control quality was deemed an unnecessary irrelevance.

In the immediate post-war years General McArthur was put in charge of regenerating the Japanese economy. Through a series of events Deming was invited to Japan to provide a lead in training the Japanese industrial leaders in statistical methods. His ideas were quickly taken up and developed by a culture very sympathetic to open management and teamwork. Extensive training in statistical methods and problem solving followed. The result was that by the mid-1960s Japan had at its disposal a well-trained workforce more than capable of leading the country towards global economic leadership in key sectors of industrial activity.

Meanwhile Deming was little known in his home country, until in 1981 he appeared on an American NBC documentary *If Japan can, why can't we.* The film included material showing Deming consulting with the Nashua Corporation in the USA. Not least of those who watched the documentary were personnel from the Ford Motor Company, and subsequently Deming worked closely with Don Peterson, the President of Ford, in implementing the Ford version of his '14 points' within the company. Deming's philosophy became a corner-stone of the Ford world-wide quality improvement programme.

In emphasising the need for management change it is easy to overlook the fact that both Deming and Shewhart built their reputations as statisticians. Shewhart devised the control chart, and Deming, until his death at the age of 93 in December 1993, spent his time travelling the world persuading thousands of the need to understand variation. He was at odds with business schools in the West because of their unwillingness, or inability, to teach statistics based on readings over time rather than the classical statistics which have traditionally been taught. Myron Tribus (35) has similarly expressed concern that the business schools provide future managers and executives with little exposure to the Deming philosophy. It is not the purpose of this book to provide its readers with material on management education. Nevertheless, it will become evident that in applying SPC in software development, as much as in any other area, management style in the organisation has considerable implications for the success of the project.

SPC has now moved on. No longer should it be seen as a technique uniquely associated with the automotive industry and, more specially, Ford. No longer is SPC applicable only in production areas. SPC has now been applied in electronics, health care, food, chemical and other industries, although it has to be said, still mainly in manufacturing areas.

The most encouraging development of late has been the extended use of SPC into administrative areas of manufacturing industry and, even more so, the use of SPC in purely administration and service organisations. Insurance companies, banks and other service organisations are recognising the considerable scope for applying SPC in improving their processes. This is a natural development, as is the use of SPC in software development, but it takes time. This book includes various case studies showing how the organisations involved are making, or could in future make, use of particular types of control charts, and suggests scope for further possibilities. The studies do not suggest that the organisations have these control charts operating on all their processes and that SPC is understood throughout the entire workforce. This can only be achieved over many years. They do show how the chart has been utilised in a way which is particular to that organisation and which provides much promise for further and wider applications in the future.

We have made several references already to SPC but we have not as yet actually defined what we mean by SPC.

■ 1.3.2 A general definition of statistical process control

Before considering the term in its entirety, it is best to examine each word independently.

'Statistical' in this context has to do with data, and more particularly its collection, representation and analysis when relating to a time sequence. It has little to do with proving mathematical relationships and nothing is to be gained by following this line.

A 'process' is any activity. Some may be more repetitive than others and therefore provide more data, and more quickly, but this does not invalidate the fact that SPC can be applied in a wide range of activities.

'Control' is used in a statistical sense, i.e. is the variation in the process stable and predictable?

Control is concerned with correctly interpreting patterns of points plotted on a time scale and taking appropriate actions as a result. Control in itself is not sufficient. It is a requirement for our various processes to be under control in the first place, but a necessary part of SPC is working on our processes to improve them. Control, as understood in this context, has nothing to do with controlling people in an authoritative sense.

SPC requires data to be collected from the process and used to check first on whether the process is stable. If so, the process can be predicted, and the pattern of natural variation of the process used not only to monitor the ongoing performance, but more especially to indicate how the process can be improved. The process can relate to any organisation, any function. Specifically, as far as this book is concerned, the process will relate to software development, although other processes will be associated directly or indirectly. For example, administrative processes such as invoicing must be controlled and improved if an organisation is to improve its service to the customer. Equally, software development depends on acceptable materials such as languages and specifications, appropriate tools such as compilers, as well as highly trained software engineers.

The application of SPC in software development, however, is new. The technique has been applied with considerable success in the more traditional automotive-based industries for some 12 years or so in the West, and for a much longer period than that in Japan. It has been increasingly used in service and administrative functions and works because the principles are independent of the application. Measuring the process is clearly not restricted to machining components and can be applied just as effectively in software applications.

▨ 1.4 An SPC Model for Software

It was Lord Kelvin who said, many years ago, that without measurement, no information or knowledge can be gained. In the software industry, where we are struggling with metrics, the need for information from the data that is captured as a matter of routine, is vital for the future survival of the industry.

Because of the wide variety of industries, languages and development methods within the software development sector, we cannot generalise about the issues for any one company. If, as Deming stated, we can begin to understand variation that occurs in any one process, then we begin to understand how to control that process by eliminating unnecessary or special causes of variation. In software development this means reducing

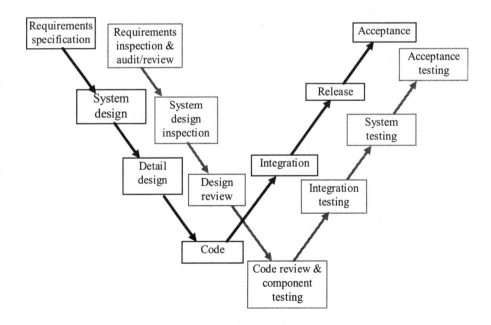

Fig. 1.2 The W model.

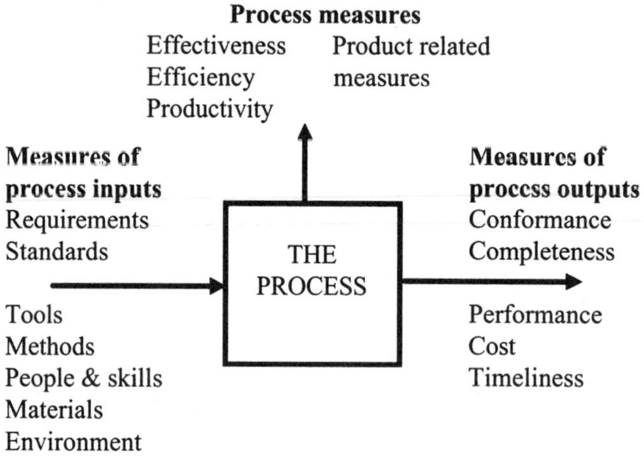

Process measures

Effectiveness   Product related
Efficiency   measures
Productivity

Measures of   Measures of
process inputs   process outputs
Requirements   Conformance
Standards   THE   Completeness
                       PROCESS

Tools   Performance
Methods   Cost
People & skills   Timeliness
Materials
Environment

Fig. 1.3 A general process model.

the variability of the process by using a mechanism for minimising the number of defects left in a product on delivery. This has the consequence of reducing the cost of development, improving the cost estimation process and increasing the profitability of projects.

But what varies during the development process? The obvious measures are cost, time and the number of defects found. However, these do not provide us with sufficient information to control the process, so the aim is to find the characteristics that vary in each part of the development cycle.

In a typical cycle as defined by the W, or double V, model as shown in Fig. 1.2, each step is a process in its own right. Any process has inputs and outputs, as well as internal controls, as shown in Fig. 1.3, and it is these that are subjected to preventative quality control.

An example of this for the outset of a project is demonstrated when considering the first step to be taken. This step is usually defining the user requirements, and the input, process and output metrics for this process are generically defined as:

■ INPUTS
1. the customers' knowledge and understanding of the business problem
2. the suppliers' understanding of this problem
3. the standards that the customer requires the system to comply with

4. the suppliers' internal standards for gathering and documenting requirements
5. the guidelines for content of a requirement specification for a product of the type being considered
6. the ability and experience of the supplier.

▓ THE PROCESS

1. the gathering rate at the meetings
2. the meeting metrics — unresolved questions, misunderstandings, technical understanding discussions, prepared answers, changes
3. the production rate of the document
4. the document error rates.

▓ THE PRODUCT

1. the review metrics
2. the acceptance metrics.

Control of this first process then depends on two factors:
1. Confidence — a measure of the relationships between the various parties involved in the development process; at this stage this is between the supplier of the specification and the customer.
2. Completeness — a measure of the product. At the first stage the product is a requirements document and it is the completeness of this that establishes the risk for the whole of the future project.

Whether or not the requirements definition is aimed at being absolute (totally clear and unambiguous) or only an outline of eventual requirements, the control metrics derived from the different stages are:

▓ INPUT METRICS

1. confidence that a supplier has in the customer before starting on a project or embarking on a further project stage
2. confidence that the customer understands the requirements and the consequences of those requirements.

■ PROCESS METRICS

1. confidence that the developer has understood the requirement and understands the business consequences
2. the risk of taking on the project indicated by the confidence in the time/cost estimates and the technical judgments made at the outset.

■ PRODUCT METRICS

1. the completeness and defectiveness of the specification.

All activities from this point onwards rely on the statement of requirements. There are other inputs to the process such as the technical capability of developers, the development tools, the language being used, and the environment that the development is to take place in (building, staff relationships, etc.). Without knowledge of the confidence in the relationships between the developer and the customer, the probability of success is greatly reduced. This is not peculiar to software development. For many years, accountants have used statistical analysis methods for establishing confidence in capital projects, and software development can be compared with some of the largest construction projects of this century. The techniques can also be applied to the more humble project of just a few man months, but with appropriate scaling of the activities.

The confidence measures are used to measure every product and process throughout the development cycle, as well as many of the maintenance and reliability measurements after completion of development. The measurements are used to control the process and are gathered using questions related to the stage of development. Examples in the gathering and development of requirements are:

1. How many of the expected requirements had the customer already considered prior to the first meeting?
2. How many requirements were left for future discussion after the meeting?
3. How many of the standard model requirements (assuming that such a model is applicable) were left unanswered at the meeting?
4. How many questions resulted from the presentation of pre-planned and documented answers?
5.. How many questions resulted in technical discussion and development of understanding?

▧ In other stages of the development cycle the questions will change. A few questions at the completion stage of a project (maybe at the acceptance test stage) are:

1. Did the computers perform?
2. Did the compiler and language introduce more defects?
3. If an engineer is left to get on with it, does better and quicker code result?
4. When a developer says 80% complete is there still 80% to go?

These questions are formulated for a project or an operational group within the development company to identify the areas of risk that are being taken and to calculate a value for this risk based on confidence measurement. This subject is covered in detail in Chapter 8.

These are not the only measures that are used for process control. Most companies are already measuring the process and the product, and these measures provide an understanding of confidence and, from analysis, enable signals to be observed indicating that a control input is required.

Once control based on these signals has been achieved, the work is not complete. Any quality system must have a target of never ending improvement or the laurels that are being rested on will whither and die. The Deming cycle, more properly named the Shewhart improvement cycle, shown in Fig. 1.4, provides a model for keeping one step ahead of the competition and for keeping the improvement cycle going. It is up to management to ensure that the rate of change is controlled so as to remain competitive.

For a project-based company, the question of what to change in the process is critical. For a product-based company, however, the question of which changes to make next to the product is one key part of keeping ahead of the competition. The main competitive advantage is gained from delivering a slightly better product, more cost effectively and with fewer defects. For both types of company this is achieved through the proper use of quality control. Initiatives and standards such as ISO 9000, and the IT industries own interpretation, ISO 9000-3, and schemes such as the EFQM Award and the Malcolm Baldrige Awards, all provide part of the jigsaw for process improvement. Process maturity models such as that provided by the Software Engineering Institute, the SPICE methodology, as well as initiatives such as the Lattice method and the various development cycle models provide further elements of the jigsaw as shown in Fig. 1.5. Some of these models have embraced statistical methods as part of the strategy.

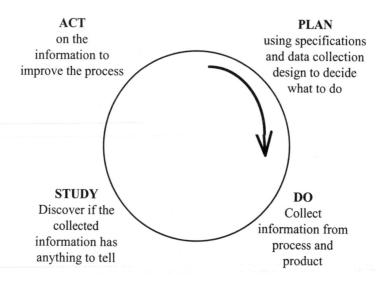

Fig. 1.4 The Deming or Shewhart quality improvement cycle.

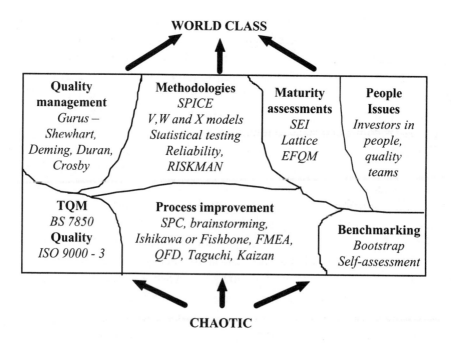

Fig. 1.5 The jigsaw of quality and process improvement.

■ 1.5 SPC and Quality Initiatives

■ 1.5.1 SPC and TQM

TQM (total quality management) can be defined in various ways. For those who are steeped in quality systems, TQM and ISO 9000 are often interpreted as being the same. Devotees of SPC, or customer satisfaction, may make the same claim.

Whilst it is true that ISO 9000, SPC, or any other tool, technique, or current management philosophy, all make their contribution to improving the competitive position of the organisation concerned, it is the combined effects of these components in a company-wide improvement initiative that will mark the progress of the organisation.

TQM could be interpreted as integrating the various elements as pieces of a jigsaw. Many pieces will be required, and some of these can be identified from Fig. 1.5. This book covers the subjects that specifically use statistical methods such as benchmarking and SPC. The following table provides references to subjects that may be part of a quality programme allowing the reader to find a greater depth of understanding of related subjects than is possible in a book of this length.

Statistical process control (SPC)	Chapters 4–7
Statistical quality control (SQC)	Chapter 8–9, 11
Benchmarking	Chapter 8
Statistical Project Management	Chapter 10
Statistical Inspections	Chapter 12
Statistical Product Acceptance	Chapter 13

Failure Mode and Effects Analysis (FMEA)	(36)
ISO 9000	(26)
Improvement groups	(37)
Investors in People	(38)
Quality Function Deployment (QFD)	(39)
Taguchi methods	(40)
Quality Teams	(41)
Kaizen	(42)
Poka Yoke	(43)

The size of each piece, reflecting the relative importance of each aspect, will vary from one organisation to another, depending on how the organisation sets up its quality improvement programme. In some organisations, perhaps there has been a major thrust on problem solving. Others will have gone first for some sort of certification, be it ISO 9000, or an internal scheme which is operated within the industry concerned. Whatever the choice, it would be foolish to neglect the importance of, at some stage, implementing programmes based on reducing process variation. Whatever the nature of the organisation, or the product, there is a common theme. All organisations have internal processes, which involve internal customers and suppliers. A person, section or department will be a customer of another person, section or department and at the same time a supplier to others. These customers and suppliers react to each other across all traditional levels of hierarchy, as shown in Fig. 1.6, and their interrelationship more closely represents the activities of an organisation than does the traditional organisational tree based on status within the organisation.

A first step in improving these processes is to simplify them as far as possible. Flowcharting provides a particularly useful and simple method for clarifying the individual parts of a process. After the process has been simplified, there is really no alternative to measuring it, and the most effective way of doing this is to use a control chart. Some organisations feel that SPC has nothing to do with them. They have different processes to others, their product is unique. Techniques which may be successful in other industries will not operate in their organisation, they claim. Software development has similar problems. No claim is being made that SPC is the only approach that can be used in quality improvement. However, not making use of the technique is to ignore a major component of any improvement programme, and the software development industry can surely apply SPC techniques with equally impressive results.

■ 1.5.2 SPC and ISO 9000

Within ISO 9000 there is only one reference to statistical methods, but several to process control, and the reference to statistical methods does not make their use obligatory. Section 4.20 of the standard (1987 version) only requires statistical methods 'if applicable'. Most companies put 'not applicable' and consequently never explore the benefits that they could be obtaining by effective measurement in many areas of the company. The 1994 version of

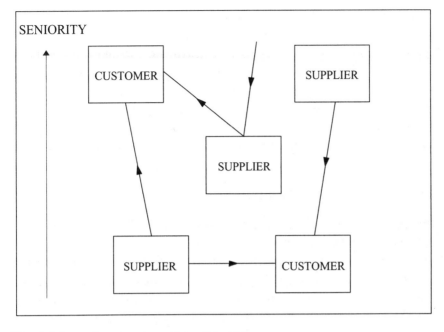

Fig. 1.6 Internal customer–supplier relationship.

ISO 9000 changes the wording slightly to 'where applicable', but this makes SPC no more a mandatory requirement than in the old version. However, under the process section (4.16) the fact that the process must be 'capable' has been recognised, although there is no mandatory requirement to measure this capability. One established method of capability measurement is to measure the variance of the process and product metrics and compare these on a continuous basis with the historical values. This at least will show whether the processes are stable and provides the basis for measuring continuous improvement.

This only reflects the state of the art. SPC has not yet become an obligatory control for all industries, although as an automotive supplier, a company is unlikely to be able to retain market share without SPC applied to manufacturing, administrative and financial activities.

The purpose of using SPC in areas other than manufacturing is that it gives a quick measure of when something has changed in a process. If there is an increase in error rates on invoices the effect on the business can be greater than delivery of defective product, and the result can be equally devastating for the company, and this is true of software too!

While SPC is not a mandatory requirement for a quality system that conforms to ISO 9000, there are few ways of achieving process improvement other than actually measuring the processes, products, activities and progress. The most cost-effective way of measuring is to take representative samples over time rather than attempting to achieve 100% inspection. Once this idea is adopted then SPC naturally takes its proper place as the method of gathering, analysing and presenting information for process improvement.

ISO 9000-3 is the version of the standard for the software industry.

▧ 1.5.3 SPC and ISO 9000-3

In this standard (28) all reference to statistical methods has been removed, but process control is still considered an important part of the quality system. However in many software companies statistical techniques are being used, and as such, auditors will be obliged to take the view that if they are used in a way that effects the quality of the product, then they must conform to the quality management standards. This means ensuring that their use is properly understood, that the charts have been properly designed, and proper documentation exists for controlling the use of the charts. Also work instructions are required to ensure that actions are defined and followed when a chart indicates that a special event has occurred and the process is consequently referred to as being 'out-of-control'.

Proper chart management and quality documentation will make the use of SPC techniques financially effective by ensuring that the charts are properly designed. Measurement theory is used to choose what to measure, how to measure and how to interpret the results.

One of the purposes of SPC is to obtain control of processes that, without charts, change each time the process is repeated making it unpredictable. While charts in themselves will reduce the variability of a process by obtaining this control, the process of continuous improvement, which is the aim of any reasonable implementation of ISO 9000, requires continuous analysis of the charts to find causes within the data and minimise process variation. By eliminating the causes the process should remain 'in statistical control' for ever and if the process is able to reproduce the product well within specification and with very little variation — it is said to be capable — charting becomes far less useful. However, this requires a leap in faith that few can take and is probably not achievable in a project-oriented business. New causes may arise requiring new control methods to be implemented. But the goal of reducing the amount of charting required will ensure that the company remains prepared for new causes, but minimises the overhead of this state of readiness.

Process improvement leads to business maturity, which means understanding the processes in the business sufficiently well to be able to decide what management actions to take to stay ahead of the competition. In a very mature company it may mean being able to take a process and replicate it anywhere in the world with full confidence that the same results can be obtained, regardless of local conditions and cultures. There are many levels between the ability to replicate processes and the start-up condition of a new process, and selecting the economic level to operate at is a critical management skill. In many industries benchmarking has become the way forward — comparing one company with the competition to ensure that up-to-date methods are used in successfully providing the competitive edge. In the software industry there are various benchmarking methods available based on models of maturity of the organisation.

■ 1.5.4 SPC and maturity models

The main benchmarking methods, include the Malcolm Baldrige Award (29) for quality and the European Quality Awards presented by the EFQM (30). Other process improvement methods are available including SPICE (47). In 1991 the Software Engineering Institute (SEI) set up a model (31), shown in Table 1.1, to provide a stepwise method of improving software development processes. The method describes five steps of maturity which aims to show how a company is achieving its quality objectives.

The assessment against the model tells customers where the company is in terms of providing a reduced risk of defective code. It is broadly based on the principles of Deming although the first two levels are about getting the management structures right. The fourth and fifth levels about process improvement and statistical techniques are expected to be used in the model at this stage.

SPC will certainly satisfy the SEI model in terms of metrication providing it is applied to process metrics that are seen to reduce the risk of defectiveness. Table 1.1 shows the model combined with statistical measures.

Other models that are available include the Bootstrap model (32) shown in Fig. 1.7 and the Lattice model (33), shown in Fig. 1.8. The Bootstrap

Table 1.1 The SEI maturity stages.

Maturity level	Stage	Development activities and controls
1	Initial	Chaotic and ad hoc. No quality management or process control, unpredictable cost, timescales and performance.
2	Repeatable	Development process is based on procedures for project planning and management. Statistically the delivery timescale distributions are of the same shape and at the same mean level.
3	Defined	Procedures and tools used for software development. Reliable cost and timescales but performance still not predictable.
4	Controlled	Basic metrics used and resources available to gather data. Statistical measures for product quality and product distributions show reasonable control.
5	Optimising	Process database available and a program of process improvement is in place using Deming principles.

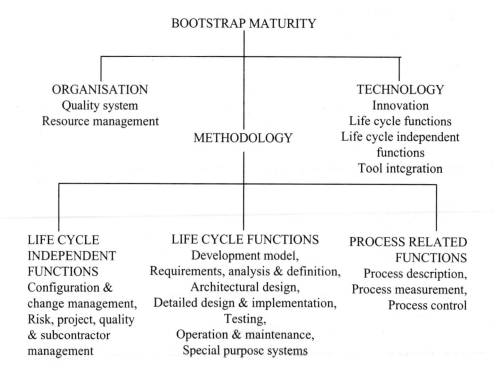

Fig. 1.7 The Bootstrap model.

model provides a mechanism for assessing individual parts of the process and generating a benchmark profile for an individual company. It is a two-dimensional model in that a rating is provided for specific parts of the process but not for the relationships between these parts.

The Lattice model develops this idea into a three-dimensional model providing a six-level improvement process enabling a company to change from an ISO 9000 registered organisation (seen by the model as the minimum requirement for a quality system) to the position of a world class survivor. The model in its basic form is applicable to any industry and provides not only the six steps of maturity growth, but also an activity model within the organisation to enable individual processes of the company to achieve quality improvement. In any one of the base elements of the process model there are essential inputs and outputs. The inputs fall into standard process model categories of people, machines, materials, methods and environment. The outputs are products or actions or less tangible but equally desirable outputs such as experience and knowledge.

Each of the base elements of the model can be individually developed using the process improvement cycle. Statistical control techniques are used to measure the inputs and outputs and to provide input to the process improvement activity. This makes the Deming/Shewhart process improvement cycle and the use of statistical control techniques fundamental to the model.

A second function of the Lattice is to provide a model for a benchmarking process. Because the processes can be improved separately, a benchmark profile for an individual company can be produced. This allows only the essential parts of the process to be improved to a higher maturity level rather than an overall maturity being achieved as required by many of the other benchmarking models.

The aim of these models is to provide a framework for improvement measured as a reduction in the cost of the product to the producing company. The 'cost of quality' is the metric that causes process improvement in this area.

■ 1.6 Quality Costs

The cost of quality within any development cycle is a variable that is inevitable, but at the same time can be minimised. There are two extremes,

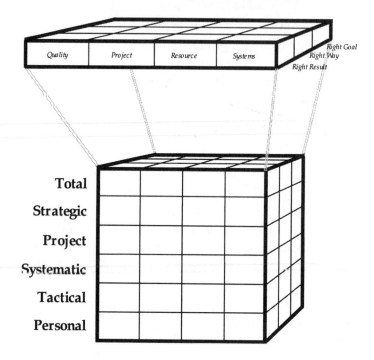

Fig 1.8 The lattice model.

based on either a completely controlled, stable and defect-free operation or an 'artistic' style of development where no control is used.

In a controlled operation, costs typically relate to the following activities:

1. prevention (process control)
2. measurement (audit)
3. analysis
4. process improvement
5. maintenance.

For an uncontrolled operation, costs are associated with the following:

1. measurement (testing)
2. rework (corrective action)
3. over-run
4. customer non-acceptance
5. maintenance.

Of course, no organisation can achieve a totally controlled situation, but few are likely to survive long without some of the elements relating to control, such as process improvement.

Quality costs can be measured (44). However, too much emphasis on analysing quality costs in detail can be non-productive. In the wrong environment, for example, quality costs are used by management as targets with no resources being provided to enable these targets to be achieved. Of more concern are the costs which cannot be measured, those which Deming refers to as the 'hidden costs'. For example, the risk of delivery of a defective software product that is going to fail in many months' time cannot be directly measured. Another example is the cost of the debug cycle completed on-line by developers. The question of when development stops and debugging starts makes measurement of this cost difficult. However quality improvement will aim to reduce this activity and hence reduce the overall development cost.

There are many other hidden costs – the de-motivational costs of tracking difficult defects, and the frustration of continually being told that the product is 80% complete. Fig. 1.9 shows how the cost of quality increases as a development progresses.

Costs associated with detection or corrections at the end of a project are much greater than those associated with prevention. This means maximum benefit is obtained from catching causes early in the cycle and correcting them before defects are generated. This is why recent developments which aim to provide a model for testing throughout the development cycle (the W model), provide cost benefits as well as product improvement benefits. This is also true of simultaneous engineering models such as prototyping and rapid application development (RAD), which provide methods of verifying requirements and specifications throughout the development cycle. It should be said that the different development cycles are not exclusive. As shown by the Lattice model, the maturity required is dependent on the importance of a function and the customer requirements, and consequently each of the models has a place in different development areas. The methods all aim to minimise the cost of quality as shown in Fig. 1.10, but for different development environments different tools are appropriate.

▮ 1.7 Software Development and Customer Relationships

How many times has a system been delivered only to find that it has not met the fundamental requirements of the customer? The industry has too often obtained a reputation for poor delivery because of the state of the

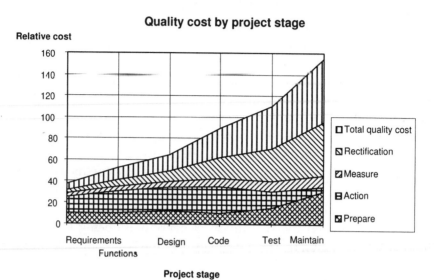

Fig 1.9 Quality costs through the development cycle.

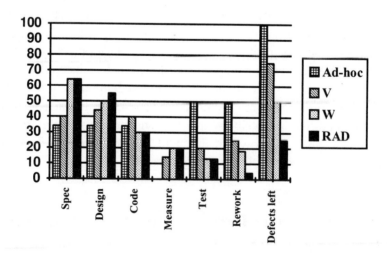

Fig 1.10 Comparative cost/performance graphs.

relationships between customers and developers — the starting point of this chapter.

Whenever code is developed, a customer somewhere has a requirement for that code. Of course both the customer and the supplier have different views of the development process — one may be trying to maximise product attributes for minimum cost while the other is trying to achieve the opposite. However a compromise is usually reached regarding the technical capability of the product. Most projects fail not because of lack of agreement, but because of the failure of the development process to deliver. There are a few well-advertised and spectacular exceptions to this, but these are generally because there is a lack of understanding regarding the risks that are being taken.

Relationships that allow customers and suppliers to understand the risk that is being considered in a major development project should rely on measurement and not feelings for the projects. However we do not advocate throwing out all the techniques without any consideration — intuitive management does have its place. It is usually that much better when it is working from the basis of the measured capability of an organisation to deliver. This capability is a measurement of project progress, both in the technical capability and the completeness of the product, and this provides the reliable facts to support management decisions.

▓ 1.7.1 A Supplier's View

One of the benefits obtained from SPC is that measures of many of the variables of a project are available for keeping track and estimating the risk of a project throughout the life cycle. These measures include timescales, technical conformance and completeness, as well as the defectiveness of the final product. Even in product-oriented companies, such as the standard packages sold for administrative or scientific computing, the ability to indicate the capability of the producer could provide marketing benefits that make ignoring SPC difficult.

This book outlines some of the techniques that provide measures of process control. The biggest argument to date against using statistical control in the development process is that sampling will never find the single defect that causes the whole system to crash. This of course is true, but considerably truer (and statistically more valid) is the fact that ad hoc testing has an even smaller probability of finding that error. Since we now have tools that can generate test cases that it would take years to run, we have to find strategies of selecting cases and using test results for process improvement. This is the heart of statistical control.

Incomplete testing, projects that overrun due to a lack of information, risk taking without measurement of risks, and a process that has a high probability of introducing such an error, all lead to an argument for using appropriate metrication with statistical control. There is no financial possibility of ever catching the one error by any method (100% testing is impossible), so statistical methods provide the best means of giving your customers what they have requested, or what you may perceive that they require. Thevenod-Fosse (45) in recent studies has shown that using appropriate statistical selection methods can actually improve the detection capability of the test process. Her recent papers report finding a defect in critical software that had already been accepted and delivered. The major defect was not critical, but would have caused failure of the software. Statistical modelling coupled with SPC would have reduced the original risk for the software purchaser.

■ 1.7.2 A Purchaser's Perspective

If you are about to purchase a major software product, or are a large scale purchaser, you have it in your hands to request that the developers control the processes and provide measures for their control. Once purchasers demand such information then process and product quality improvement will follow.

Our difficulty is establishing what information to demand. So many of the metrics available are based on the development cycle and cannot be correlated between competing products. How then can you decide which is the better product? Often this is based on 'look and feel', but if test coverage and statistical capability were available these metrics could provide an index of how tested the product is. The British Computer Society (BCS) proto-standard (46) on component testing of software, currently under development, provides some of these measures and this provides purchasers with metrics that can be demanded. Other statistics that can be requested relate to the statistical capability of the company to produce. Metrics such as errors per 1000 lines of code or errors per module or even a chart of errors against module size will provide measures that enable a purchaser to decide whether a supplier has the ability to provide what is needed. Another useful measure is product reliability. By continuous testing an estimate of the product reliability can be made. Each of these factors alone provides only a small part of the confidence required by you, the customer. The combination provides a picture of the ability of a company to specify, develop and deliver.

If we take the Ford program mentioned earlier in the chapter, then we can see that suppliers who have survived have been those with both a demonstrable and measured ability to deliver combined with a program for process improvement. However the step that Ford had to first admit was that the products being delivered were not of adequate quality to ensure that they could deliver their own product competitively. If your software effects what you can deliver, then the quality of the process that is producing the product is of prime importance to your company and measures such as capability are fundamental requirements. Note that capability is a statistical measure, not a subjective view of a successful history.

By insisting on this information the maturity of the industry will improve as it has in manufacturing and the construction sectors.

▓ 1.8 Summary

- The work of Shewhart and Deming is highly relevant to introducing SPC into software development.
- SPC makes use of a control chart to monitor, and improve, a process.
- Many measures are available to enable the various software development processes to be improved.
- SPC is just one element of a TQM programme. International standards such as ISO 9000, and national standards such as TickIT, make reference in varying degrees of the use of statistical methods in quality improvement.
- Process maturity models provide a method of moving from a quality oriented company (quality standard registered) to a world class company. Various assessment methods are available including Lattice, SEI, BOOTSTRAP and SPICE.
- Quality cost analysis can be carried out, and may be of benefit, but it is unwise to concentrate only on costs which can be measured.
- Information gathered from the process can be used to inform the

customer about the quality of the development process in order to gain a competitive advantage.

- Software purchasers can request process control, product audit and testedness information.

This chapter has provided a general look at quality and statistical methods. The software industry is finding appropriate metrics, but many of the metrication programmes fail due to a lack of understanding of measurement and quality matters. Statistical methods are at the heart of understanding the information gathered from a metrication programme and should be considered an essential tool for quality improvement.

2 Software Control Using Metrics

2.1 Introduction

The use of metrics is the key to the quality and maturity improvements that most organisations seek. It provides the key to establishing relationships between suppliers and their customers and it is also the only effective method of obtaining management control of the development process.

Methods for metrication of a software development cycle are divided between measurement of the process and measurement of the product. One thing that most metrication projects have in common is a process improvement cycle. This cycle is an afterthought, the information being used to conduct a post-mortem on a project to find out why it went wrong and how it could have been done better. A post-mortem of this kind usually finds no key indicators, no common causes of variation and defects, and no way of establishing any improvement in the process for future development.

So why is this? What is wrong with the metrication process?

As we will see later, the success of a post event analysis depends largely on the *control status* of the process when the metrics were being collected. That is the cause of variance that are observed during the development process. The metrics are unlikely to correlate with any single root cause if the state of control is 'chaotic' (a term defined as lacking in process definition by the SEI maturity model (31)), or even defined chaos (the state where processes are defined but not controlled), with many external causes for variation in the activities.

The managing director of a software company complained that analysis of all the key indicators for projects completed over the previous three years showed there was a different cause for the overspend and the defectiveness of every project. All projects were different in technical composition, resource utilisation, language, code and development environment, as well as being developed under a changing management structure, and with a variety of different clients. The probability that the projects were being controlled in a similar way was so remote as to make the search for root causes impractical. This situation is the lowest level of process maturity at the project level. The company did have much higher levels of maturity at the development process level. The processes for software development were defined and procedures existed for many of the activities. Configuration management, control of the use of programming constructs, and development process definitions were all in use. Note that these factors did not provide any evidence of an improvement in the quality of the software produced at project level. It is not these controls that provide consistency of the end product, but the measurement and control of the activities of the project. This particular company requires methods of metricating the process and establishing controls over the project activities – they had reached a level 1 maturity as defined by the SEI model.

To improve on this requires a greater understanding of customer requirements, project risk, and product conformance management as well as methods and metrics to control the processes. To usefully provide comparison of the many different projects requires a common method of measuring the state of control at the level of both the developers and the project managers. This means ensuring that the engineers are all equally trained both in the software development process requirements and in understanding the variance of the metrics that reflect both product and process quality. The variances can then be normalised across projects for comparative purposes. To obtain any improvement in the company performance requires the third level of measurement of success. This is provided by measuring the company development strategy.

It is these three levels of metrication that provide statistical control information for managing software projects in different types of organisation. Which level any company should concentrate on, when metrics should be collected, and the selection and use of these metrics are the subjects to be covered in this chapter.

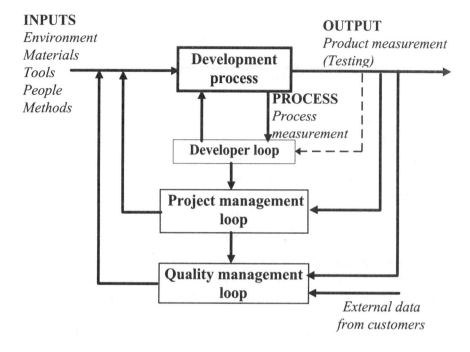

Fig. 2.1 The three control loops for any quality control process.

■ 2.2 The Collection and Use of Metrics

The general improvement cycle uses the metrics described here along with other process and product metrics to provide feedback to the people who are managing, developing or in any way servicing the clients' requirements.

There are three different loops in any quality system, illustrated in Fig. 2.1. The loops each have a separate but interlinked function of controlling different levels of the requirements set out by the company in the quality policy. The aim is to continuously improve at a rate that will assure success in the market for the company.

The Developer Loop – This is the real time loop that controls the every day activities of the development team. The metrics are collected by and provided directly to the developers themselves so that process and product improvement can be ongoing during the development process. Part of the activity can be a totally private loop where the only person who knows how the measures are helping is the person receiving and using the metrics.

In addition, metric inputs from external sources are used such as the measurement of confidence (see Chapter 9), the defects detected by customers, testers, and other team members.

The loop is classified as using information on an hourly or daily basis. The information is summarised and provided to the project management loop.

The Project Management Loop – This is the loop that team managers and leaders use to make sure that the risks of the project are kept in check. Metrics come from a summary of what the developers are using and from inspections, reviews and audits. They also include the management data gathering activities such as time sheets and progress reporting.

The loop cycle time is usually between weekly and monthly and the summary information is provided to the management loop.

The Quality Management Loop – The managers receive summary control information as well as error and fault reporting and quality non-conformance reports from all projects (or groups of similar projects). The loop is not specifically concerned with the current project and clients, but the strategic development of the company. Some of the input to this loop is from external sources such as competitors and marketing departments. The information is used to learn lessons from projects and ensure that preventative actions are taken to remove all root causes of variability and failure. The activity is usually completed once every month or every quarter.

■ 2.2.1 Information reporting

In each of these loops the information collected measures the control status of the process. That is, the metrics are analysed for the amount of variation occurring, and this is used to determine how stable and repeatable the process is. Different figures obtained for each time period may only indicate that the process is varying, perhaps within expected bounds of operation. Without this analysis of variance there is no way of knowing whether the change in a metric has some exceptional or special cause or whether it is the normal operating capability of the company.

In order to determine the difference between normal operating capability and exceptions, the reports must include details of metrics analysed for special events. This means that a common reporting method is required throughout the organisation. This minimises the risk of incorrect interpretation by staff and ensures common interpretation of the data. The common reporting method may include time charts and histograms for developers and supervisors, and a method for displaying both the current value and the historical range of values for managers.

Table 2.1 shows the types of charting expected in each of the loops and these are discussed in detail in the later chapters cross-referenced in the table.

▨ 2.2.2 Inside the development loop

The charts used by the developers reflect their need for information to be provided quickly so that minimum time is lost between an out of control event and the opportunity for a corrective action. The developers consequently are required to keep charts regarding the state of control of their processes. Typical methods of achieving this include charting the

Table 2.1 Reporting types in the three loops.

Loop type	Report types	Purpose of report	Chapter
Developer	$\bar{X}$-R charts	Maintenance of control state	4, 5
	Histograms	Control state data	4
	Cause-effect diagrams	Finding and	8
	Defect maps	removing causes	
	Defect cause maps	Finding which	
	Pareto	causes to remove first	8
Project management	$\bar{X}$-R charts	Time, completeness Conformance,	4, 5 8
	Histograms	risk, and	
	Cause-effect diagrams	confidence	
	Defect maps	management	
	Defect cause maps		
	Pareto	Process improvement	8
Quality management	Trend line graphs	Company	6
	Pie and bar charts	capability	
	Pareto	improvement	8
	Distribution graphs		7
	Star charts	Competitiveness	7
	Process improvement tools	management	8

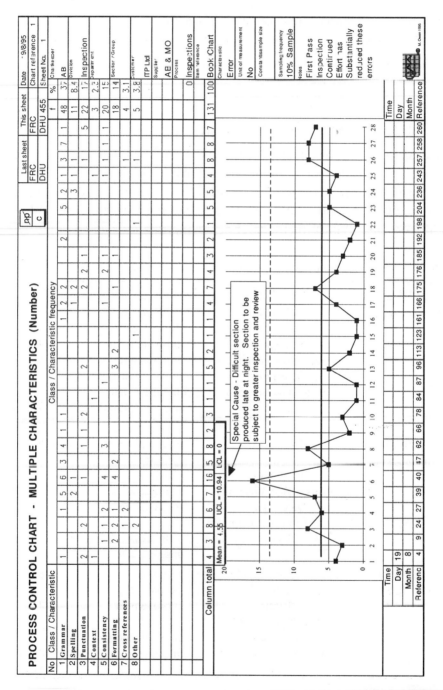

Fig. 2.2 c chart for errors in this book.

number of lines of code per module. Individual developers are the most likely people to be repeatedly producing similar code. Consequently, this metric, along with factors such as cyclometric complexity, will provide a very quick indication if any one program is going out of control.

Developers may include specifiers, designers, test designers, testers, coders, auditors, reviewers, and authors of technical or user documentation. In fact anyone involved in the activity of producing part of the product rather than managing its activity should be using the charts shown to produce the documents.

A typical example of the c chart, shown in Fig. 2.2, provides the errors per page resulting for a first pass sample inspection of this book. (Note that this is not the error level of the version you are reading, just an early draft!) The out of control point displayed caused the section in question to be reworked, and a cause to be sought. The net effect is a reduction in time to write the sections as the project progressed, with a more consistent style enforced by the charting process. This is the type of control that can be used for specifications and technical documents during the development process. It is also an effective way for an individual involved in the development process to improve his or her own performance.

▓ 2.2.3 Outside the development loop

The two outer loops, supervisory and managerial, use summary information from the developer loop, and data gathered from the management information and the customer/supplier interface. The information from the developer loop may be sensitive since it can reflect the performance of individual team members. For this reason, it is more usual to summarise information about project teams, with both the mean and range values being reported. The detail information is still in the data, but presented in a form that assists a manager in dealing with the performance of the team, rather than being the cause of friction with individual members.

The manager is not particularly interested in whether one individual is producing as well as the rest of the team because each team member will have days when performance is better or worse. Highlighting the worst days of an individuals' effort will only cause the project to deteriorate, but the control of the overall performance is essential to the success of the project.

The use of performance metrics such as error rates, inspection efficiency and the ratio of rework to accepted product, must be based on this group

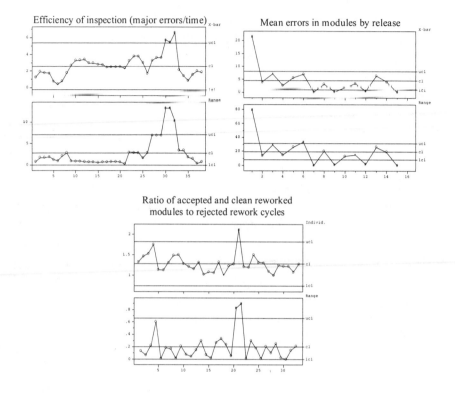

Fig. 2.3 Metrics plots for mean and range of project indices.

rate. The weekly rate for the project team on one software development activity is provided in Fig. 2.3. This shows how variable the project is for a number of the metrics. Note that charts such as these are useful for comparative metrics and a quick scan of a project. The plots are used to control the project as will be demonstrated in the following chapters of this book.

The quality process metrics are combined to produce indices for the whole of the organisation enabling capability to be calculated. This index is used to drive process improvements based on charts of the history of metrics for many similar projects across the site.

This information is not charted using the same methods as provided in the supervisory plots. The managers require only a snapshot and comparison with immediate past history, so a new form of diagram is provided. This has been developed from the star chart or Kiveat diagram as it has more recently become known (48). This form of diagram displays a single measurement for a number of different metrics and plots them with the axis of each metric starting at the centre of a star and radiating outwards. Each of the current values of the metrics are joined to create a polygon representing the current status of the set of metrics. The diagram used in statistical control is derived from this, using the last value from the statistical control chart for each of the variables. This may be a single measurement or the mean of grouped data. The statistical control limits provided by the charting process are drawn onto the diagram and these limits are used to bound each axis.

In addition the *range* of the grouped data (the largest in the group minus the smallest) can be represented on the chart as a maximum and minimum line. The previous values for the metrics can also be provided to show how the process has changed.

By adding the statistical limits, the range and the last set of data, the diagram now provides information about the state of control as well as providing a comparative summary. An example of the modified diagram is provided in Fig. 2.4 which is further explained in Chapter 7.

This then completes the metrics cycle, with managers providing the outer control loop that will keep the organisation ahead of the competition and improving to survive.

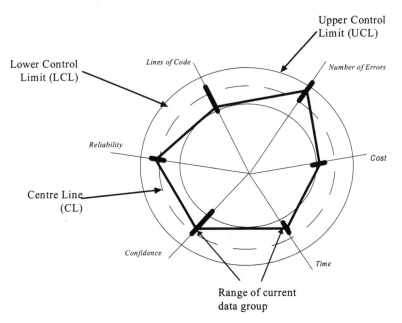

Fig. 2.4 A statistical version of the star chart or Kiveat diagram used to provide metrics to managers.

■ 2.3 Metrics through the Development Process

In a book such as this it is impossible to list all the metrics available. There are many books on metrics available including the works of Halstead (23) and McCabe (22), and books by Fenton (20) and Ince (21). Which metrics are the best for any individual organisation is left up to the reader to decide. However there are some general metrics that cannot be ignored.

■ 2.3.1 Use of metrics at the different project stages

For each stage of the development different metrics are required, and, as we have seen earlier, they are presented in different ways according to the user of the information. Table 2.2 shows the metrics used at different stages and the purposes of these metrics and Table 2.3 shows how they may be collected and how they relate to either the product or the process.

Of the commonly available metrics the most frequently used are time, cost and defects. These are usually collected at the end of the development process (during testing). They are usually limited to the number of defects found and the amount of time the project has taken for each stage of the project. Fig. 2.5 shows the results from a CAD graphics project. The defect data shows that the test and correction phase successfully brought the defects detected down to a level that they believed could be delivered. The metrics regarding how thoroughly the testing was completed were not

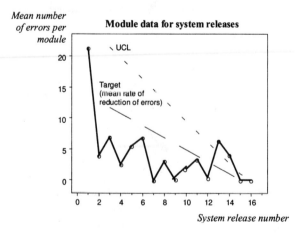

Fig. 2.5 CAD project mean number of defects per module for each release of the software.

gathered. The extra time taken to complete the tests and correct the product for the errors found, when added to the development time, made the project late. The only measure of how well the development team did their job is this indirect measure of the time taken for corrections.

Metrics such as the cost per line of code, and other productivity metrics, have largely been discredited because of the variation observed. This variation has not been correlated with a cause and consequently the metrics have lost credibility and are no longer widely used. Complexity metrics have fallen victim of the same problem. The correlation of defectiveness, conformance or cost with module complexity has led some experimenters to believe that the metric is of little use in the control of the process.

■ 2.3.2 Metrics at project initiation

At the start of a project there are few metrics available to calculate the risk of the project, and to select the appropriate development method (see section 2.5). The only metrics available must be collected at meetings between the customer (internal or external) and the specifier of the product. The metrics are used to identify risk and are based on method of assessment. We will see in Chapter 3 how confidence measures are taken.

The confidence measures are used in a similar way to the intuitive measures used by a sales representative. Since the development team are often removed from the reality of the customer, the measures are used to ensure that no non-essential risks are taken. Of course, most development companies will try and ensure that developers are close to customers and their requirements. In practice, however, an expert developer cannot be expert in the customers' requirements as well. Many major software companies use risk assessment forms during the estimation process for a project aimed at providing the assessment of the probability of success. These are categorised by customer history, development team history and the probability of success based on the intuitive feel of the estimator.

Once this level has been completed the measures can be made of the documents produced. These are based on the standard activities of measuring readability, accuracy and completeness. It is also useful to measure conformance to the internal standards and the error rates based on inspections of the documents (see Chapter 11). The error rate is used to establish a new level of risk based on the process of the proposers.

Table 2.2 Metrics through the Development Life-cycle.

Process stage	Metrics	Purpose of collection
Pre-project definition	Supplier confidence	To establish the development method
	Customer confidence	To identify project risk
	Document readability	To remove misunderstanding and early defects
	Accuracy	To identify errors at earliest stage
	Completeness	To identify missing requirements
Requirements definition	Supplier confidence	Tune the development method to match the abilities of the developers
	Customer confidence	Remove causes of concern early in the cycle
	Document readability Accuracy Completeness	} To enable the removal of defects early in cycle
	Conformance	To remove errors of omission
Design	Customer confidence	Remove causes of concern even at this late stage
	Supplier confidence	To ensure that technically the system is likely to meet requirements
	Completeness Conformance	} To remove errors of omission
Code	Language use	To control compiler usage to known error free areas, and to constructs that minimise error generation
	Size	To minimise chances of error generation due to incorrect partitioning of system
Test	Complexity	To measure probability of defectiveness
	Effort	To measure probability of defectiveness
	Defectiveness	To measure defectiveness rate
	Testedness	To measure the effectiveness of testing
	Coverage	To measure the amount of testing completed
Accept	Defectiveness	To measure defectiveness and only deliver at an acceptable level
	Completeness	To measure completeness of system
	Conformance	To measure conformance of systems and deliver at an agreed level
	Customer confidence	To measure customer confidence in system
Maintain	Defect correction rate Defect introduction rate Customer confidence	} To measure effectiveness of maintenance
Upgrade	System defectiveness	To measure status of start point
	Supplier confidence	To measure customer confidence in original system and track this for improvement
	As for pre-project	Go to start of new project

Table 2.3 Commonly available metrics.

Type	Product metrics	Metric source
Size	Lines of code/module	Compiler/editor
	Modules/function	Compiler
	Functions/system	Specifications
	Data types/areas	Specifications/compiler
	Variables	Compiler
Complexity	McCabes	Test tools
	Path count	
	Call count	
	Data types	
Conformity	Completeness	Audit/review
	Functional differences	Customer audit
	Supplier confidence	Customer/supplier mtg.
	Customer confidence	Customer/supplier mtg.
Defectiveness	Defect count	Test tool/test actions
	Function failures	Test tool/test actions
	Data faults	Test tools
	Machine or system failures	Test activities
	Reliability	Reliability tests

Type	Process metrics	
Time	Lines/day or hour	} Time sheets and
	Module/month	} module checks
	Review time	Review time
	Stage time	management
	Preventative/total time	Project management
	Corrective/total time	Project management and Quality cost analysis
Cost	Systems utilisation	Systems management
	Cost per line or module	Project management
	Cost of correction	Project cost analysis
	Cost of failure	Quality cost analysis
Defectiveness	Error count	Test tools and results
	Error rate/module	Test tools and results

▓ 2.3.3 Development cycle metrics

The development cycle requires metrics that will provide information about the success of the process to deliver a product of a quality that will give the desired confidence levels. The metrics available cover a wide range of factors, and the list that follows may be used to start a selection process.

The one fact that must always be considered when initiating a metrication programme is that there are no 'right' metrics. The measures chosen must be analysed for effectiveness. If process and product improvement are resulting from the measurement then the metric may be beneficial. This must be providing that the cost of collection is less than the likely cost of quality for a product that has not been so improved.

A simplistic approach to the calculation of the quality cost will lead to no metrication whatever in most instances. The most essential cost to estimate is that of failure of the system in the field and failure of the process to deliver a conforming product.

The use of metrics means continually developing and changing as the process becomes more mature and less prone to causes of out-of-control occurrences. The most useful metrics to start measuring and controlling are:

(1) lines of code per module
(2) complexity
(3) effort per module.

with product metrics of:

(1) defectiveness
(2) language usage
(3) conformance.

These metrics provide the basis for process improvement, but will not enhance a process that is already well controlled by procedures and guidelines. Neither will they provide control of a process where the engineers are particularly well skilled. Indeed the reliance on highly skilled and motivated engineers results in a distortion of the metrics because of their willingness to work until the product is right. Time recording becomes distorted and the difference between source generation and defect detection (debugging) becomes less clear.

While this method of working is seen as beneficial to many companies, it is a short-term phenomena. Using staff with fewer skills who will still be required to meet the same levels of quality will indicate to the company the true effort required. This will also allow true metrics to be recorded and the true cost of the process to be analysed. Mechanisms for reducing these costs can then be identified.

These costs are required for each phase of a project. The measures listed above apply equally to the documents produced at the early stages of a project and the software testing phases at the final stages.

■ 2.3.4 Project management metrics

The aim of these metrics is to provide managers with information that will help them to make decisions supporting reduced time-scales and costs for the development cycle. The aim is still to deliver products that conform to the requirements and inspire confidence in the users.

The metrics of time and cost are produced throughout the project and we are familiar with using them as control parameters throughout the development cycle. Conformance and confidence control the project by providing a visible measure of the risk that is being taken, even if the project is on time and within budget. This is because these metrics take into account the acceptance of the product by both those developing it and the final customer.

The largest risk taken in a project is the difference in understanding between the customer and the supplier, and this is controlled by measuring the understanding whenever review meetings take place. If the prototyping V model is used for development, then this frequency is increased, and the measure can be readily tracked to the end of the project. The recommended rate for this is dependent on the life cycle of the project, but should never be more than 4 weeks apart.

Conformance is a physical measure of how much of the software written currently conforms to the specification. Often testing is limited to finding those things that do not conform. This concentrates the activity on the few things found early.

The aim of conformance measurement is to take each system requirement and compare it with the actual system. The developer and the customer can both take a view on how well each function conforms. This is not just a logical value, but a numeric judgment based on a conformance percentage. If the function being checked consists of 10 entry items and each item has an input range of possible values, then the conformance measure is taken once all of these items have been checked. The measure is then given by:

$$\text{Conformance Index} = \frac{\text{Number of conforming items}}{\text{Number of possible items}} \%$$

This index requires a model of the software at the start that will enable all possible input and output screens to be defined and tested. The time taken to do this makes the task impossible and so a statistical view is taken of the index. This will be covered in detail in Chapter 10.

Finally the confidence index is a measure, used by both the developer and the customer, that indicates a probability of failure even though all tests may be successfully completed.

At the start of a project the confidence of both the customer and the developer is expected to be low. As the project progresses the increase in confidence is rapid and convergent as each party begins to understand the needs of the other.

The measure of confidence is based on three factors:

(1) the differences observed in the requirements by each party

(2) the differences in interpretation understood by the parties

(3) the coverage of the system achieved in the meeting.

These differences are measured by asking a number of questions of the developer and the customer about each of the functions under discussion. This involves preparing a formal review meeting between the parties. This review may not impede the progress of the meeting in any way since a reviewer will ask the questions as each of the subject areas is covered in the agenda. The reviewer also observes the discussion taking place to provide a third-party judgment.

The methods of producing the conformance and confidence index are discussed in detail in Chapter 3.

■ 2.3.5 Completion metrics

When should a product be delivered? The answer to this question is a varied as are the number of different types of product being developed. This is equally true of the metrics that can be used to decide whether a product is fit for delivery.

Using the metrics previously identified, criteria for delivery can be chosen based on the history of the company of successfully delivering products. The measures obtained are statistically analysed and the values used to determine target and maximum levels that should be expected at the delivery point of a project.

A further metric is the rate at which the defects are being found in the software that can indicate one of two things:

- The test method efficiency is reducing and a new test method is required to find the defects left in the code.
- There are fewer defects left to be found.

To tell the difference between these two metrics it is required to measure the efficiency of the test method being used. The most usual metrics for this are the change on rate of defect detection, the ability to detect seeded defects, and the coverage achieved by a test method. While these methods are not absolute measures of test efficiency, they provide adequate information. When test efficiency experiments can be completed, better information will be available and the appropriate test methods can be selected. Even under these circumstances the efficiency would depend on the same set of inputs to the test process as we used for inputs to the development process. The training, skills, method of using the tests, ability to interpret the results, spread and type of defects introduced by the organisation all contribute to the test efficiency.

▓ 2.4 What these Metrics Mean

When a measurement is taken from a process that is expected to be consistent and repeatable, as arguably the software development process should be, the results plotted as a distribution can be expected to follow one of the standard statistical formulae depending on the type of metric and the nature of the measurement. However the credibility of the measurement does not rely on this relationship nor on the ability to correlate the metric with some other variable.

When metrics are first collected the values do not usually create a single continuous distribution or match one of the standard formulae. This is often then cited as a reason why the metric cannot be used. By analysing the causes of the differences in the distribution, insights can be obtained that show how some of the measures may be partitioned into separate causal regions. These causal regions may be either based on the product or on the process.

An example of this is the number of lines of code in a module. A particular large software house designs code typically with between 50 and 150 lines of functional C or C++ code. However there are two further regions. There are a few modules with only small numbers of lines (4–20 typically) and a few with many lines (200 and above). Analysing the programs shows that most of those with small numbers of lines are all simple utilities or setup functions. Most of the long programs fall into two classes – initialisation functions and case (switch) functions. Fig. 2.6 shows an example of such a distribution.

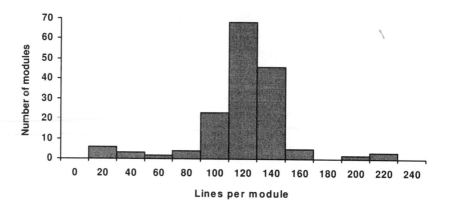

Fig. 2.6 An example of the distribution of lines of code per module.

If we exclude the values relating to the types of modules that are expected to have either exceptionally small or large number of lines, then a single distribution might be expected to result. We can then suggest to developers that they should produce modules with a length around a value that is based on the mean of normal development practices. The measurements will then be caused to form a single distribution. If there is then a correlation between defectiveness and length of code, it will become apparent from any exceptional data, rather than from modules that fall within the expected region.

The relationship between lines of code and the defectiveness of a module is far from conclusive with studies (1,2) both proving and disproving the theory. However this only goes to show that the metrics used in one organisation will not necessarily be applicable to another. However by using techniques to control the process so that the variation is controlled and minimised, the opportunity for analysing relationships is made available. Most of the studies are based on processes that are not repeatable and consequently cannot be expected to provide results that will relate to the defectiveness of the product. The example in Fig. 2.6 includes modules that have high levels and low levels of defects in each of the distributions. This is because some of the code naturally falls into one or another category such as mathematical, logical, file access or switch, but does not reside in the same distribution as others in its class. This may mean that there is an exceptional cause for the defectiveness level for that module. Fig. 2.7 shows the distributions for the main category of code. As can be seen, there are still two separate distributions suggesting that there are two different processes. In fact the case is proved by the fact that two different groups of software engineers produced the code. By analysing one of the distributions for exceptions in error levels the causes of increased or reduced error rate can be used to determine how the process can be improved to improve its effectiveness.

The result of this study is to provide the project team with training on the ideal length for each different type of module. This may be dependent on the make up of the individual project teams. Any exceptions that now exist will have a special cause – a reason for not adhering to the guidelines, and the consequential difference in product quality can be countered with increased care in the production process. Alternatively, if the change results in better code, it can be used to amend the guidelines to improve the process for the future.

The values can now be used to produce a control chart as we will see in later chapters. Also, correlation of the lines of code and defectiveness data will be feasible since it is based on one defined process and one defined product class. The exceptional values caused by different processes and classes all being grouped together have been removed.

By correlating the defects found against lines of code the graph shown in Fig. 2.8 results. These results are for two companies and for a selection of code that has been subjected to statistical control with removal of exceptions. These graphs show clearly that a relationship exists between these two variables for the majority of the code, although the minimum is at a different place. This is probably dependent on the development process. The

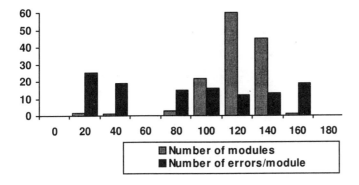

Fig. 2.7 The distribution of lines of code and errors for one class of modules showing the variation due to the lack of process control.

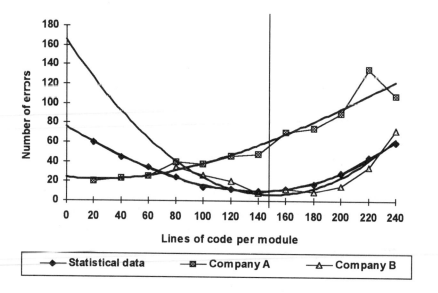

Fig. 2.8 Distributions of the number of errors per module vs. the module size in lines of code.

statistical company B data is for non-critical software. Company A data is for operating system software that is much more critical in terms of the number of customers and the knock-on effect of a failure.

The actual minimal point of these graphs is not expected to be the same for all companies. A clear example of this is a change in process caused by a team not working to the same quality standards and without the same management control. This team has a much larger defect rate and consequently the minimum is both at a different point and at a different level.

A process that results in a single distribution of the metrics is a process that is 'in control'. The causes of exception have been removed and the process has a capability of consistently producing with metrics at known metric levels. However the spread of the metric may also be of concern and so the process may not be capable, i.e. it may result in error rates that are unacceptably high.

The first step to achieving this condition is to select the metrics to be measured. The choice of metrics is dependent on the type of development process to be used. This in turn is dependent on a number of criteria that must be satisfied before the start of a project.

▓ 2.5 Choosing a Development Process

The choice of development process is often not considered at the start of a project. Most companies believe that the methods in use are appropriate for all projects and will provide satisfactory results. This is like suggesting that the mode of transport for getting from one place to another should always be the same. The criteria for the journey are critical to the choice of transport method, and so it is with the software development method. There are many development methods, some which only vary in detail and others that are quite fundamentally different.

The second criterion for the choice of development method depends on what is expected from the development process. Is it purely a process for producing a product, or does the organisation wish also to learn about its effectiveness and efficiency? The choice of development process will affect the long-term future of the company for two reasons:

(1) Without measurement the company will never understand the process better and will consequently find competitive advantage difficult to maintain.

(2) Without process selection the company may never know the commercial success that could be available from more effective processes for particular projects.

We will consider here the choice between the following development processes:

- The V model, which is traditionally passed through once to complete a development cycle. This provides the stages of development, including simultaneous preparation of acceptance specifications for each stage.
- The W Model, which again is passed through once with the same steps as the V model but has a second V that provides continuous product review to support the development activities,
- The X Model which includes the W model, but also has a process improvement cycle to continuously learn the lessons and optimise the process as outlined in the previous section,
- The simultaneous engineered or RAD model. This is the repetition of many V, W or X cycles simultaneously and sequentially being completed.

The following sections provide some of the metrics to be used in the selection of a process. They particularly identify the need for a method for selecting a process based on measures of the initial inputs to a project. It is not important whether the development is for a new product, the enhancement of an old product, the maintenance of an existing system, or for the development of a bespoke one-off or small volume user system. The selection criteria are based on the input metrics for the project alone.

■ 2.5.1 Selection based on project initiation metrics

The input metrics for a project are based on the information available at this point and are usually limited to a proposal or a simple requirement statement rather than a detailed specification. Consequently it is necessary to consider the risk that is being taken by all parties in initiating the development as well as measuring how well the problem is understood.

The measures required at the start of a project are common to all development projects and require an understanding of the processes that the company is capable of using. A company familiar with developing a shrink-wrapped product for the volume market may not have a process capable of developing bespoke mission critical software. However the mission critical software company may not have a process that is capable of success in an environment where the requirements are not fixed at the start of the project.

The first step in this process is to profile the input information. The Ishikawa or fishbone diagram, Fig. 2.9, developed by Ishikawa (49) in the 1970s for analysing causes and effects (see Chapter 8), provides a method of categorising causes of a particular effect. In this case the 'effect' is the development process to be selected for the project. In any specific development method there are different expected causes of project failure. These are identified and can then be rated for importance and according to the company's capability of using each of the particular processes and methods.

These causes are identified using the six basic categories of risk, confidence, materials, methods, tools and environment. Each arm will include detailed items that relate to the company carrying out the study. Fig. 2.9 provides a starting point for analysing the processes and the company capability. Hence this process considers all the different process tools available, the different platforms that a system might run on, the people and skills available, as well as the confidence measures resulting from an

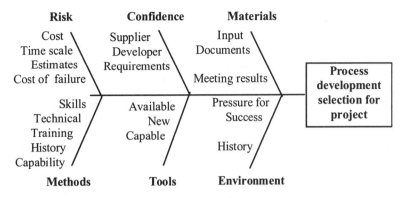

Fig. 2.9 Ishikawa (cause and effect) or fishbone diagram for initiating a project.

initial meeting with the customer (see Chapter 10). The selection for most organisations is between a multitude of different detailed techniques, and between either:

(1) the simultaneous engineering or RAD method, or
(2) the single pass methods including the V, W and X models.

▓ 2.5.2 The simultaneous engineered (SE) or RAD choice

Research work within manufacturing industry has provided a process where the manufacturing system design is developed alongside the product design, thus preventing many of the difficulties of translating a design into a finished product. In software development, finding a solution to the problem of the need to develop products from impossible designs has been one driver for the new generation of development tools. These tools rely less on the knowledge of the designer and more on knowledge from the whole team involved in the project.

The work has also led to the development of the prototyping loop. This attempts to shorten the development cycle between the specification agreed by the customer and the presentation of a working model for agreement by the customer. This shortened loop has a safeguard in its measurement system. It can be recalibrated as a result of measuring the customer confidence in the prototype, thus enabling the measurement errors to be reduced in their scope for accumulation.

Fig. 2.10 shows a prototyping loop based on the W model of software development. The inverted W is the external activity required to ensure that the project is meeting the confidence and conformance criteria of the customer. It is the model for the inspection meetings required to assure this. Note that the audit and review activities (the second V of the W model) are still present, but the formal customer review and audit process (the inverted W model) will take priority over the internal activities

For a prototyping development activity such as that described as rapid application development (RAD) or simultaneous engineering (SE), the X model is continually being repeated until the last elements of the system are 'finished'.

The choice of this development method is based on the input metrics all having values that increase the probability of failure of a single-pass method such as the V or W model. The need of the project is to build confidence of delivery of a system that the customer is sure will provide the features required. The project process must be a mechanism to build that confidence throughout the process.

A second reason for choosing this method of development is that the historical capability of a company to provide a solution is not as high as the customer would like. The method reduces this risk by allowing the customer to assure progress in confidence as the product is being developed.

■ 2.5.3 The single pass choice

To complete a development in a single pass requires a maturity of process development and knowledge of expectation that must be high. The risk of failure must be minimal and this requires a knowledge that the company can continually produce with minimum risk of failure. Methods of assuring this are provided by the reviews, inspection and audits of the second V in

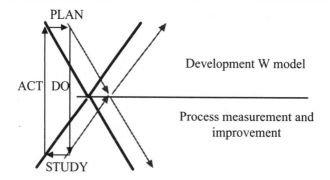

Fig. 2.10 The X model.

the W model.

For this type of development process to improve, a secondary activity is required which is provided by the Deming process improvement cycle. The X model then is used, not as an input into the current project, but to provide inputs to future or parallel project cycles.

■ 2.6 Summary

- Metrics provide a practical management tool to control software development commensurate with the quality aims of ISO 9000 registered companies and process maturity development based on the SEI, EFQM and Lattice models.
- A complete picture of the process is obtained by measurement of both product and process metrics enabling causes of variance to be detected and removed.
- Measurement of confidence at the start of the development cycle allows the selection of a development process suited to the risk of the project.
- The key management metrics for software are the development time, the total cost of development, and the conformance of the product. The confidence that the customer ultimately places in the product is the most significant indicator.
- The process improvement cycle is used during development to improve an individual project, and then generically to remove causes of variance throughout an organisation by allowing one project to learn from the experiences of others.
- The process and product metrics throughout the development cycle provide inputs to the process improvement activities.
- The completion metrics enable product delivery to be based on the performance of the process, the probability of process failure, and the management statistics. The confidence that the potential customer has in the project is the best delivery metric but must be reinforced by internal measures.

This chapter has provided the basis for using metrication in the software development cycle. The following chapters will build on the models provided here. However, to gather metrics an efficient mechanism is required otherwise the cost benefits will be lost in the increased effort of the metrication and process improvement programmes.

3 Design of Statistical Data Collection

3.1 Introduction

We have seen the importance of metrics to the control of the development process, but to be effective, an efficient method of collecting the chosen metrics must be designed. This Chapter provides rules for ensuring that a method of collecting process or product metrics will provide information for analysis which in turn will provide an improved understanding of the process. In most organisations the methods of collecting data will depend on the structure of the development teams. It will also depend on the teams' acceptance of the use of metrics and their ability to make use of the metrics to improve their own development capability. As we saw in Chapter 2, there are three key stages during a project for the useful collection of metrics:

(1) Prior to the start in order to establish the starting values for the project.

(2) During the development stages to provide control of the processes and the product improvement required to achieve release criteria.

(3) On completion to ensure that the process has successfully produced a product that conforms to the customer and company requirements.

The metrics collected at the start of a project are project risk and confidence. These metrics provide a starting point for the metrication program as discussed in the last chapter.

Once the project is under way these two metrics are tracked by measuring each of the outputs from the project, such as documents, code or test scripts. These metrics show that the project risk and confidence are continually trending toward a value that is acceptable for delivery. In addition both product and process metrics provide control of the individual process stages.

A number of metrics, including risk and the confidence, must be within a satisfactory range for the product to be considered as complete. The process and product metrics provide this release information, but in addition provide information about how the process performed. This data is then available for future process improvement programmes.

All the metrics collected through the project are summarised for a management review that has the task of learning lessons and preventing future additional quality costs occurring. These statistical summaries summarise similar projects as well as comparing activities across different types of projects. To achieve this we require methods for comparing different projects and individual activities. The methods described at the end of this chapter include normalisation, partitioning and variance analysis of metrics to establish common comparative metrics for a development organisation regardless of product or activity type.

The following sections provide guidelines for each of the stages of measurement, for successfully designing the processes of collecting and analysing the data. The first stage of this is understanding the different types of metrics in statistical terms.

■ 3.2 The Types of Metrics

For the purpose of control charting, the two classes of metrics are:

(1) **Variables** – measures of a product that can have any value between the limits of the measurement. They are usually close to a target value and the range of values may be limited to greater than zero. However, measurements of differences from a target may lead to negative values, and temperature for instance may have a positive and negative range.

(2) **Attributes** – characterised as counts of things which may or may not be present in the product (such as defects). These generally have a positive value.

These two standard categories come from the analysis of the distributions expected from the different types of measurement. A variable will provide randomly distributed results about some mean value and if a total population could be collected, then the resulting distribution would be normal. The mathematics describing normal distributions applies to these distributions, for example, the measures of the centre of the distribution such as the mean and the measure of the spread defined as the standard deviation.

If it is possible for the feature not to be present at all, that is the metric is equal to zero, then for a total population the distribution is likely to be binomial and the measure is an attribute. The mathematics relating to this distribution requires much larger samples, but the measures of spread and mean can still be calculated as we will see in Chapters 5 and 6.

The mathematics of distributions is used for calculating means and estimating the spread of the distribution, but beyond this the analysis of distributions is not helpful for control purposes. This is because the purpose of statistical control is to continuously improve the process and this generally implies that the metrics will become more stable and have narrower distributions over time. The aim of statistical control is to continually alter the shape of the distribution by minimising the spread and optimising the mean for any individual metric. An estimate of the current shape and mean value of the current distribution provides the mechanism for achieving this. The standard statistical method of identifying a representative sample of a complete population is not useful since we have no knowledge (because it is continually changing) of what the population might be. The method to use is to take small groups of data and estimate the current mean and the spread of the distribution from this limited set of data.

The use of groups of data combined with the fact that an attribute value can be zero requires the group size for attribute data to be larger than for variable data. This is to ensure that there is adequate useful (non-zero) information available for controlling the process. It is because of this requirement for different sample sizes that we treat the two types of metrics differently on the control charts.

■ 3.2.1 Variables

The main characteristic of variables is that they are measurements that can have any value within the capability of the measurement system and potentially produce a single distribution centred about a non-zero value. Examples of variables in software development are time, complexity, lines of code per module (LOC/M), number of paths per module, function points or modules per system, mean errors per day and cyclometric complexity.

There are three classes of variables defined by the restrictions on the range of values that they can take, which are:

(1) **Variables with infinite resolution and accuracy** – those for which the range of values is infinite (e.g. time, cost, complexity) and for which the accuracy and resolution are bounded only by design or physical limitations of the instrumentation.

(2) **Variables with fixed resolution and accuracy** – variables whose range of values is limited by their nature (lines of code per module, numbers of paths, function points) and whose accuracy and resolution are fixed by the nature of the measurement.

(3) **Variables that are mathematically or logically derived** – those for which the range, accuracy and resolution is dependent on the source metrics from which they are derived, and the accuracy and resolution of the mathematics used to derive them. Examples are errors per module, cyclometric complexity, Halsteads effort estimate.

Table 3.1 provides the characteristics of a few variables used in the software industry together with their classifications.

Table 3.1 Examples of variables and their characteristics.

Variable	Characteristics
Time	Variable resolution and accuracy
LOC/M	Fixed resolution and accuracy
Complexity	Mathematically derived variable with accuracy dependent on mathematics and resolution dependent on source measurements
Lines of code per day	Mathematically derived variable with accuracy dependent on mathematics and resolution dependent on source measurements
Mean error rate (errors per module)	Fixed resolution and accuracy. Accuracy dependent on mathematical function and source of measurements

▓ Variables with infinite resolution and accuracy

Measurements of this type have their accuracy and resolution determined by design. Examples in software development are time and completeness. The design of the measurement method controls the accuracy, resolution and variability of the measurement activity to minimise their effects on the result. An example using time measurement of a development activity can be used to demonstrate the principles and we will see later how the design of the measurement takes account of both resolution and accuracy.

▓ Fixed resolution and accuracy variables

A measurement of this type is usually a count to determine the 'size' of something. It is differentiated from errors and events because it defines the presence of the item being measured, for example a module is measured by the number of lines it contains. These measures are always of fixed resolution – less than one line of code is not a meaningful measure. The accuracy with which a measurement can be made is also limited to the resolution of the measurement technique, although this is often influenced by process variables such as the layout of the source. For the example of lines of code, the design of the measurement system must refer back to the defining document for source layout so that the measure is based on this standard. One source of variability for these measures is the lack of a standard for the item being measured and consequently the accuracy of the measurements is compromised.

▓ Mathematically derived variables

These variables can be derived from both of the previous types through complex formulae. Many of the metrics derived for software, including McCabes and Halsteads metrics, are derived from simple measurements of the software through complex formulae. These types of metrics are subject to two sources of accuracy and resolution. The first is the source errors due to the accuracy and resolution of the source measurements. The second source is the accuracy and resolution of the mathematical functions used. In the worst cases it is combined with both a fixed and a variable resolution and accuracy measurement which leads to high variability of the derived variables and consequently to unreliability of the metrics. Most calculations rely on the accuracy of computers to provide minimal errors. However, if a time measurement is involved in the calculation and a complex formula is involved, such as that for the Halsteads effort estimate, the accumulated error from the measurement can reduce the mathematically derived measurement to little more than a rough estimate.

In all circumstances where these types of calculations are used, the calculation for the accumulated errors should accompany the design of the data collection and metric derivation system. These techniques are not the subject of this book, and would require a major chapter to explore in full. Examples of error analysis are available in various mathematical texts on applied mathematics such as (50). We will see the effect of these causes of variation in section 3.3.

▓ 3.2.2 Attributes

Attributes can only be observed and counted rather than measured. It is the fact that an attribute may have no observable occurrences that makes it different to a variable. A variable will always exist (e.g. lines of code) but an attribute (e.g. defects) may not be detectable. Because attribute metrics may be present at specific levels we have to plan a mechanism for detecting them dependent on the volume expected within the item being searched. The most usual example of this is defects which can only be detected providing a strategy is used that is capable of detecting all occurrences of the type of defects expected. As we will see later, a strategy for detecting all the occurrences is usually impossible or impractical, and so different detection strategies are adopted. Chapter 12 provides details for sampling during testing and we will be considering the general rules for taking samples later in this Chapter.

▓ Classes of attributes

Attributes are usually considered in classes so that they may be analysed either as individual counts or as the accumulated number for all classes. In the case of errors in software the classes may be causal, such as language, design, coding and compiler errors. For any one class there is a probability for any development team using a particular language, a particular target computer, and under a specific management regime, that a number of these errors will occur. For any one of the error types a distribution can be produced (Fig. 3.1) over a period of time. If the process is improving then this improvement should result in both the mean level and the spread of the distribution reducing.

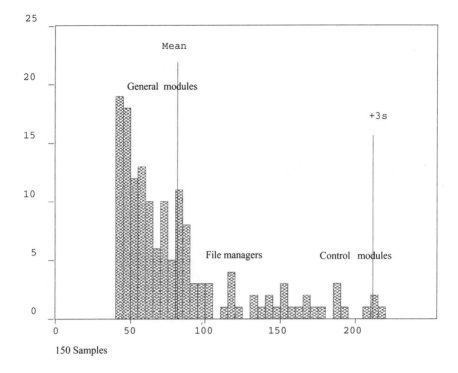

Fig. 3.1 Distributions of types of errors.

■ Effectiveness of attribute detection

This should be true for any one of the attribute classes as well as for accumulating related attributes. To observe this reduction a common method of detection must be adopted which, for attributes, means adopting a method of ensuring that the probability of detecting the attribute is equal for each repeated attempt. In order to achieve this metrics are required that will measure the effectiveness of detection.

For physical attributes the use of manual inspection has been shown in various studies to have a probability of consistent results from a single detection pass of only about 80% (51). An example might be where a manual tester is observing differences from a written specification or even a guideline screen. This is relatively easy to corroborate – try using a group of people to detect the number of occurrences of the letter 's' on one page in a book in a 5 minute interval. The very simple rule of detecting the letter 's' will result in a distribution with a mean of 90–95%. By making the rules more complex by detecting only a letter 's' that follows an 'e' the efficiency reduces dramatically. Errors in software are defined by even more complex rules and consequently we cannot expect to improve on these detection levels. For those who wish to try this exercise use this section (effectiveness of attribute detection) and look at the results at the end of this chapter (section 3.10)

Fig. 3.2 shows the distribution results for a controlled study of this nature, where the 20 testers were all provided with the same product. This product had been carefully inspected by a control (a person not normally involved in the process, but who consistently found more errors that the rest of the team). The results are illuminating in terms of the variability of the results and the change in variability with time. Some of the testers were provided with the control at the start of the day and others at the end of the period of testing. The results show that there are clear differences in the ability of testers to detect defects. This is a study that any individual can complete by looking at the errors in a document. On each repeated inspection of a document new errors will be found. If a period of a 10–15 days is left between each repeated inspection of the same document, and the inspection is carried out at different times of the day or after different types of activity, the variability of inspection can be discovered. Even for the most professional and consistent of inspectors, a distribution will result.

If the inspection is immediately repeated after completion of the first pass then the number of errors found can be expected to improve. However, the improvement is often nullified by the 'expected results' syndrome of the tester, and by rapid deterioration of the effectiveness of this type of manual observation activity.

The main factor governing the effectiveness of attribute measurements is the ability to ensure a consistency of measurement. Consistency may be improved by automation providing that the input to the automated system is controlled so that it is consistent. It may indirectly be measured using variables such as coverage, time and rate of inspection. The use of classification systems also improves consistency providing that the people generating the classifications can discriminate effectively and so care is required in the design of the discrimination system.

■ Sampling to improve effectiveness

Finally for any attribute system to be effective a method of ensuring equality of the measurement is required. This involves producing a strategy for sampling the product to be measured in such a way that the expected levels

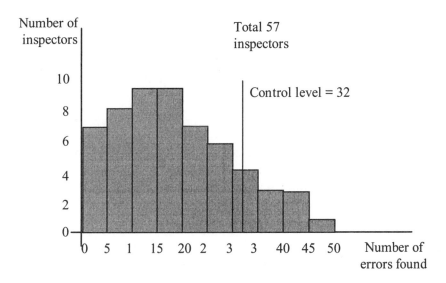

Fig. 3.2 The efficiency of the inspection process.

of attributes will be detected. There are guidelines for sampling in most standards authorities (BSI (52), ASQC, ASM, DIN). However, for software where the main attribute to be measured is defects, then the method of sampling is dependent on identifying the testable events. Chapter 12 will detail how this achieved. Any test plan that includes branch testing as well as coverage testing will test most of the code several times. This is achieved because each different test strategy not only covers particular code once, but is expected to cover a number of areas of code that are covered by other tests. This overlapping provides an opportunity to discover defects that are not found by a straightforward sampling from a single 100% pass through the code (if one could be found anyway). So for software testing, the sampling plans are based on the probability of defects occurring. The plan is also dependent on identifying tests which provide a probability of greater than one for detecting a particular type of defect. This is particularly true for defects that might be considered as dangerous or critical.

Consequently if there is a probability of only one defect then a 100% sample is required which may only be a 20% sample from the total test suite. If however the distribution developed shows that there is a likelihood of 10 errors in every 100 paths, then a sampling level of just 3% will provide a control chart adequate to detect this level. Consequently, the development is at the 'normal' level of error generation.

■ 3.2.3 Variables or attributes?

Table 3.2 provides guidelines for which software metrics to treat as variables and which as attributes. The choice of whether a metric is to be considered as a variable or an attribute is dependent entirely on whether the feature has a probability of being present. Most metrics must be present for the item to exist and consequently have a probability of unity or higher, whereas defects may not be present and have a probability of less than unity. Hence metrics that would naturally be considered as a count of something and might at first consideration be considered as attributes (such as lines of code per module) are more properly classified as variables.

While there is only one type of attribute, there are three types of variables. The only difference between a variable such as time and the counted variables, such as lines of code per module, is the difference in resolution available. The fact that half a line is not practical is not an issue since the design of the data collection system often renders other small resolution measurements impractical also (e.g. 1 second of development time or a complexity of 0.1). In any measurement system the limiting factor is always the resolution that can be achieved and this is may be limited by the variable itself or by the measurement system.

■ 3.2.4 Conversion of attributes to variables

When making measurements the design of the measuring system is critical to the usefulness of the data collected. A variable has the properties of always being present and always providing some information about the product and the process, whereas zero defects is ambiguous. Either there are no defects or we have not found any, or we haven't tried to find any! At least one other metric is required to qualify attribute data. Defect data should always be accompanied by a variable measurement such as testedness, coverage, or some other metric that describes why the value should be believed as a statement of the occurrence of the attribute. In manufacturing this data is taken to be the method of sampling used to detect the defects.

Some metrics can be converted from one type to the other. An example of this is converting defects to defectiveness. It is useful to know how many defects have been detected in a module. Equally useful is the defectiveness .of code which is a measured value obtained as the ratio of the number of defects to the length or complexity of the code. This can have any value

Table 3.2 Software development metrics as variables or attributes.

Project phase	Measure	Variable or attribute	Metrics
Start-up	Risk	Variable	% with target of 100
	Confidence	Variable	Supplier and customer % with target of 100
Inspection	Document quality	Attribute Variable	Errors/page Error rate in errors/day
Development	Effort	Variable	Time, pages/day Lines of code/day
	Errors	Attribute Variable	Error rate/team Re-key effort per day
	Completeness	Variable	% with target of 100
	Size	Variables	Number of pages, functions, lines of text, lines of code, paths
Testing	Halsteads metrics	Variable	Effort, language use, size
	McCabes	Variables	Complexity
	Testedness	Variable	Coverage
	Test effectiveness	Variable	Defects/module
	Defects	Attribute	Count
Acceptance	Defectiveness	Variables	Number of defects per module, function, or system
	Completeness	Variable	% with target of 100
	Conformance	Variable	% with target of 100

over zero and consequently is treated as a variable. Note that it is unlikely that the value will ever be zero. It is always possible to redefine an error so that even the most minor deviation from the requirements or standards are flagged as defects. Note also that the second variable data is still required to qualify the original data, and may be used as part of the equation. An example is defectiveness, which can be defined as defects found divided by coverage achieved. Extrapolation of this for 100% coverage is covered in Chapter 12, but in general extrapolation should be used with great care. Attributes cannot generally be said to be distributed evenly through a product and consequently other techniques are required to analyse the nature of the distributions before extrapolation can be used.

Conversion of an attribute to a variable is beneficial for the purposes of looking at the control status of a process and identifying major changes. If, for instance, the defectiveness is charted, calculated from defects found divided by coverage, then out of control situations on the chart identify when events outside the normal have occurred. The charts can detect when a product is exceptionally good, or testing coverage has not been achieved, and will ignore the 'normal' changes in defectiveness that are a natural feature of the capability of the developers.

▓ 3.3 Designing the Data Collection Activity

There are three elements to the design of a data collection system:
    (1) Selection of appropriate metrics.
    (2) Design of a collection method including accuracy, resolution, sample period and the grouping of data.
    (3) Choice of appropriate tools or methods to analyse the metrics meaningfully.

The choice of metrics has been discussed in Chapter 2, but once this choice has been made the source and stability of the metric must be understood.

▓ 3.3.1 Distribution analysis

A metric that has been chosen as a measure of a process or product should be produced by a common process. This is achieved only by gaining control of the process by removing any special causes from the process which cause variation of the metric. A process without any constraint of this type is unlikely to result in a single distribution and it is said to be out of control. Fig. 3.3 shows the distributions for errors per line of code from a particular project. The modules in each of the separate distributions may result from different types of module or different processes. Whichever is the case there are likely to be special causes present for the modules that are totally separated from the main distributions. Partitions can be defined to identify the different types of product or process.

Corrective factors can then be applied to the modules in the different partitions so that, all other factors being equal, modules that should belong to the higher or lower distribution will appear in the main distribution.

Applying correction functions may be appropriate when attempting an overall analysis, but more usually if only a small number of functions fall

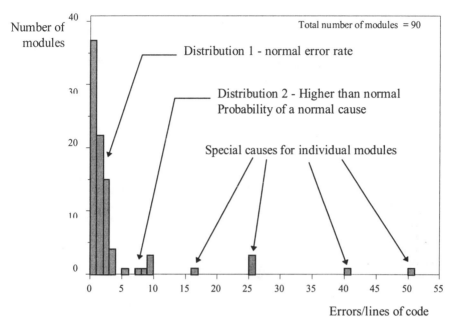

Fig. 3.3 Complexity distributions.

outside of the main distribution because of some known contributory factor. In the majority of cases the causes of the multiple distribution are unknown. It is probably not beneficial to attempt to apply corrections because of the difficulty in establishing clear boundaries between the different types of product, processes or causes. For instance the complexity of all modules involving a particular software function will not necessarily be the same. It is best then to treat all modules as if they came from the same distribution. If a special case arises while establishing reasons for the out-of-control situation, any known contributory factors such as the type of the module should be examined first.

■ 3.3.2 Accuracy and resolution

Measurement systems must be designed to provide the accuracy and resolution required for the data to be useful and not misleading. The resolution required of a measuring system must be three times greater than the standard deviation of the distribution of the data if any useful information is to be gathered about the variance of the metric. Hence, Fig. 3.4

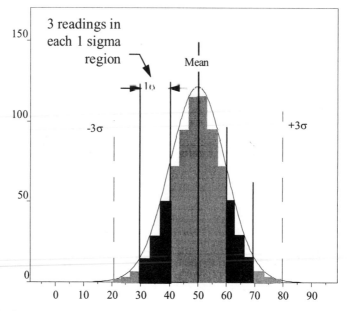

Fig. 3.4 Distribution showing the minimum resolution required.

shows that the resolution required is 18 times the $\pm 3\sigma$ values (where σ = standard deviation) and this will ensure that:

(1) The measurement error is insignificant compared to the main distribution.
(2) If there is a frequency component to the variability of the metric sufficient resolution is available to detect the full range of values without aliasing.

The accuracy required on this value is at least the same as, if not better than, the resolution since this determines the error distribution if the individual measurements were repeated. If the measurement is taken only once then the reading could be anywhere within the accuracy band, which must be at least as small as the resolution band. Fig. 3.5 shows the effect of accuracy and resolution on the overall distribution.

Accuracy and resolution are best explained by example. Accuracy of a measuring system is its ability to consistently read a value that is close to the true value. If the value of cyclometric complexity is actually 8, but the automated tool consistently produces a value of 6, then the measuring system is inaccurate. Equally the process may be inaccurate. For instance, if the target value for the number of lines of code per module is 150 and the measured mean is consistently 120, then the process is considered inaccurate. Another example of process inaccuracy is the time for the estimating process. If the target time for a particular project type is estimated as 3 months, but the measured elapsed time is consistently 4 months the estimating process is considered inaccurate.

The resolution is the measure of how many discrete values can be discerned within the range of variance observed. For the project time scale example, if project times are measured to the nearest week and the distribution has a spread of 1 month then the measurement system is of inadequate resolution. An adequate design for a measurement system that will measure a process that is expected to have results covering a range of one month requires a resolution of at least 1/18 of a month or 20/18 days = 1.11 days (assuming 20 working days in a month). The accuracy of measurement must be greater than this to ensure that the measurement is within the same distribution. Fig. 3.6 shows the separate effects of high and low accuracy and resolution on the distribution of a measurement.

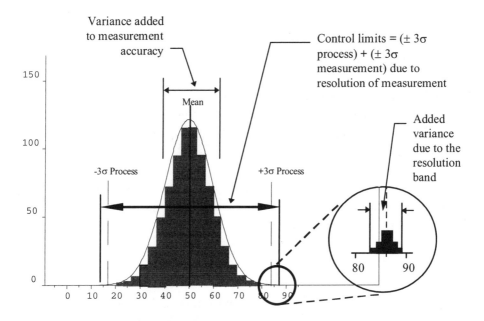

Fig. 3.5 Distributions showing the effect of accuracy for a single measurement repeated several times.

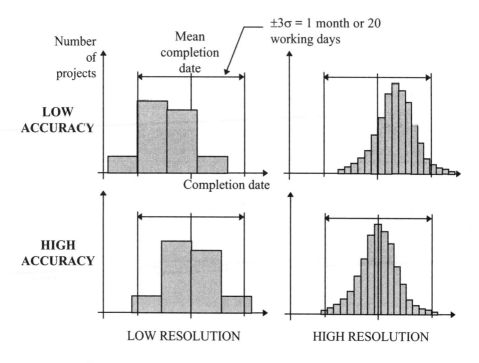

Fig 3.6 Distribution for accuracy and resolution in time measurement.

The rules then for defining the accuracy and resolution of measurement of a variable are:

(1) The accuracy should be at least equal to the resolution of measurement and 3 times better if possible.

(2) The resolution should be at least 18 times greater than the spread of results expected.

To achieve this it is necessary to know what the spread of results are likely to be in order to establish an appropriate measurement system. A few examples are provided in Table 3.3.

■ 3.3.3 Collection methods and tools

The method of collecting data depends on the metric. The tools and methods were discussed in Chapter 2, but whichever method is chosen it must be compatible with displaying the data on a statistical chart. For most purposes this can mean collecting the data and importing it into a spreadsheet or a

Table 3.3 Metrics, their range, accuracy and resolution

Metric	Units	Range	Resolution	Accuracy
Confidence	%	0–100	1	0.1
Completeness	%	0–120	1	0.1
Size	LOC	5–300	1	1
Effort	hours	100–100,000	1	0.1
Time	days	1–100	0.2	0.02

database product. However whichever data collection method is used it is important that the users understand the charts since they can provide information to support project and management decisions. It is often useful to allow the people collecting the data to manually generate the charts so that they can learn why the data is collected and analysed in the way that it is. We will see in Chapters 5, 6 and 7 the details of how to generate and analyse SPC charts.

The type of chart used is dependent on whether the data being collected is a variable or an attribute. Where the information is coming from an automated source such as a test tool, the program should be able to calculate the SPC limits, the mean value and provide the mechanisms for sub-grouping the data.

The volume of data that could be collected during each of these activities in any medium-sized project makes collection time a critical element of the project timescale. Analysis time for this data can become even less possible. If there is no time available to analyse the data within the project time frame then the collection activity becomes redundant and any process improvement is lost.

▓ 3.4 Measurement and Sampling

There are two main reasons for sampling the data. The first of these is that a distribution, however far from a 'normal' binomial distribution, will appear closer to that ideal if the information is grouped and the means of the groups are plotted. The second reason is that, with test and development tools, it is possible to gather vast quantities of numbers in a metrication programme. It is much more difficult to make any sense of this data, and so sampling is a way of gathering and presenting information to support decisions for process improvement.

▩ 3.4.1 Sampling for distribution normalisation

The usual method of normalising the distribution is to use the central limits theorem which states that:

> The distribution of the means of samples of data from a single distribution will produce a new distribution centred about the mean of the original and with a spread related to that of the source.

This theorem allowed all the early users of SPC to conclude that the chart based on sampled data could have lines drawn at three standard deviations from the mean. The probability of an event outside these limits would then be given by standard tables for normal distributions.

In most applications we are unable to represent the full distribution in any way, far less understand what a 'normal' state of the distribution should be. The relationship between sampled data and the individual distribution cannot be determined. However, most small samples of data from processes, such as software development, provide a distribution that is normal within the limits of accuracy and resolution of measurement. It is also normal within the knowledge of what a full population should look like. This means that grouping data can provide a means of determining whether one group is similar in its attributes to another. From a control viewpoint this is all that is required of the data.

▩ 3.4.2 Sampling for data reduction

To reduce the volumes and make data useable for management and control purposes, the collection process must be based on sound statistical design. This should go without saying, but many projects are initiated either based on a specification that has not been measured, or the measurement process is based on unsound principles.

Many project failures are put down to incorrect or incomplete specifications. However, it is not this that is the cause, but the failure to identify and put in place project activities that will correct or complete the specification. This action must be down to the managers of the project, and this is the reason that measurement at this early stage is so critical to the success of a project.

The measurement process at any stage of a project provides information that managers, software engineers and all involved in taking even the smallest decision in the project are going to rely on. The basis of the measurement must consequently be correct. A document that is 1000 pages long or a program that has millions of permutations of operation can never be fully inspected and measured unless the time available is limitless. So methods of sampling have been developed that reduce the data collection effort while still providing a view of the product and the process that enables management decisions on quality to be taken with confidence.

The probability of a statistical sample being an accurate reflection of the whole of a product is dependent on the relationships between the product and the process that produced it. A random selection taken from a product and assessed or measured can only successfully be extrapolated to the whole if the distribution follows a known and understood set of rules. In most software development activities the rules are not understood or known, primarily because the project has no controls that ensure any form of distribution of the particular metric being considered.

An instance of this is observed by analysing the contributory factors to the errors introduced when developing a specification. The factors may include the experience and knowledge of the producer, the knowledge and experience of the information supplier, and the actual production process such as ideas management and organisation, typing skills, document production tools, language skills, etc.

If these contributing factors are all controlled in some way then the distribution of any metric will be single and continuous and can be used to control the process. If the distribution for introducing errors can be identified then the average rate can be calculated and, for any particular product the error volume can be estimated. This knowledge can then be used to decide when the product is complete since the number of errors can be estimated, sought out and removed before agreeing to release of the product. (Note that each subsequent process will have its own error rate and consequently a release must be based on the information from all previous processes.) Because most software development processes do not have a single distribution, control is a matter of deciding when the distribution has changed for the worse.

Fig. 3.7 is an example of the error distribution found in software that clearly shows that it is neither a 'normal' nor a single distribution. The process that generated this distribution clearly was not 'controlled'. The variation includes what are termed 'special causes' which have the effect of making the distribution other than normal and may produce multiple

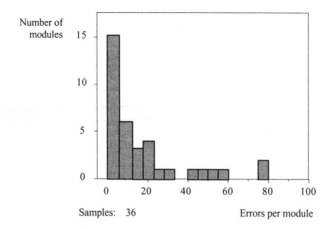

Fig. 3.7 Distribution of errors found in software code.

distributions. However, the main distribution, in the range 0–35, can be used to control the process if the particular types of module can be identified and the higher level distributions eliminated from the control process.

Most software development activities will not produce just one distribution. For instance there are many reasons why complexity should be in one of two or three distributions centred at different values. These reasons may be language and its use, function, optimisation, experience of developer, or functional standardisation of coding. Each of these factors may cause a particular module to fall in one or another of the distributions, but it is not only these causes that have that effect. There may be other influences and consequently a distribution resulting from a measurement can only be analysed in this way if the expected type of distribution is known. This factor has seriously limited the ability of companies to use metric information to control processes – the distributions always look different and rarely provide a correlation that is useful.

■ 3.5 Sampled Distributions

The distribution of the population for many of the metrics may never be known – how many software errors make a population! In these cases and even for measurements where an expected population size can be estimated, the problems of the distribution can be overcome by sampling and grouping the data. For a variable such as complexity the data is gathered at the time

VARIABLE:	Complexity		Chart Started:	10/2/93	Initials:		AB

Ref:	1	2	3	4	5	6	
1	24	18					
2	128	76					
3	37	56					
4	5	26					
5	14	42					
ΣX	208	218					
X	42.6	44.4					
R	123	58					

Fig 3.8 Recording sample data.

of testing (the measure is taken from a testing tool) and recorded as shown in Fig. 3.8.

The characteristics of the distribution for this data, shown in Fig. 3.9, are the mean values for the individual samples $\overline{X}$ and the standard deviation, SE. They are calculated as follows:

$$\text{Sample mean } \overline{X} = \frac{\sum x}{n}$$

$$\text{Grand mean } \overline{\overline{X}} = \frac{\sum \overline{X}}{\text{Number of samples}}$$

and for a population distribution the standard deviation is given as:

$$\text{Standard deviation }(\sigma)\text{ of distribution} = \sqrt{\frac{\left(X - \overline{X}\right)^2}{n}}$$

For any continuous distribution of a whole population the sub-grouped data has a relationship with the whole population that can be calculated using the mean value and the standard deviation. This can be demonstrated using a distribution for a typical software metric shown in Fig. 3.9 – the errors found in the releases of software. This is a distribution of all the individual readings taken.

The data is divided into subgroups of 5 as it is collected and the means of each group are used to create the distribution. Fig. 3.10 shows the resulting plot.

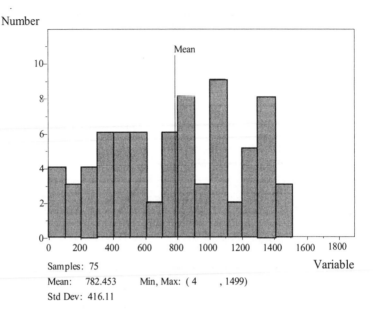

Fig 3.9 Distribution of a metric.

The standard deviation or standard error as it is frequently known, for this sampled distribution is:

$$SE = \sqrt{\frac{\left(\overline{X} - \overline{\overline{X}}\right)^2}{n-1}}$$

and the 3 sigma limits are: ±3 SE.

The standard deviation of the population can be estimated from the range of the sub-group data using standard tables for the constants (see Appendix B) and the formula:

$$\hat{\sigma} = \frac{\overline{R}}{d_2}$$

where $\overline{R}$ is the mean range for all the sub-groups and d_2 is a constant from the statistical tables.

From the sample plot the distribution appears to be closer to a 'normal' distribution and has its mean centred on that of the population mean. This is true for almost any population distribution that is continuous and consequently allows us to use the sampled data distribution as the reference

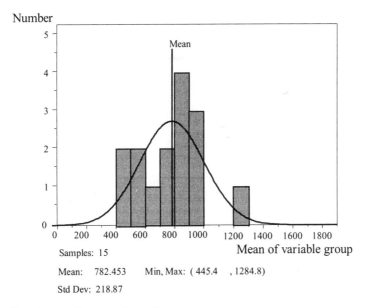

Fig 3.10 Distribution of means of samples.

for future comparisons. It provides the 'normal' distribution that all future samples will be expected to fall within and any that do not can be treated as being influenced by some external cause and investigated.

▨ 3.6 Project Management Examples

Measurements used in software projects are shown in Table 3.3 and some examples of these show how the importance of the sampled calculation is to the measurement of the development process. The examples also show the effects of information from different distributions being combined into one and how these might be split to provide a controlled process.

▨ 3.6.1 Process confidence and risk

Projects are managed by assessing the individual factors that influence the project for whether they might increase either cost, time or functional risk. Confidence, on the other hand, is the analysis of the understanding that each of individual involved in the project has. It is the analysis of risk of failure to understand one of the issues that affects the project. This risk of not understanding the implications of a technical, management or cost

Table 3.4 Risk and confidence factors.

Process risk factors	Process confidence factors
Development time	Customer/supplier relationship
Development method risks	History of success of project team
Skills risks	History of tools in use
Equipment risks	Stability and maturity of process
Specification stability risks	

decision can put the whole project back by reducing the level of confidence that an individual may have in the project. It is interesting to note that it is this confidence (coupled with knowledge), rather than an actual risk assessment, that is used by many people to decide whether to sell or buy on the stock exchange.

Measurement of project risk and confidence is carried out by analysis of the factors associated with the project as shown in Table 3.4.

The distributions of data collected from these types of risk measurements are shown in Fig. 3.11. The risk and confidence factors are recalculated at every stage through the process from information gathered at review meetings. The aim is to establish the growth of these factors through the project. The resolution and accuracy achieved for these factors is largely dependent on the skill of the assessor and so it is important to keep people with these skill levels throughout the project. If the variations seen in the range and mean change the shape of the distribution on every occasion then the measurement process can be suspected. If however the mean and range remain within the population estimated values, then the actual values can be relied on to inform of project progress.

▓ 3.6.2 Product confidence and risk

Product confidence and risk associate totally with the technical, timeliness and cost aspects of the product rather than the project. The analysis of risk

Table 3.5 Product risk and confidence factors

Product risk factors	Product confidence factors
Time to market (too late/too early)	Customer specification understanding
Specification risks	Developer specification understanding
System failure risks	Tester specification understanding

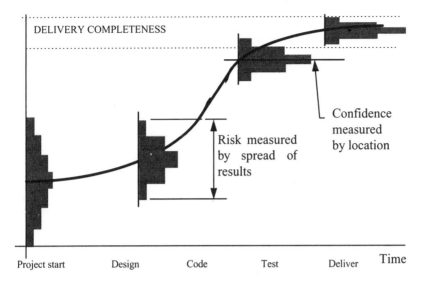

Fig 3.11 The risk and confidence distributions.

in technical terms is the probability of failure of the project due to the technical decisions being made. The project confidence is determined by the relationship in understanding between the members of the project team including the customer and is provided by assessing the factors shown in Table 3.5.

The factors provide distributions that once again should remain uniform in size and shape from each reading. Special causes such as a change in the project or the failure of the measurement system can be suspected if the measurements cause radical changes to the distribution shape.

■ 3.7 Product Quality Examples

■ 3.7.1 Document quality

The first stages of a project involve the generation of many documents including specifications for the product and the tests, project and quality plans, and resource reports. To measure these documents a method known as Fagan inspection (53) has been in use for many years. However this method of gathering statistics about documents relies heavily on the defective areas being in the parts of the document that are inspected. The process of measurement uses time and volume as control variables in order to ensure that the inspection process finds as many of the defects as possible. The measurement of document quality has three main elements:

(1) usability
(2) accuracy
(3) understandability.

These are usually measured using comparative methods such as readability metrics and language analysis. Examples are:

(1) word usage counts
(2) sentence length averages
(3) readability
(4) Flesch reading ease, which is calculated from average number of word syllables and average sentence length.

There are a number of other grading methods usually expressed as a school grade level for ease of reading. They may also be measured by comparison with other specifications, previous documents, standards and related documents.

The main techniques for analysing documents were established in the software industry by Fagan, but have been in use in the publishing business for many generations. The principles of Fagan inspections are covered in more detail in Chapter 11. The technique relies on the time taken for the check being relatively short compared with the time taken for a complete document check, but relatively long for the time normally taken to check individual pages. An example illustrates the point. For a check based on a complete 320 page document the time taken may be 16 hours. This relates to a check rate of 1 page every 5 minutes. A Fagan inspection would recommend checking only 8 pages and taking 4 hours to complete this, giving a full 30 minutes to every page.

Fagan inspections, even as modified over recent years to be more statistically valid, do not recommend a sampling method for analysing the document, or a method of control of the document generation process. As we have already seen, the error distribution in a document probably does not follow a normal distribution. Consequently the analysis recommended by Fagan is not statistically valid since, in most cases, it overestimates the numbers of errors by orders of magnitude. However it is useful to do this since it causes a continued search for new errors.

There are two factors sought during a document inspection:

(1) the background error rate for the whole document
(2) the exceptions to this error rate.

The statistical method requires a model of the document in terms of the criticality of its contents and a generation method that will guarantee consistency.

█ 3.7.2 Software quality

The measurement of software quality is based on both conformance of the development process and tests of the software at each stage of its development. The stages included are prototype, module, system and finally customer acceptance. The measurement process is either a review of the product or process, a formal audit, or a test activity. Each of these activities provides an input into the qualitative measurement of the software product.

The relationship between process control and product quality is often not appreciated and consequently is not considered when designing a metrication process. However there is clear evidence that if the design and development processes are controlled using statistical methods then the product resulting will be likely to meet the functional requirements at the cost and within the timescales expected.

Evidence of this is shown by looking at the correlation between the software process metrics and the product metrics of defectiveness, timeliness, and cost. Fig. 3.12 shows that the higher the variation for the development process, the higher the end defectiveness of the product, the cost and the variance of delivery.

This example is extrapolated from several sets of metrics observed in different organisations. It provides representative shapes of curves, not actual data, but given that this correlation exists, then the optimum operating positions can be selected for the different process variables. If optimum levels are chosen then a method of maintaining control of the process is required and a measure of product quality on exit from the development process will show how well the control mechanism has worked.

█ 3.8 Company Management through Project Statistics

Each of the above metrics can be used to provide an indicator of success of a project for senior management. However to successfully run a company the managers do not require the detail of every metric for every module

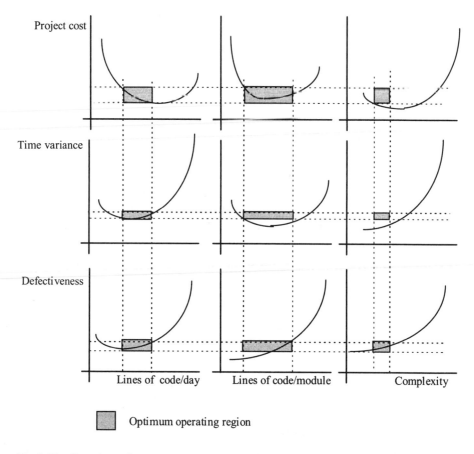

Fig 3.12 Correlation between process variance (complexity, length of code, lines per day) and the product measures (defectiveness, time variance, cost).

and every developer. Most of the individual metrics are used by the individuals involved in the activity to improve their own processes. By appropriately combining metrics, a picture of the capability of the company can be developed that is used by management for a number for different purposes such as:

(1) motivation
(2) project control
(3) commercial competitiveness
(4) preventative control actions
(5) training management.

However, it is important that these still take a statistical view of the processes and products, reacting only to out-of-control situations. The techniques for displaying and using these metrics will be detailed in Chapter 7.

An issue that arises when carrying out analysis for management is how to compare the different projects, products and processes. In order to show how a process is being affected the techniques that can be used include:

(1) normalisation
(2) partitioning
(3) variance measurement.

These are techniques that enable managers to make sense of the differences between the metrics allowing like with like to be combined and compared. The company then has information that can be used for understanding and improving its processes.

▓ 3.8.1 Normalisation of metrics

The results from the measurement of product complexity provide an example of normalisation. The process for each development is essentially the same for a particular set of modules and so the time taken to produce the code is normalised against the length and complexity of the code. The normalised value for any one module is given by:

$$\text{Normalised module development time (MDT)} = \frac{\text{MDT} \times \text{length} \times \text{complexity}}{\text{mean time} \times \text{mean length} \times \text{mean complexity}}$$

This time is plotted on the control chart for the process in order to establish whether it is in any way exceptional (see Chapter 5).

▓ 3.8.2 Partitioning

Whenever a relationship is sought between products and the development activities, the data correlated should only relate to products and processes of the same type. Take the development of modules for example. If the metrics for the activity are controlled such as:

- the length of code is controlled to a target value
- the development team is the same size and experience level
- the same tools are being used
- the code type is the same (mathematical, control, data movement, etc.),

then the module can be expected to be in the same distribution for time and cost, i.e. the module is in the same partition.

When establishing a metrication program the number of partitions expected may be a few tens. Pareto analysis, the principle of ranking occurences or costs, is used to identify the partitions and only those with a significant number of entries are considered worthy of treating this way. Any identified partitions that have too few entries are either to be treated as specials (with the consequent difficulty in finding a way to control them) or they are normalised to fall within the bounds of the nearest compatible partition.

Any partition generated should be expected to produce enough data to generate a control chart. The rules for this are that the time scale is chosen to be close to the rate that the event occurs at and there should be at least five entries for each time scale. For instance a module is generated every 7 working days by one group, so the time scale can be selected as 35 working days. If there are other compatible partitions then the time scale may be reduced. If however the group produces only one module every 3 months then the chart loses its significance and the partition should be subsumed into one of the others using a normalisation technique.

Examples of partitions are usually found in projects where there are obvious differences. For instance, an organisation with an experienced team producing complex real time code and a second team providing the equally essential user interface code would generate two partitions. In an example of graphical modelling of chemical processes the partitions in the metrics were from the different teams on the project:

- those devising the chemical algorithms,
- the team developing specialised and optimised code,
- the developers of the network functions,
- the team developing databases and the data manipulation functions,
- the developers of the user interface who produced the graphical user interface (GUI).

The metrics for these teams could not be expected to be the same since the effort is being used in different ways. The highly experienced chemical analysis teams are not trained software engineers, but are essential to the success of the project. The network and data manipulation engineers could not be expected to be experienced at producing efficient and effective user interfaces. This team requires cognitive skills, and they could not be expected to produce efficient and effective database solutions.

This broad method of partitioning can be further developed by looking at the distributions of the metrics for code. The first step is to take the obvious partitions such as the activities of the teams. The next step is to consider experience and ability, and the third is to consider process maturity. An undefined process with no pre-defined goals is unlikely to produce consistent metrics for the code. A process which is clearly defined and with clear goals for the metrics of the process may not produce better results but is likely to be consistent. The effect of inconsistency has thus been removed and it is then possible to concentrate on effectiveness.

▦ 3.8.3 Variance measurement

The normalisation and partitioning techniques provide data from the metrics that can be compare within disciplines and partitions. The principle is always to compare like with like. However one common attribute of all processes is the variation that occurs for each of the measured parameters. An example might be the difference between the largest and the smallest modules of a particular type or the difference in the time scales taken to create similar types of module.

There are two ways of considering this variance. The first is the formal definition taken from the distribution of the metric which has a standard deviation σ. (See section 4.5.2.)

Variance is calculated as σ^2, which for most purposes can only be calculated from an estimate of the standard deviation. This method is used to compare single variables of a comparable type, i.e. those within the same partition.

The second way is to calculate the differences from the mean of the values and use this difference as a measure of the degree of variation occurring. For every measurement taken the value can be converted to a percentage of the mean value for the process and so the variation across partitions can be compared. This enables project teams to be compared and, since reducing variance is the feature that provides increased effectiveness, can be used as the basis for the process improvement project.

An example of this is the lines of code per module example. Taking the historical data for three partitions given in Table 3.6, the next three readings are: 94, 182, 126.

The three readings represent differences of +14, −23 and −17, but when they are considered as percentages of the mean they represent +17.5%, −11.2% and 11.9%. On a control chart for all processes the maths function result might cause concern, whereas the other two may be within normal statistical operating limits.

Table 3.6 Lines of code per module example.

Partition	Mean
Maths functions	80
File management	205
GUI	143

■ 3.9 Summary

- There are two types of measures; variables which are continuous and attributes which are counts of the exceptional presence of an item.
- To manage the volume of data if all software metrics are collected, a method of statistical sampling is used so that the company does not become overwhelmed by data rather than being provided with information.
- The relationship between the population of a metric and the sampled and sub-grouped data is not significant to the control of the process. Sub-grouped data is used to control the process in order to rapidly detect changes in the process.
- The risk of a process or a project can be measured and related to the controllable external and internal factors.
- Confidence is a measure of the understanding between different people within the project and is consequently a process risk factor. It does not specifically relate to the technical, cost or time scale risks since it is psychological.
- Measurement of both documentation and the software products as project outputs provides real time control metrics for the development process. Data collection may be automated or manual, and will probably be a mixture of both.
- The data is combined to provide company capability using normalisation, partitions and variance measurement.

Collecting information from a software process can be a rewarding exercise and can provide quite unexpected results. The interest in a particular measure can in itself change the state of control and consequently assist the metricator in the task of analysing the information for trends, differences or major influential causes. However in order to observe these changes tools are required to display the information in real time enabling preventative and process improvement steps to be taken.

Table 3.7 Results from manual inspection.

Method	Count	Average number	Number of lines	Estimate of actual number	Time taken (min)
Every line	187	3.978	47	187	15
Every 5th line	43	4.3	10	202	3
Every 10th line	17	3.4	5	160	1

▒ 3.10 The Manual Detection Exercise

In the section 'Effectiveness of attribute detection' (section 3.2.2),, ignoring the headings, there are 187 occurrences of the letter 's' in the 47 lines of text. Usually a group of people asked to inspect this page for the letter 's' over a 5 minute period will provide a result that will give a reasonable distribution with a mean of around 175–180 and a range of about 10. There will be a few that will get more than 187!

If you have enough people (groups of 20–30 for each test provides good results), divide them into three groups and ask the first to count every occurrence of the letter 's'. Request that the second group count the occurrences on every fifth line (ignoring the headings, e.g. lines 1, 6, 11 etc.) and the third group to count the occurrences on every tenth line (e.g.1, 11, 21). The results should be as given in Table 3.7.

For the same section there are 34 'es' combinations. For this test the same groups will get a wider range of results as the occurrence of an 'es' combination is more difficult to detect.

A further test can be completed to detect the letter 's' only when it has two or more letters before and after it (excluding spaces and carriage return characters). For this combination there are 64 occurrences and the result can be expected to be much wider and with a mean of only about 54–58.

Try this with your own group using your own example. For variation try it at the start and at the end of day, also with the most skilled engineers and the least, the oldest and the youngest. You can also try it under extreme pressure (you have two minutes and if you don't get it right you are fired!), and in a free and friendly atmosphere (take all the time you want), and observe the differences. The results can surprise you, but if you understand variation in processes you can see the effect of the inputs to the process on the outcome. You can also see that manual inspection is rarely 100% effective and effort is required to maximise its effectiveness.

Another note worth considering is that the sample provides a good estimate of the whole. However this does rely on the fact that for each sample at least one observation is expected. The sample rate is determined from a calculation that will ensure at least one observation in each sample from 97% of the samples.

Part II
Statistical Techniques

Part II provides the main statistical tools for recording, plotting and the analysis of metrics. Chapter 4, describes the tools for **data collection** and general statistical analysis with the theory of why this form of statistical measurement is valid for the metrics of software.

Chapters 5 and 6 deal with the charting process for **variables and attributes** and Chapter 7 provides some of the **specialised statistical techniques** with indications of where they are appropriate and how to choose the method appropriate to a task.

Chapter 8 provides the tools for using the information gathered to gain the benefits from the process, that is **process improvement** achieved through the increased maturity that knowledge of the process brings. Finally, Chapter 9 shows how to use **assessments and maturity measurement** to close the long term process control loop.

4 Collecting and Analysing Data

4.1 Introduction

In Chapter 3 we considered the difference between variables and attributes, especially in the context of software development. We also discussed distributions which corresponded to certain software parameters, and the point was made that if processes are not under statistical control, then it is not possible to correlate metrics which may be available.

Both these topics will be expanded further in this Chapter, together with a study of other basic statistical ideas which are necessary to develop specific control charts which will be covered in Chapters 5, 6 and 7.

Data collection is covered in section 4.2, and this leads on naturally to measures which specify the location and variation of a set of readings. A very important measure is the standard deviation, used extensively in classical statistics and equally important in process analysis. However, the way in which it is calculated is critical, as is an understanding of the relevance of the standard deviation to a control chart.

Having set up a chart for a process, it is then used to check that the process is under statistical control. Four rules are available for this analysis, and familiarity with these rules is essential if a control chart is to be interpreted correctly. Detail of these rules is provided in section 4.6 and this provides a good basis for the detail of specific control charts for variables and attributes which appears in subsequent Chapters.

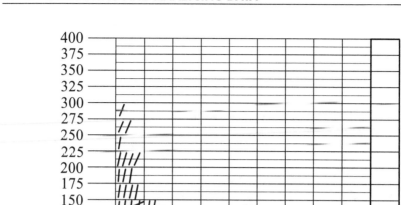

Fig. 4.1 Data sheet for number of lines of code.

▨ 4.2 Data Collection for Variables

Fig. 4.1 shows a typical check sheet for collecting variable data. The data refers to lines of code recorded for a typical software development from the source code of a C program.

The figures on the left-hand side of the diagram represent the size of the individual modules.

Fig. 4.1 shows the advantage of building up tally marks. A better, more visual representation of the process is made available which provides a lot more information than would be obtained from a stark tabular layout of all 50 readings, as shown in Table 4.1.

Table 4.1 Number of lines of code.

51	129	121	115	68	119	62	210	169	180
125	258	269	117	96	83	87	99	116	92
218	72	126	63	139	194	57	168	135	176
101	83	122	226	220	79	93	85	82	108
76	74	150	146	279	59	111	148	172	203

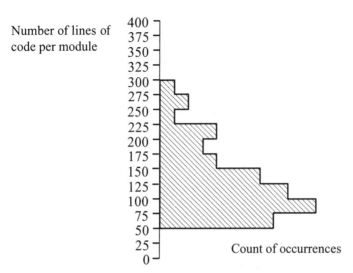

Fig. 4.2 Histogram for number of lines of code.

By drawing a series of rectangles whose heights correspond to the number of readings in a given interval, the tally marks shown in Fig. 4.1 can be used to produce the familiar histogram shown in Fig. 4.2

Typically the number of class intervals is about 10 – 12 in practice. Too many or too few class intervals provide histograms which are respectively too complex or lacking in detail. For guidance, we have already seen in Chapter 3 that measurement theory predicts the lowest resolution for the width of a class interval.

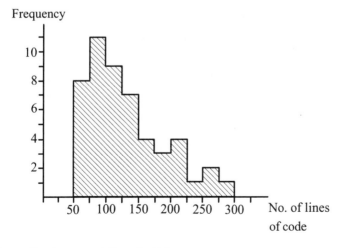

Fig. 4.3 Conventional representation of a histogram.

There are other tips for choosing class intervals, but it is better not to dwell too much on the detail of setting up histograms because they are not particularly useful, as we shall see.

Histograms may be familiar to you, but the layout of the one shown in Fig. 4.2 may seem unusual. Most histograms tend to be drawn with the measurement axis horizontal and frequency plotted vertically, as in Fig. 4.3.

From now on we shall draw a histogram with the measured scale vertical, as in Fig. 4.2.

To see why, we need to interpret our sample of 50 readings represented in the data block shown in Table 4.1 as readings taken at sequential times, recording horizontally from row to row. Suppose we interchanged any two readings. Doing so has no effect on the histogram. The final histogram is independent of the order in which the readings were taken as any variation over time is not picked up. However, if we plot the readings over time, as shown in Fig. 4.4, which is based on the 10 readings in the first row, then it is clear that changing the order of the readings changes the pattern.

Since variation over time is common to all our processes, then we must use the horizontal axis to represent time, and if a histogram is to be drawn then it appears with the measured scale vertical.

Histograms are of some value, mainly in crudely assessing the capability of a process, i.e. the ability of a process to satisfy customer requirements. In software development they are used particularly to characterise objects into classes, as shown by the lines of code example in Fig. 4.5.

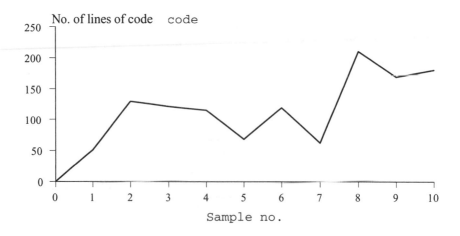

Fig. 4.4 Run chart for number of lines of code.

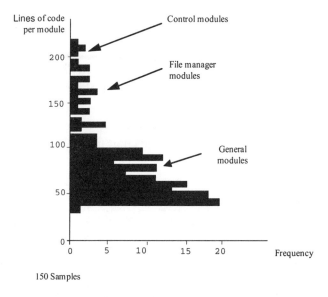

Fig. 4.5 Lines of code per module for one software development company.

Fig. 4.6 shows the inability of a histogram to detect time-based sequences. Many different patterns of performance over time can result in the same final histogram. In other words, if only the histogram is known, we cannot tell which pattern over time the process has actually followed.

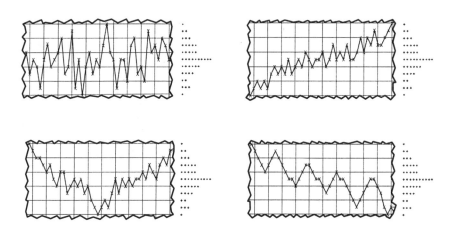

Fig. 4.6 Limitation of a histogram.

■ 4.3 Data Collection for Attributes

Because attributes are defined on an acceptable/non-acceptable basis, the data collection sheet is different to that shown in Fig. 4.1. As for variables, time is to be plotted horizontally and a typical data collection format for attributes is shown in Fig. 4.7.

In this case the data refers to software defects. Six main categories of defect are recorded. Fig. 4.8 shows a run chart for the total number of defects.

CHARACTERISTIC	NO. OF ERRORS														
Typing	1		3		1		1	1	1	1	2		1		1
Spelling	3	2		1	2	7	1	2		3	6		1	4	3
Grammar	3				2		2		1		3		2	2	1
Function		5	2	1		2	2	4		1	2	1		3	2
User			1			1		1		1			1		1
Consistency	2			1			1	2			1		2		
TOTAL	9	7	6	3	5	10	7	10	2	6	14	1	7	9	8

Fig. 4.7 Section from data collection sheet for software defects.

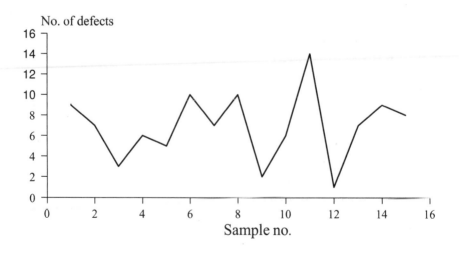

Fig. 4.8 Run chart for number of defects.

CHARACTERISTIC											f	%	RANKING
Typing	1		3		1		2		3	1	19	13	*4*
Spelling	3	2		1	2	7	4	3	1		46	33	*1*
Grammar	3				2			1		1	20	14	*3*
Function		5	2	1		2		3	1	2	35	25	*2*
User			1			1		1		1	8	6	*6*
Consistency	2			1					1		13	9	*5*
TOTAL	9	7	6	3	5	10	6	8	6	5	141	100	

Fig. 4.9 Data collection sheet showing totals and priorities.

Instead of plotting the total number, the option is available to plot Fig. 4.7 for each classification of defect. Hence with 6 classifications, 6 run charts could be generated corresponding to each defect type.

In practice we tend to plot the overall level first, then the next level of priority. How is this choice made ?

Fig. 4.9 provides totals for each classification over a given period, usually 20 readings in time sequence. Issues relating to number of samples and sampling frequency are covered in Chapter 3. By ranking the totals it is seen that 'spelling' is the major problem, followed by 'function'. This is an example of the Pareto principle, the process of ranking occurrences and its use in conjunction with a control chart in this way provides a very important tool for process improvement. The resulting chart, which combines the tabular layout in Fig. 4.9 with a control chart, is called a multiple characteristics chart and is discussed in Chapter 6.

▦ 4.4 Measures of Process Location

The lines of code data that was collected, and subsequently analysed in section 4.2, was designed, as seen in Chapter 2, to represent part of the development process.

The mean value for this set is given as:

$$\bar{X} = \frac{\sum X}{n} = 130.62$$

More generally,

$$\overline{X} = \frac{X_1 + X_2 + X_3 + \ \dots \ + X_n}{n}$$

$$= \frac{\sum X}{n}$$

where n is the number of readings in the sample and $\overline{x}$ is known as the sample mean.

This is one of three types of average value. The others are the median (the middle item in the group when ranked in order of magnitude) and the mode (the most frequently occurring value). For our set of 50 readings the median ($\tilde{X}$) is 113 and the mode (**X**) is somewhere in the class 100–125. The median and the mode do have their uses in classical statistics but they are not used within an SPC framework. All control charts to be discussed in this book will only make use of $\overline{x}$.

It will be seen that we calculate $\overline{x}$ in two particular situations.

In generating a central line for a control chart $\overline{x}$ corresponds to the mean of the first 20 values used to set up the chart. All charts will therefore require a calculation similar to that just carried out using n = 20.

Sometimes the values being plotted will themselves be mean values. The ($\overline{x}$, R) chart, described in detail in Chapter 5, requires the calculation

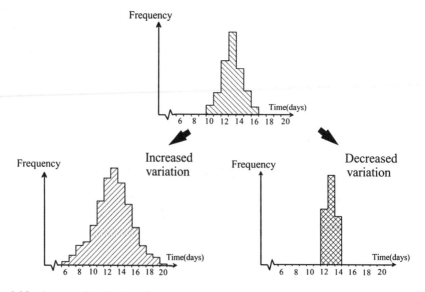

Fig. 4.10 Increased and reduced variation.

of a mean based typically on a sample size 5, and hence it is calculated from the formula:

$$\text{Mean} = \frac{\sum \overline{X}}{5}$$

The mean itself is not sufficient to adequately represent a set of numbers. Fig. 4.10 shows three different distributions, all with the same mean of 13.5 days.

Knowing the mean does not help in deciding whether the process variation has changed. We would prefer to have a process with the narrower variation, as shown, and we therefore need other statistical measures in addition to $\overline{X}$ in order to measure variation.

▨ 4.5 Measures of Process Variation

There are two common measures of variation – the range and the standard deviation.

▨ 4.5.1 The range

By far the simplest measure of variation is the range, defined as the difference between the greatest and the least value in a set.

For example, for the five values, 2, 1, 3, 7, 4, the range, denoted by R, is calculated as $7 - 1 = 6$.

X_1	5	2	-1	1	3	4	-2	3
X_2	1	3	3	4	2	-3	-3	-2
X_3	2	7	2	3	2	2	-1	4
X_4	3	3	-2	5	3	5	-5	-1
X_5	6	4	5	3	4	2	-1	-4
$\sum X$	17	19	7	16	3	10	-12	0
$\overline{X}$	3.4	3.8	1.4	3.2	0.6	2.0	-2.4	0
R	5	5	7	4	2	8	4	8

Fig. 4.11 Data section from ($\overline{X}$, R) chart.

The range is used extensively in variable control charts. It is easy to calculate and a perfectly adequate measure of variation when the sample size is small, typically 5.

Fig. 4.11 shows a section of an ($\overline{x}$, R) chart. $\overline{x}$ and R values are plotted as will be shown in Chapter 6.

The range is also important in another way in that it can be used to determine the standard deviation. This point will be referred to again in Chapter 6.

Even though the range does have the advantage of being easy to calculate, it is limited in that its value does depend only on the extreme items in the set.

Fig. 4.12 shows how the range neglects an increasing number of readings as the sample size increases. For example, in Fig. 4.12(b), all but two of the many readings which are available are not utilised in determining the range. Useful information is being thrown away. There has to be a more accurate method of measuring the variation, and this is given by the standard deviation.

▨ 4.5.2 The standard deviation

The standard deviation makes use of all the numbers in a set and is generally obtained from the expression:

$$S = \sqrt{\frac{\sum(X - \overline{X})^2}{n-1}}$$

(a) Sample

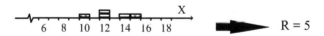

R = 5

(b) Histogram

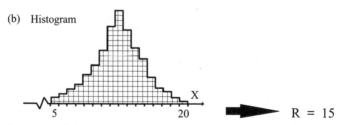

R = 15

Fig. 4.12 Limitation of the range.

We say generally, because there is a lot of uncertainty regarding which formula to use when calculating a standard deviation, and also confusion as to which symbol to use when representing the standard deviation.

For our set of 50 lines of code data, the standard deviation is calculated as 58.71.

Commonly adopted symbols for this standard deviation are s and σ.

The value determined in this way is said to be the best estimate of the standard deviation of the much larger group – the population – from which the sample came. Yet another symbol is sometimes adopted. This symbol relates to the appropriate pocket calculator used and will vary depending on the make of calculator.

Fig. 4.13 shows the statistical keys used in a CASIO *fx*-82LB together with the numerical values for the various statistical symbols. The symbol on the calculator corresponding to the standard deviation formula used so far is σ_{n-1}.

Two other statistical keys are present. σ_n provides the standard deviation of the sample using the formula:

$$\sigma_n = \sqrt{\frac{\Sigma(X - \overline{X})^2}{n}}$$

In terms of SPC this key is not used. This is because we are always more interested in estimating the standard deviation of the parent group rather than calculating the standard deviation of the sample.

ΣX^2 is the sum of the squared readings. This result is sometimes required in a more advanced statistical analysis.

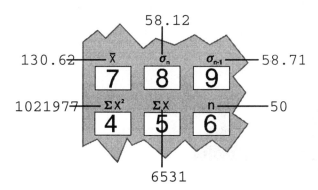

Fig. 4.13 Typical calculator display, together with numerical values.

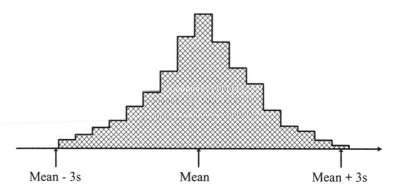

Fig. 4.14 Standard deviation and the histogram.

■ 4.5.3 Interpreting the standard deviation

Having calculated a standard deviation, what does it mean in practice?

Fig. 4.14 shows that for any reasonably symmetrical distribution the majority of the readings fall within the limits $\overline{X} \pm 3s$, i.e. the base width of the histogram is 6s for all practical purposes.

It has been suggested that all histograms should have their bases drawn on a vertical axis. The histogram, and the ±3s lines, drawn in Fig. 4.15 are thus rotated as shown.

The lines corresponding to the ±3s values now become the control lines for the process and are said to represent the natural variation of the process, i.e. the system. These lines, shown as the upper control limit (UCL) and lower control limit (LCL), must not be confused with any customer demands such as those defined in the requirements specification.

These control limits are important in at least three respects.

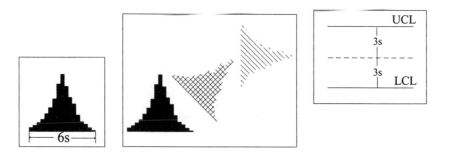

Fig. 4.15 Generation of control limits.

(1) If a process is unstable, then the pattern of points will provide certain signals. These special causes, as they are called, require action and need to be removed if the process is to be made stable.

(2) If a process is stable, i.e. special causes are not present, then the control lines can be drawn ahead to allow for ongoing monitoring of the process.

(3) Having obtained a stable process, improvement is necessary and improvement means narrowing the ±3s band by reducing the variation, as shown in Fig. 4.16.

This will require management action, as opposed to operational action (described as process maturity level 3 in section 9.3.1).

▓ 4.6 Rules for Interpreting Special Causes

Three stages are involved in process improvement.

The first step is to collect data and set up the control chart. The specifics of this will be covered in the following chapters when the different types of control charts will be discussed.

Next, the process is checked for stability, i.e. are there any special causes present? If so, they must be addressed and appropriate action then taken. Rules are available for detecting special causes and they will be considered in this section.

Finally, when the process is under control, it is checked for capability, i.e. can the process satisfy any customer requirements which have been laid down? Capability will be dealt with in Chapters 5 and 6.

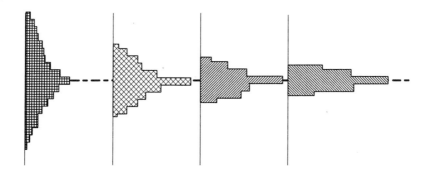

Fig. 4.16 Process improvement.

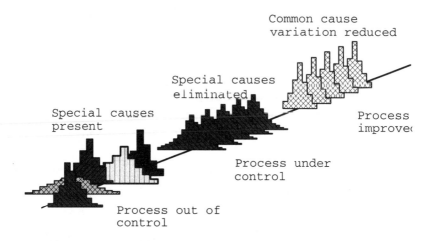

Fig. 4.17 Three stages of process improvement.

The three stages are shown graphically in Fig. 4.17.

For now, we need to consider issues relating to control, not capability. The two are not the same and the distinction is important and must be clearly understood. Control has nothing to do with capability and is entirely concerned with stability and predictability.

Four rules are available to decide on whether or not a process is under statistical control.

Rule 1 Any point outside one of the control limits.

The presence of a point either above the upper control limit or below the lower control limit, as shown in Fig. 4.18, is an indication of a special cause. This rule takes priority over the others and it is worth explaining how the rule was first formulated.

When Shewhart first developed the control chart in the 1920s, he was faced with the problem of whether to react to a point which seemed suspicious or whether to leave the process alone. There is nothing unusual about this. Managers are still facing the same problem. They are typically presented with complex tables of figures and attempt to make a judgment on process performance. Shewhart's first step was to plot the results. It is depressing that some 60 years later we have still not learnt the lesson that more information is to be obtained from a graphical representation of data than from a mass of figures.

In plotting a run chart over time, using typically the first 20 readings as a basis, Shewhart also calculated the mean value and drew in a horizontal line. He then decided to use decision lines to enable appropriate action to

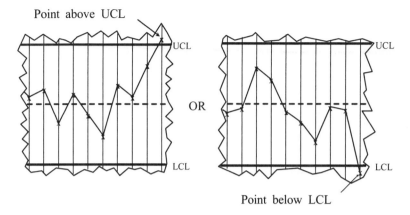

Fig. 4.18 Point outside a control limit.

follow. These lines would be placed at fixed positions out from the central line. Where should they be located? If Shewhart placed them at a distance of ±6σ, for example, then he would at least make sure that there would only be a response to a point when it was almost certain that it represented something unusual. If, on the other hand, the lines were placed very much closer to the central line, for example at ±1σ, then the reverse would be true. There would be a danger of responding to points which were actually part of the common cause variation and not special causes. How could the risks be eliminated? Well, they cannot, but they can be minimised. Shewhart proposed that this can be achieved by setting the decision lines at a distance of ±3σ on either side of the mean. This rule has operated successfully for the last 60 years, is simple to use, and has nothing to do with properties of the normal curve. In fact using the normal distribution, and associated probability levels relating to areas in the tail beyond ±3s, could be misleading. Shewhart argued that until a process was actually measured by taking readings from it, then no assumptions could be made regarding its performance.

A point outside the control limits, therefore, is an indication of a special cause and experience has shown that it is well worthwhile allocating resources to determine the reason for this special cause. Without this knowledge, the process is out of control, is unpredictable, and therefore the control lines cannot be projected ahead to monitor the process.

The other rules for detecting special causes are used to support this first rule.

Seven points above
centre line

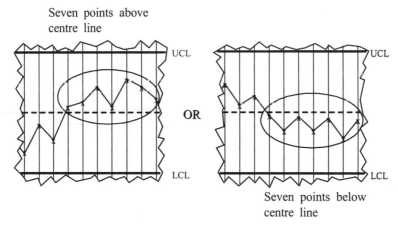

Seven points below
centre line

Fig. 4.19 Run of seven, rule 1.

Rule 2 A run of seven points in succession, either all above the central line or all below the central line, or all increasing or all decreasing as shown in Figs. 4.19 and 4.20.

Some organisations use an alternative based on a run of eight, rather than a run of seven. The principle is the same. A run of seven points in succession can occur by chance 1 in 128 times. Therefore care must be taken in jumping to a conclusion that there is in fact a special cause present when a run of seven occurs.

Rule 3 Any unusual pattern or trend.

Fig. 4.21 shows an ideal process in that a natural random pattern is

Seven points in a
downward direction

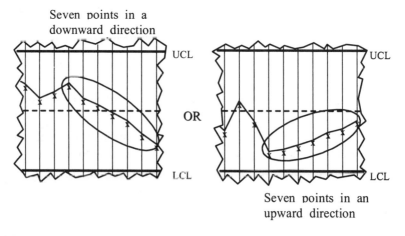

Seven points in an
upward direction

Fig. 4.20 Run of seven, rule 2.

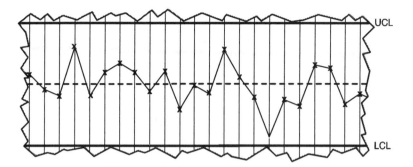

Fig. 4.21 Natural pattern for a process.

present. If such a pattern is to be expected, but does not occur, then a special cause is present. Several unusual patterns can be seen in practice. For example, the process may be cyclic or may drift, as shown in Fig. 4.22. Sales figuress often have a tendency to follow this rule. There are ways of coping with both these situations and Chapter 7 will provide the detail.

Rule 4 The proportion of points in the middle third zone of the distance between the control limits should be about two-thirds of all the points under observation.

This rule is based on properties of the normal curve, which shows that the area under the curve between ±1σ is 68%, i.e. about two thirds. The rule should be applied with some flexibility and can be used in two ways in particular. For example, if very few points are in the middle third zone, as shown in Fig. 4.23, then it could well indicate that the process is a combination of two or more batches. Equally, if all the points are in the middle third zone, then something has happened which has resulted in

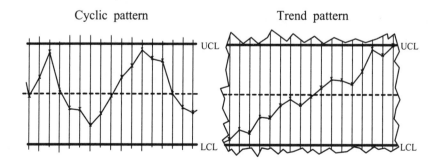

Fig. 4.22 Some unusual patterns.

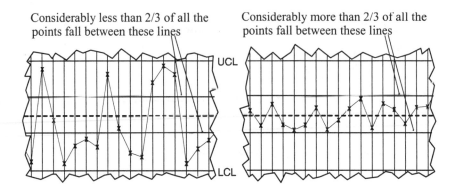

Fig. 4.23 Middle third rule for detecting special causes.

process improvement. This factor should be identified, and providing it is a genuine reason for a reduction in the variation, then it should be made a permanent feature of the process.

■ 4.7 Summary

- A histogram does not detect variation over time and therefore does not provide as much information as a control chart.
- Attribute data collection is closely associated with the Pareto principle.
- All control charts make use of a central line, corresponding to the mean of typically the first 20 readings.
- The range is a simple measure of variation, used in the $(\overline{X}, R)$ chart.
- The standard deviation is the basis of all control charts.
- Reducing the standard deviation is primarily a management responsibility.
- Four rules are available for detecting special causes.

This Chapter has explored the background and the basis of statistical charting for the purposes of controlling processes. The next two Chapters build on this information to help you understand, design, and use appropriate charts in different software development circumstances.

5 Control Charts for Variables

5.1 Introduction

Control charts for variables fall into two categories – those which allow for samples and those which are based on individual readings. A distinction is necessary and this will be brought out in section 5.2.1, which provides guidelines on how to make this choice.

Mainstream approaches to introducing SPC into an organisation have tended to concentrate on charts based on samples. The ($\overline{X}$, R) chart, considered in section 5.3, provides material on how to deal with samples. Whilst this type of chart can be used to great effect, it is inappropriate in those situations where the information is based on single readings. Hence the need for another type of chart – the (X, Moving R) chart – and the material in section 5.4 covers this in some depth. Many interesting and highly relevant applications of SPC using single reading analysis are becoming increasingly available, and some of these will be identified.

Control of a process is not the same as capability, and this needs to be well understood. Detail on capability, and its relevance to software development, appears in section 5.6.

■ 5.2 Chart Types

■ 5.2.1 Samples or individuals?

The choice of the appropriate variable chart depends essentially on the volume of data and the resources which are available to handle it.

For example, Table 5.1 shows a set of typical values of lines of code per module, over a sequence of months, from one particular development team producing approximately 1/2 million lines of code per year. The table is a section from Fig. 4.2, but the approach in dealing with the data is now different to that adopted in Chapter 4. The numbers are easy to handle and, more importantly, sufficiently few in number as to allow for each item to be utilised in generating a control chart.

Table 5.1 Typical lines of code values.

51	129	121	115	68	119	62	210	169	180
125	258	269	117	96	83	87	99	116	92

What happens if the number of items is increased? Suppose we are dealing with large numbers of test cases for modules, e.g. as in the nuclear power industry, so many that it is impractical to handle each one? The only realistic option is to sample at regular intervals, and to use the evidence provided by the sample as an indicator of how the larger group from which the sample came is operating. This is true for the case of reliability testing where a sample has a clear relationship to the whole population of test cases. However, for software development processes, the relationship between the sample and the population will only be true once the process has achieved SEI level 4 (or better), i.e. it is a repeatable and stable process. (See section 1.5.4.)

Fig. 5.1 shows the two approaches and the corresponding control chart to be used.

A decision as to which type of chart to use may also depend on resources. If these are insufficient to handle every item, samples should be utilised and the ($\overline{X}$, R) chart used. If it is possible to assess each item, then the corresponding chart to use is the (X, Moving R) chart. More detail on what is meant by 'Moving R' appears in section 5.4.

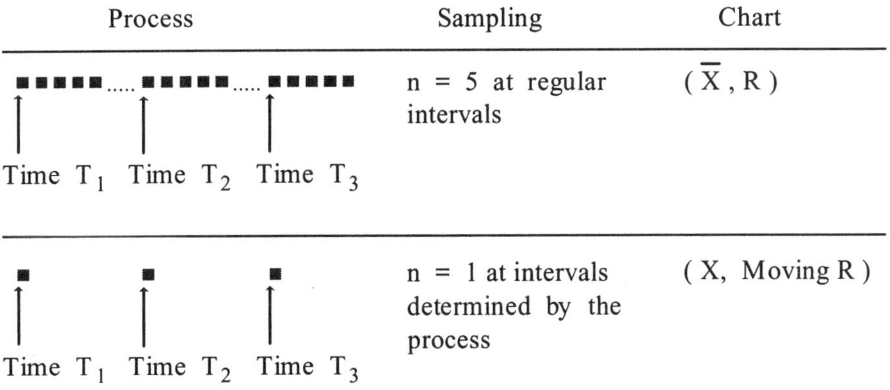

Process	Sampling	Chart
■■■■■ ..... ■■■■■ ..... ■■■■■ ↑　　　　↑　　　　↑ Time T_1　Time T_2　Time T_3	n = 5 at regular intervals	$(\overline{X}, R)$
■　　　　■　　　　■ ↑　　　　↑　　　　↑ Time T_1　Time T_2　Time T_3	n = 1 at intervals determined by the process	$(X, \text{Moving } R)$

Fig. 5.1　Options for variable charting.

■ 5.2.2 Number of samples

Both the $(\overline{X}, R)$ chart and the (X, Moving R) chart, as well as attribute charts, use the first 20 readings from the process to determine the control limits. This is a guideline figure. Experience of a particular process may suggest other figures. Some processes may require a longer time to provide a complete set of 20 readings and hence initial control charts may be set up using fewer samples. If historical data is available, then this can be used to provide the 20 readings necessary for the charts.

For the $(\overline{X}, R)$ chart, the readings are means of 20 successive samples. For the (X, Moving R) chart, the readings are the 20 successive X values.

■ 5.2.3 Frequency of sampling

For the $(\overline{X}, R)$ chart, the generally adopted rule is that sufficient samples should be taken over a long enough period of time to allow for the natural variation of the process. Automatic testing results therefore require a different approach to manual coding figures. Both examples have a common requirement that the process should not be changed whilst these initial 20 samples are being collected. Tampering with the process, as it is called, is a typical reaction based on a lack of understanding of variation coupled with a misguided belief in one's ability to improve a process by tinkering with it. So in software development we should not change the environment, people or software tools whilst collecting metrics for setting up the chart.

■ 5.2.4 Subgroup size

A sample size of 5 is generally used, not least because it is an easy number to handle mathematically. It represents a balance between taking individual readings, where the trend is masked by the natural variation of the process, and taking larger samples, where by so doing we increase the variation within the sample. This means that the range is not a good measure because it is dependent on the extremes in the sample, and to overcome this the range is replace by a chart of standard deviations for each sub-group. This chart is otherwise treated as an ($\overline{X}$, R) chart.

■ 5.2.5 Setting up a control chart

Setting up a control chart requires consideration of other issues. Who is the customer? Who understands the process? Who collects the data, and how? The intention in this chapter is to concentrate specifically on the detail of the chart, but it would be unwise in practice to progress too far on this area if the other related requirements have not been looked at.

Setting up a control chart requires a logical approach summarised in Fig. 5.2.

DEFINE THE PROCESS

COLLECT THE DATA

CALCULATE SAMPLE STATISTICS

CALCULATE CENTRAL LINES AND CONTROL LIMITS

SCALE CHARTS

PLOT RESULTS

DRAW IN LIMITS

INTERPRET CHART FOR CONTROL

REACT TO SPECIAL CAUSES

ASSESS CAPABILITY

IMPROVE THE PROCESS

Fig. 5.2 Sequence for setting up a control chart and using it to improve the process.

This procedure should be followed in all cases and will be referred to in detail for the ($\overline{\text{X}}$, R) chart in section 5.3. In subsequent examples it will be taken as read.

▨ 5.3 The ($\overline{\text{X}}$, R) Chart

▨ 5.3.1 Data collection

Twenty samples of size 5 are taken from the process. If the sample size is not determined directly from the nature of the activity (e.g. as in a 6 man development team) then it is best to use a sample size 5.

The working example uses 20 samples of 5 based on the number of lines of code for a typical software development programme. Five readings are taken systematically from the sequential listings which are available and the results are shown in tabular format in Table 5.2.

These figures are transferred to the appropriate section of a control chart, as shown in Fig. 5.3. In practice, the readings will be recorded directly onto the chart. It is well worthwhile getting into a routine of recording values and completing the relevant information sections of the chart. A sensibly designed control chart should provide these reference boxes.

Table 5.2 Sample data for the number of lines of code.

X_1	8	104	61	139	63	74	93	179	112	174
X_2	81	169	129	94	156	79	147	79	74	63
X_3	117	103	50	273	57	185	45	154	193	172
X_4	156	26	103	76	51	112	168	122	93	87
X_5	135	178	142	276	183	121	152	190	174	262
Sample no.	1	2	3	4	5	6	7	8	9	10

X_1	48	88	184	94	85	121	12	122	58	95
X_2	151	103	128	119	147	112	93	139	228	146
X_3	92	125	186	74	132	126	126	117	61	59
X_4	87	140	32	64	101	123	78	85	79	39
X_5	90	73	113	149	58	110	148	124	122	76
Sample no.	11	12	13	14	15	16	17	18	19	20

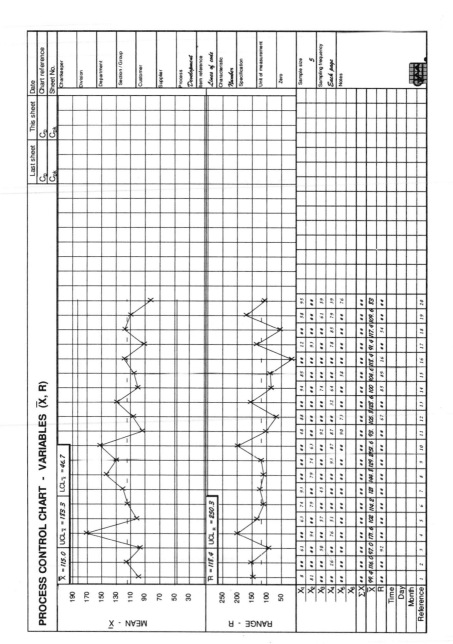

Fig. 5.3 Control chart for number of lines of code with data entered.

■ 5.3.2 Calculation of central lines

The central line for the $\overline{X}$ section of the chart, is obtained from $\overline{\overline{X}} = \dfrac{\sum \overline{X}}{20}$

Similarly, for the range chart, $\overline{R}$ is obtained from $\overline{R} = \dfrac{\sum R}{20}$

Hence for our particular example:

$$\overline{\overline{X}} = \frac{2299.2}{20} = 11.5$$
$$\overline{R} = \frac{2368}{20} = 118.4$$

Lines are to be drawn at these values, spanning the first 20 points only and using the adopted convention of a broken line for each of these central lines. However, before actually drawing these central lines, we need a scale for the vertical axis, and this can only be set up when numerical values for the UCL and LCL are known.

■ 5.3.3 Calculation of control limits

For the ($\overline{X}$, R) chart the upper and lower control limits are located 3 standard deviations out from the central line $\overline{\overline{X}}$.

Hence, $UCL_{\overline{X}} = \overline{\overline{X}} + 3$ standard deviations

The calculation of this control limit has been considerably simplified by making use of predetermined constants, obtained from the reference table in Appendix B. A section of this table appears in Fig. 5.4.

Statisticians have shown us that 3 standard deviations is equivalent to $A_2 \overline{R}$, where A_2 is an index which depends on the sample size. (See Appendix C.)

Reference to the table shows that with a sample size 5, $A_2 = 0.577$.

Therefore, $\qquad UCL_{\overline{X}} = \overline{\overline{X}} + A_2 \overline{R}$

In a similar way, $\qquad LCL_{\overline{X}} = \overline{\overline{X}} - A_2 \overline{R}$

We know that $\overline{\overline{X}} = 115$ and $\overline{R} = 118.4$

Hence $\qquad UCL_{\overline{X}} = \overline{\overline{X}} + 0.577 \times \overline{R}$
$$= 115 + 68.3$$
$$= 183.3$$

Sample Size	A_2	d_2	D_3	D_4
2	1.880	1.128	0	3.267
3	1.023	1.693	0	2.574
4	0.729	2.059	0	2.282
5	0.577	2.326	0	2.114
6	0.483	2.534	0	2.004
7	0.419	2.704	0.076	1.924

Fig. 5.4 Section from table of constants used in obtaining control chart limits.

Also,

$$LCL_{\bar{X}} = \bar{\bar{X}} - 0.577 \times \bar{R}$$
$$= 115 - 68.3$$
$$= 46.7$$

Fig. 5.5 provides a summary of the sequence involved in obtaining the control limits.

Reference boxes allow these values to be recorded on the control chart, and knowing these values enables a suitable scale to be set up for the $\bar{X}$ values. These values can now be plotted accordingly and lines can be drawn spanning the first 20 readings. For control limits we adopt the convention of using solid lines. At this stage the predetermined $\bar{X}$ line should also be drawn in, using a broken line.

For calculating the limits for the R chart, a slightly different approach is adopted.

The upper and lower control limits are obtained using the constants D_4 and D_3 and multiplying these values respectively by the mean range $\bar{R}$.

Thus, for the upper control limit, $UCL_R = D_4 \bar{R}$

Referring to the tables we see that with a sample size 5, $D_4 = 2.114$.

Therefore $\qquad\qquad UCL_R = 2.114\bar{R}$

We know that $\qquad\qquad \bar{R} = 118.4$

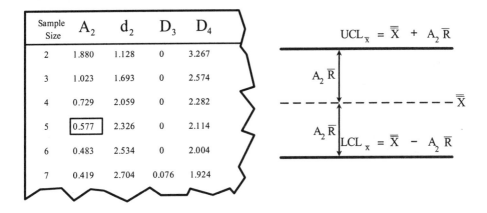

Fig. 5.5 Table of constants and a control chart for n = 5.

Hence
$$UCL_R = 2.114 \times 118.4$$
$$= 250.3$$

For a sample size 5, $D_3 = 0$
Therefore

$$LCL_R = D_3\overline{R}$$
$$= 0$$

Again there are boxes available on the chart to record these values. The R values are plotted, and lines are drawn as before corresponding to the control limit and also the central line, using the previous convention.

The final result appears in Fig. 5.6.

■ 5.3.4 Control status

The four rules for the presence of special causes are now applied to the process and it is found to be under control. As a result, the central lines and control limits can now be projected ahead to monitor the process, hence enabling predictions to be made. Unless some change takes place, then the sample readings will fall naturally within the distance between the control limits. Improvement can only take place by action, primarily at management level as well as operational level. Improvement in this example can be interpreted in two ways. Firstly, we need to reduce the variation in the number of lines of code.

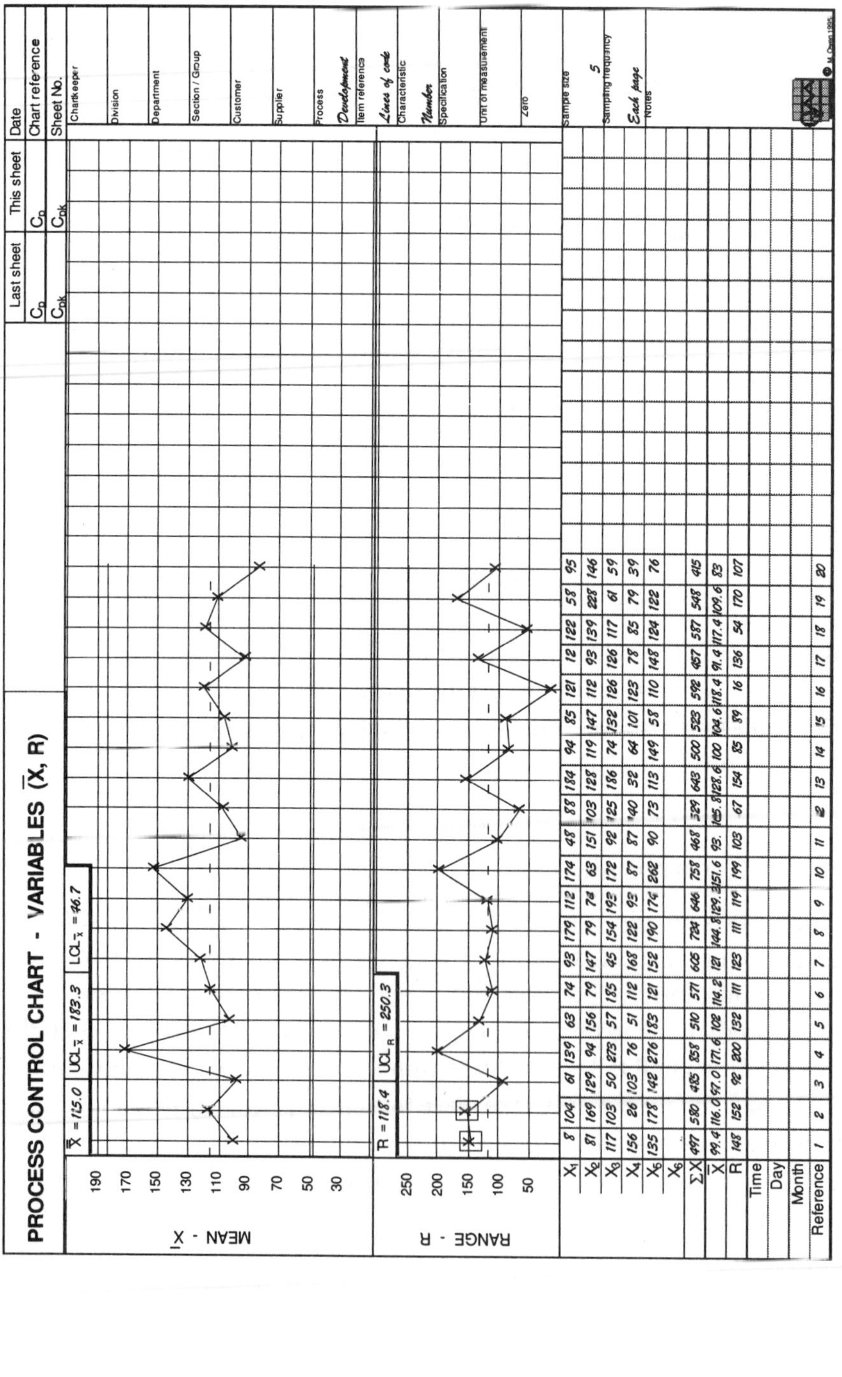

Fig. 5.6 Final control chart for number of lines of code with data entered.

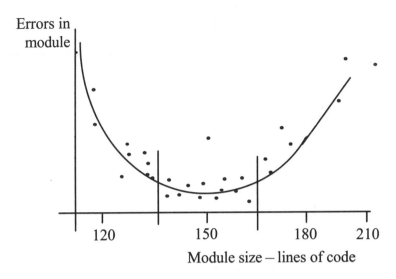

Fig. 5.7 Graph showing the relationship between module size and the number of errors.

Secondly, since there is a relationship between the number of lines of code in a module and the number of errors in a module, shown in Fig. 5.7. It shows that for a given process, an optimum size will minimise the number of errors.

■ 5.4 The (X, Moving R) Chart

■ 5.4.1 A moving range

In many respects this chart is much easier to set up. Because we are considering only single readings, there is no need to calculate R. (In fact we cannot calculate it because with only one reading, a value for R is not possible.) Instead we use a moving range as indicated in Fig. 5.8.

The working example is based on inspection times for a particular type of specification document, measured in hours. The numbers recorded are the mean times/page for successive inspections. As usual 20 readings are taken and the results are as shown in Table 5.3.

Fig. 5.9 shows the control chart to be used with the 20 readings recorded. in the appropriate data boxes with the moving range data evaluated and recorded.

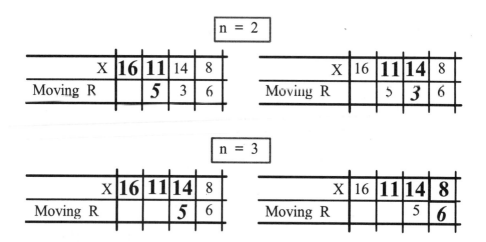

Fig. 5.8 Moving range calculations for n = 2 and n = 3.

Most traditional applications of the (X, Moving R) chart tend to use a sample size 2. One reason is that we do not need to wait as long for 2 readings as for 3. In most software development areas, this is not an issue. However, whether we use 2 or 3 or indeed any other sample size, the moving range section of the control chart does not tell us a great deal. This point will be best explained after we have drawn a control chart using a typical set of readings generated in software development.

Table 5.3 Data for document inspection times.

Time(hr)	1.56	0.31	0.86	0.52	2.00	1.16	3.05	0.48	3.48	2.58
Sample number	1	2	3	4	5	6	7	8	9	10

Time(hr)	5.09	1.37	0.74	0.76	0.8	8.30	0.43	2.07	1.30	0.43
Sample number	11	12	13	14	15	16	17	18	19	20

PROCESS CONTROL CHART - VARIABLES (X, MOVING R)

	Last sheet	This sheet	Date
			Chart reference
			Sheet No.
			Chartkeeper
		Division	
		Department	
		Q.T. Quality	
		Section / Group	
		Customer	
Cp		*Sales* Supplier	
Cpk		*ATO1* Process	
Cn		*Inspection* Item reference	
Cnk		*Specifications* Characteristic	
		Mean time/page Specification	
		1/2 hr per page Unit or measurement	
		Hours Zero	
		Sample size *2*	
		Sampling frequency *Each document*	
		Notes	

INDIVIDUAL - X

$\bar{X} =$ $UCL_x =$ $LCL_x =$

MOVING RANGE - R

$\bar{R} =$ $UCL_R =$

Reference	1	2	3	4	5	6	7	8	9	10	11	12	13	14	15	16	17	18	19	20
Month																				
Day																				
Time																				
X	1.56	0.91	0.86	0.52	2.00	1.16	1.25	0.55	0.34	1.43	0.84	1.89	8.57	3.00	0.90	2.51	8.72	0.63	0.02	0.04
Moving R		0.49	3.49	2.58	5.09	1.37	0.74	0.76	0.80	8.30	0.43	8.07	1.30	0.43						

Fig. 5.9 Control chart for document inspection times.

■ 5.4.2 Calculation of central lines

The central lines are obtained from $\overline{X} = \dfrac{\sum X}{20}$ and $\overline{R} = \dfrac{\sum R}{19}$

Note that we only have 19 R values. We need the first 2 of the 20 X values to give us the first moving R value, and hence we can only start recording the moving ranges after at least 2 values for X.

Hence for our particular example,

$$\overline{X} = \frac{37.29}{20} = 1.86$$

$$\overline{R} = \frac{38.39}{19} = 2.02$$

These values are recorded on the chart.

■ 5.4.3 Calculation of control limits

UCL_X and LCL_X are obtained from $\overline{X} \pm 3$ standard deviations.

Since we are using individual readings we cannot use $A_2 \overline{R}$ as 3 standard deviations. We may be tempted to determine $\hat{\sigma}$ by using all 20 readings in

$\sqrt{\dfrac{\sum(X-\overline{X})^2}{n-1}}$. This method is in fact incorrect because the formula does not

allow for the order in which the readings are taken. We need another approach. Instead of using the conventional formula we obtain $\hat{\sigma}$ from

$\dfrac{\overline{R}}{d_2}$, where d_2 is again available from tables.

With a sample size of 2, corresponding to a moving range of 2, d_2 is 1.128.

$$\therefore \hat{\sigma} = \frac{2.02}{1.128} = 179$$

Hence

$$UCL_X = \overline{X} + 3(1.79)$$
$$= 1.72 + 5.37$$
$$= 7.09$$

Also,

$$LCL_X = \overline{X} - 3(1.79)$$
$$= 1.72 - 5.37$$
$$= 0$$

Quite often, as here, LCL_X is negative. If a negative value does not make sense, as in this case, then we treat LCL_X as zero.

For the R chart, the control limits are obtained as usual by using the D_4 and D_3 constants.

For a moving range based on n = 2, D_4 is 3.267 and therefore

$$UCL_X = D_4 \overline{R}$$
$$= 3.267 \times 2.02$$
$$= 5.65$$

D_3 is 0 and therefore LCL_R is 0.

With the control limits now known, scales can be determined for the control chart. The sample values can be plotted and central lines and control limits drawn in.

The control chart for the inspection times is now shown in Fig. 5.10.

■ 5.4.4 Control status

The usual four rules are applied and the process is seen to be out of control in that there is a value outside the control limits. Further investigation showed that the particular point in question corresponded to a document which was unduly complicated and required more investigation than usual. We are justified in removing this value from the set of readings, and recalculating the control limits and central lines.

This still leaves a point outside the control limits (5.09 corresponding to sample no. 11). A special cause was looked for, but nothing unusual was found. In line with Shewhart's thinking, we accept that this point is in fact part of the system. Since the process is now under control for the new situation, the lines can be drawn ahead and used to monitor the process in future.

The final form of the chart is shown in Fig. 5.11.

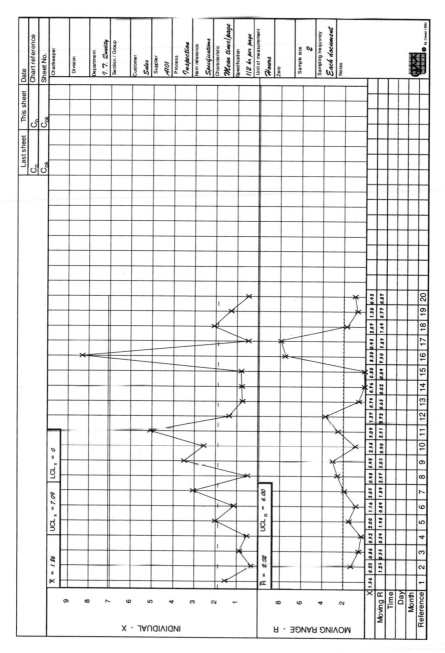

Fig. 5.10 Completed control chart for document inspection times.

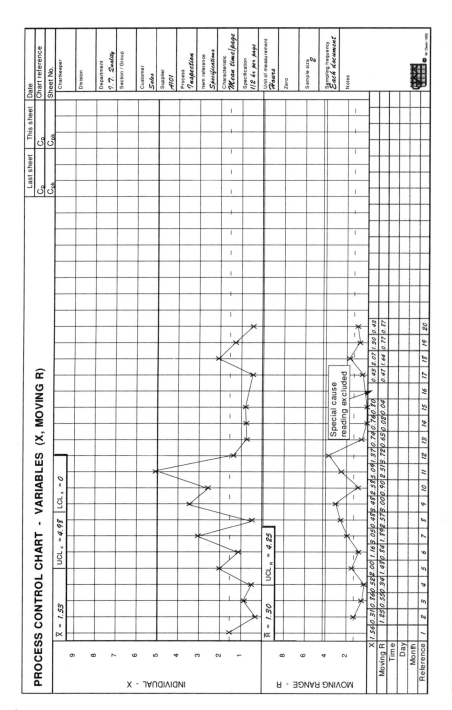

Fig. 5.11 Final control chart for document inspection times after allowing for a special cause.

■ 5.4.5 Moving R section of the (X, Moving R) chart

In practice, the R section of the chart is often not drawn. There are two reasons for this. Changes in the moving R section are really just reflecting a jump between subsequent X values. In addition, successive R values are not independent and hence the 'run of seven' rule is invalid. If we use a moving range based on a sample size 2, then in fact we need 7×2, i.e. 14 independent points in order to apply the rule.

In section 5.4.3 it was suggested that in calculating $\hat{\sigma}$ we use $\dfrac{\overline{R}}{d_2}$ rather than. $\sqrt{\dfrac{\sum\left(X-\overline{X}\right)^2}{n-1}}$. We can now see why. The standard deviation as obtained

from $\sqrt{\dfrac{\sum\left(X-\overline{X}\right)^2}{n-1}}$ does not depend on the order of the X values whereas a

standard deviation value determined from $\dfrac{\overline{R}}{d_2}$ does. Changing the sequence changes the moving range, which changes $\overline{R}$. Thus the formula for $\hat{\sigma}$, which is based on $\overline{R}$, directly reflects the order and must be used in this type of control chart.

■ 5.5 Chart Management

Charts should be formally issued at the commencement of a project with pre-determined historical limits already drawn in. This is because we expect the next project, using the same process, to have the same variation. However, if a change has been made to the process, e.g. a new computer or new hardware in general, then we would expect the process to have improved and a new chart should be set up using the rules outlined. (See section 5.3).

Relevant information about the process relating to the use of the chart should be recorded in the various reference boxes. Fig. 5.12 shows detail of the sections of the control chart used in monitoring document inspection times.

Charts should be issued and released according to projects. Important

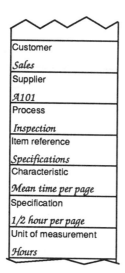

Fig. 5.12 Completed reference boxes for control chart on inspection times.

issues follow from this. The charts will indicate a need for action. Out-of-control signals will occur and the associated special causes must be investigated. Resources will need to be made available to allow this to happen. It may be that the process is stable and predictable but operating at an unacceptable level. Again, resources are required to enable improvement to take place. Collecting data and setting up a control chart is one thing. Responding to control chart signals is another matter. Working continuously on the system to reduce the variation is something else again. What we are looking for is a step reduction in the variation, as indicated in Fig. 5.13.

An appropriate improvement signal in the range chart leads to a reduction in the variation in the $\overline{X}$ chart. Further signals in the range chart are then looked for and the sequence is repeated. For this illustration the ($\overline{X}$, R) chart has been used, although the (X, Moving R) chart could be used in a similar way.

▓ 5.6 Capability

Control and capability are not the same. Capability has to do with the ability of the process to match the customer's requirements. The customer is much more likely to be an internal user of the information rather than the final

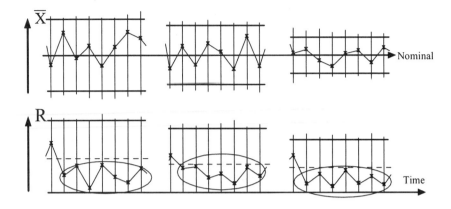

Fig. 5.13 Never-ending improvement cycle for variables.

purchaser of the software product. The notion of the internal customer, as represented in Fig. 5.14, is very important. The output of any one process becomes the input for the next process. In addition, each internal customer may have varying requirements to be satisfied, often called service level agreements (SLAs).

Control, on the other hand, has to do with the process itself, i.e. is it stable and predictable? The performance of the process, often called the voice of the process, is represented by the control chart, and, more specifically, the control limits. This performance may, or may not be, acceptable in terms of satisfying a customer's requirements, where the customer is the manager of the activity. In addition, you may find that your external customer may well require this information before they

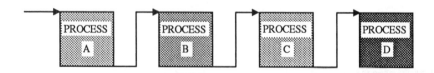

Fig. 5.14 The internal customer.

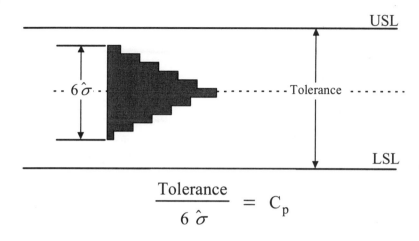

$$\frac{\text{Tolerance}}{6\,\hat{\sigma}} = C_p$$

Fig. 5.15 The C_p index.

embark on a project with you. Chapter 9 covers some of the related issues in more detail.

In typical production processes there are generally two limits quoted – an upper specification limit (USL) and a lower one (LSL). The difference between the two is known as the tolerance.

Not all situations are specified by two limits in this way. Particularly in software testing there may be only one limit, and almost certainly it will be an upper limit. For example, we may have a maximum error rate, e.g. restricting the maximum error rate to 1 per hour, a maximum number of documents to be processed in a given time period, a maximum expenditure rate or a maximum time spent in responding to a telephone inquiry.

It is possible to define capability indices (C_p and C_{PK}) which are used in many conventional processes.

Fig. 5.15 provides a definition of C_p.

A C_p index in itself is not sufficient. It gives no guidance as to the setting of the process and hence the need for the other capability index, C_{PK}. Two forms for the index are available, as shown in Fig. 5.16.

C_{PK} is taken as the least of $\dfrac{\text{USL} - \overline{\overline{X}}}{3\,\hat{\sigma}}$ or $\dfrac{\overline{\overline{X}} - \text{LSL}}{3\,\hat{\sigma}}$ and has a minimum value of C_p. In other words, if the process is running on target, then C_p and C_{PK} are identical.

Both indices are required to fully define a process. However, in many

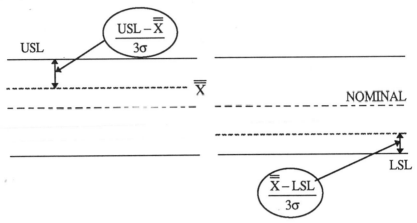

Fig. 5.16 Alternatives for the C_{PK} index.

processes only one limit is available, and in such cases only the C_{PK} index is used.

A less technical approach is often sufficient. For example, referring to the document inspection times in section 5.4.1, another inspection metric could be pages per hour. A particular inspection process quotes a USL of 1 hour. If the control chart for the number of pages per hour showed a UCL of 1.3 hours, then the process is incapable of meeting the requirements because the USL falls within the natural variation of the process.

If the optimum target is to be achieved, then the UCL must be reduced to 1 hour, and this can generally only be achieved by management action in improving the system.

Times taken to:	issue insurance policies	respond to a fax
	respond to enquiries	complete a survey
	complete a sale	deliver an item
	carry out a repair	close a corrective action
	check documents	have a meal
Cost figures such as:	sales figures	expenditures
	inventory levels	estimates
	budgets	turnover
Other single figures:	gas, electricity, water readings	scores
	environmental readings	mileage figures
	material shortages	medical readings

Fig. 5.17 Non-manufacturing applications of the (X, Moving R) chart.

▓ 5.7 Applications of Variable Charts

Whilst this book has naturally concentrated on the applications of control charts in software development, it would be unfortunate if the reader was not made aware of some of the ways in which charts are increasingly being applied in non-manufacturing areas in general. Because of its relevance to single readings, the (X, Moving R) chart in particular has been utilised in a wide range of applications, and Fig. 5.17 provides a listing of some of these.

▓ 5.8 Summary

- The measurements plotted on a variables chart may be based either on samples or individuals.
- All control charts using variable data require 20 readings in setting up the chart.
- It is advisable to commence with an (X, Moving R) chart and then progress to a ($\overline{X}$, R) chart.
- ($\overline{X}$, R) charts are not feasible for all variables because there may not be sufficient data.
- The (X, Moving R) chart is typically based on a sample size 2.
- In the (X, Moving R) chart the moving R section is not so important as is the R section on the (X, R) chart.
- Control relates to the process variation, whereas capability is a measure of the ability of the process to match requirements.
- Control charts should be issued and released in a controlled manner over many projects for the purpose of process improvement.
- (X, Moving R) charts in practice have a wide field of application both in software and management/administration.

We said in Chapter 2 that there were two types of measures and this chapter has covered the charts for variables. The next chapter describes the use and selection of charts for attributes. If you need to decide which type of measure you are dealing with refer back to Chapter 2.

6 Control Charts for Attributes

6.1 Introduction

Control charts for attributes are somewhat more complex than those for variables. This is because they have to deal with situations where either a nonconforming unit is being considered, or, alternatively, there are faults or errors within the unit. In addition, the sample size may either be constant or varying. These distinctions are important in giving guidance on the correct chart to use, and are covered in detail in section 6.2.

The bulk of the chapter – sections 6.3 to 6.6 – covers the four main types of attribute charts. Some are more relevant to software development than others and this will be brought out. A knowledge of the different types of charts is necessary in order to set up the multiple characteristics chart (section 6.7) – probably the most useful of all the attribute charts.

A further section briefly covers what is meant by attribute capability, and also provides material on some other issues relating to the choice of attribute chart.

■ 6.2 Chart Types

■ 6.2.1 Definitions

Attributes are counts as opposed to measures. They could be errors relating directly to the software development process and its management, or to the products themselves. For example, instead of measuring the time taken for a document to be processed, we now count the number of documents in error, or the number of errors in the document. Alternatively, we could be dealing with a constant number of documents or a varying number of documents. We therefore have several choices, and we will use a typical form from the management of the development process, shown in Fig. 6.1, as the basis of our analysis.

This document is a potential source of many errors, as shown in Fig. 6.2. In analysing this form, we shall first assume that we have a varying number of forms available in a given period, e.g. per month, and that we are analysing the number of forms in error. In such cases a suitable measure for the error rate is to use the proportion of forms in error, and this is plotted on a proportion (p) chart.

However, there may be occasions where the sample size is fixed, either by the nature of the work, or by taking a fixed sample size from the varying number available each month. Plotting the number of forms in error, as opposed to the proportion in error, leads to the second alternative – the np chart.

PROJECT TIME MANAGEMENT FORM								
Stage	Activity number	Staff number	Level	Activity	Estimated time (days)	Estimated cost	Actual time (hours)	Actual cost
Feasability								
	1	D.G.	1	Site visit	1	£350.00	7	£315.00
	2	F.R.T.	3	Preparation	2	£700.00	17	£765.00
	3	B.C.	2	Project review meeting	2	£700.00	14	£630.00
	4	H.McT.	2	Project review meeting	1	£350.00	10	£450.00
	5	S.R.	3	Project review meeting	1	£350.00	8	£360.00
	6	J.J.	3	Project review meeting	6	£2,100.00	45	£2,025.00
				TOTAL	13	£4,550.00	101	£4,545.00
Specification								

Fig. 6.1 Project time management form.

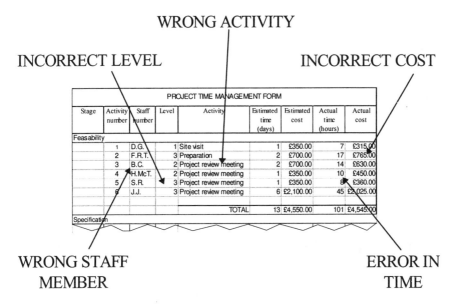

WRONG ACTIVITY

INCORRECT LEVEL

INCORRECT COST

Stage	Activity number	Staff number	Level	Activity	Estimated time (days)	Estimated cost	Actual time (hours)	Actual cost
Feasability								
	1	D.G.	1	Site visit	1	£350.00	7	£315.00
	2	F.R.T.	3	Preparation	2	£700.00	17	£765.00
	3	B.C.	2	Project review meeting	2	£700.00	14	£630.00
	4	H.McT.	2	Project review meeting	1	£350.00	10	£450.00
	5	S.R.	3	Project review meeting	1	£350.00	8	£360.00
	6	J.J.	3	Project review meeting	6	£2,100.00	45	£2,025.00
				TOTAL	13	£4,550.00	101	£4,545.00
Specification								

PROJECT TIME MANAGEMENT FORM

WRONG STAFF
MEMBER

ERROR IN
TIME

Fig. 6.2 Sources of error in a project time management form.

Reverting to a varying sample size provides us with the third type of chart. This time, instead of recording the proportion of forms in error, we record the number of errors and express that as a proportion of the number of forms available. The resulting chart is known as the u chart.

The final chart uses the number of errors in the forms as opposed to the number of forms in error. The resulting chart in this case is known as the c chart.

Using our time management form as the working example, the various options can be represented in Fig. 6.3.

▓ 6.2.2 Number of samples

In the same way as in the use of the $(\overline{X}, R)$ chart and (X, Moving R) chart considered in the previous chapter, the first 20 readings from the process are used to set up the various attribute charts, with no adjustments being made to the process during this period. As before, experience may show that more than 20 readings are required, or that fewer than 20 may provide adequate results for a short term process analysis.

np

c

Fixed number of forms and it is the *form* being assessed

Fixed number of forms and it is the *error* being assessed

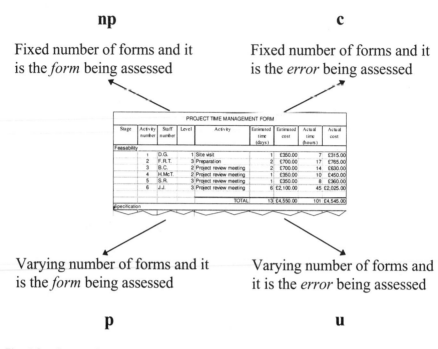

Varying number of forms and it is the *form* being assessed

Varying number of forms and it is the *error* being assessed

p

u

Fig. 6.3 Options for various attribute charts.

■ 6.2.3 Frequency of sampling

For the majority of applications, the frequency of sampling is determined by the process. For example, if the monthly number of documents under consideration is approximately 80, then it is sensible to plot monthly figures, rather than, say, weekly ones. The reasoning behind this is as follows.

We need to make sure that the sample size is sufficiently large to reflect the error rate. Attribute charts should record reject levels in the region 0 – 15 units to be effective, and this gives us a guide on deciding the suitable sample size to use. For example, if the reject rate for a document is known to be 0.03, then it means that, on average, 3 documents will be unacceptable in every 100 which are examined. Hence a sample size 100 would be suitable, and this figure can be related to the number of documents available each week or month in order to fix the final sample size to be used in setting up the chart.

In analysing forms such as the time management form, since the error rates are very small, then sampling is not useful and every form will be inspected.

▓ 6.2.4 Definition of flaw/error

Unlike variables, attributes require some clear definitions of what is meant by a flaw or an error. If these are not available then there can be no consistency in the results.

Standards are required therefore and visual aids will be necessary.

One example of this can be the grading of the seriousness of errors. A missing comma in the text part of the time management form may be unimportant, but a missing full stop in the cost figure may lead to serious extra costs at a later stage.

To chart this we can apply a numeric weighting to the cost of errors based on seriousness, as shown in Table 6.1.

By using less serious errors, or even flaws that can be delivered, the probability of detection is increased and consequently a reduced sample size is required (or at least provides non-zero error rates for a fixed sample size) for attribute charting. The weighting then provides a significance to the figures collected since frequently a large number of minor errors can be as serious as one major error. The control chart can then be run with the specification limits (not control limits which reflect the capability of the process, but the required quality limits), set so that one serious error (value of 3) or three flaws will cause a failure signal. The weighting can of course be set so that 1 error = 10 or even 100 flaws.

Training in the use of these grades will be necessary, as well as training in the process of detecting errors. All these factors need to be allowed for. Other related issues have also to be considered, e.g. the provision of a good working environment, checking on other physical characteristics such as the ability of people (e.g. colour blindness, etc.) and the process characteristics such as the efficiency of the inspection process. Of course, not all physical characteristics can be checked, but this is true of any control

Table 6.1 Weighting factors for errors.

Seriousness	Count weighting	Comment
Flaw	1	No effect on product or form
Minor error	2	Possible influence on later stages
Error	3	Influence on calculations
Major error	4	Influence on project
Critical	5	Company-wide implications

situation. The aim is to find those characteristics that can be controlled and that are frequently observed as a cause of higher than normal error rates.

Having allowed for some of the preparatory issues, we can look at the more technical ones relating to the various attribute charts.

■ 6.2.5 Control limits for attribute charts

Control limits for attributes are based on the same methodology as for variables. The Shewhart approach is adopted in that the various control limits use the ± 3 standard deviation rule, i.e. the control limits are measured outwards from the mean value by ± 3 standard deviations. The appropriate standard deviation is obtained from statistical theory. We do not use indices that vary with sample size, as in the case of variable charts. Instead we make use of the predetermined results shown in the Table 6.2.

$\bar{p}, \bar{np}, \bar{u}$ and $\bar{c}$, as shown in the table, are the corresponding means for the attributes being recorded. The square root term, corresponding to the standard deviation, varies with the type of attribute chart to be used.

In some cases, the LCL value may turn out to be negative. If such a negative value does not make sense in practice, e.g. a negative reject level,

Table 6.2 Summary of formulae used in attribute charting.

Type of chart	Control limits
p	$UCL_P / LCL_p = \bar{p} \pm 3\sqrt{\dfrac{\bar{p}(1-\bar{p})}{\bar{n}}}$
np	$UCL_{np} / LCL_{np} = \bar{np} \pm 3\sqrt{\bar{np}\left(1 - \dfrac{\bar{np}}{n}\right)}$
u	$UCL_u / LCL_u = \bar{u} \pm 3\sqrt{\dfrac{\bar{u}}{n}}$
c	$UCL_c / LCL_c = \bar{c} \pm 3\sqrt{\bar{c}}$

then the lower control limit is interpreted as zero.

Setting up the chart, and analysing it, follows a very similar pattern for each type of attribute to be plotted. Data is collected, charts set up and then interpreted. The only real difference is the formula to be used in calculating the limits.

▨ 6.3 The p Chart

▨ 6.3.1 Data collection

Twenty samples are taken from the process and used to set up the p chart.

The working example makes use of data available from inspection reports. Because of the nature of software inspection, the number of pages being inspected will often vary greatly from document to document. The data chosen for the example is based on a reasonably constant sample size being inspected, i.e. inspections for a similar type of document are grouped together. There are some important issues here relating to the stability of the process, and these will be referred to in section 6.9.2.

Table 6.3 shows the results for the first 20 data sets.

The figures are transferred to the appropriate sections on the control chart, as shown in Fig. 6.4. In practice, these readings will be recorded directly onto the chart.

The corresponding proportions are calculated and the results recorded

Table 6.3 Results from an inspection report.

No. of pages in error	2	2	2	2	2	1	2	3	2	1
No. of pages inspected	11	11	12	15	12	10	15	15	16	14
Ref. no.	1	2	3	4	5	6	7	8	9	10

No. of pages in error	1	2	2	2	1	2	1	3	2	1
No. of pages inspected	11	13	15	15	13	12	15	15	13	11
Ref. no.	11	12	13	14	15	16	17	18	19	20

in the relevant boxes.

■ 6.3.2 Calculation of central line

The central line for the p chart, corresponding to p, may be obtained from

$$\bar{P} = \frac{\sum p}{\sum n}$$

Whilst it may seem logical and sensible to calculate $\bar{p}$ in this way, in fact we use a different approach. We determine $\bar{p}$ from the two separate totals $\sum p$ and $\sum n$, where $\sum n$ is the sum of the various sample sizes. There are two reasons for this. The main one is that we need the value of $\bar{n}$ and hence the value of $\sum n$. The other reason is that sometimes there are special causes present in the first 20 readings. It is always easier to obtain new values for $\sum p$ and $\sum n$, based on the remaining values when the special cause(s) values have been removed, when the individual totals for all 20 readings are known. Hence, for our figures,

$$\bar{p} = \frac{\sum p}{\sum n} = \frac{36}{264} = 0.13$$

This value of $\bar{p}$ is recorded in the information box in the usual way.

■ 6.3.3 Calculation of control limits

The upper control limit is given by:

$$UCL_p = \bar{p} + 3\sqrt{\frac{\bar{p}(1-\bar{p})}{n}}$$

We first need $\bar{n}$ which is obtained from

$$\bar{n} = \frac{\sum n}{20} = \frac{264}{20} = 13.2$$

We assume that we have 20 samples to use, in line with the suggested value. Otherwise, we use the number of samples available, although it would be unwise to do so if we had less than about 10 samples. Even then, we would need to redefine our control limits when 20 readings were available.

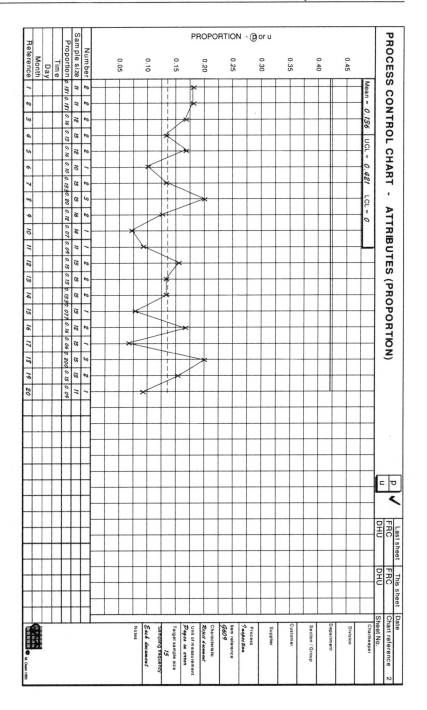

Fig. 6.4 Control chart for analysing reject documents when inspected.

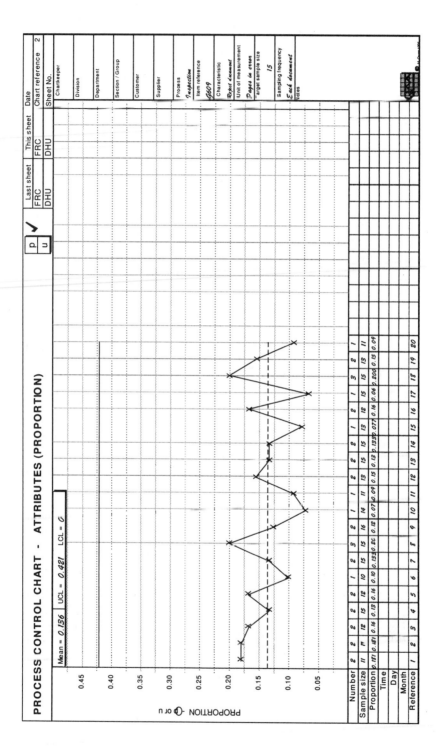

Fig. 6.5 Final control chart for proportion of documents which are in error.

Hence, knowing $\bar{p}$ and $\bar{n}$,

$$UCL_p = \bar{p} + 3\sqrt{\frac{\bar{p}(1-\bar{p})}{\bar{n}}}$$
$$= 0.136 + 3\sqrt{\frac{0.136(1-0.136)}{13}}$$
$$= 0.136 + 0.285$$
$$= 0.421$$

Similarly,

$$LCL_p = \bar{p} - 3\sqrt{\frac{\bar{p}(1-\bar{p})}{\bar{n}}}$$
$$= 0.136 - 0.285$$
$$= 0$$

In this case LCL_p is actually negative, but we treat it as 0 because a negative value does not make sense in the context of this data.

These results are recorded in the reference boxes, and the UCL value used to determine a suitable scale for plotting. The twenty p values are now plotted accordingly, and lines drawn on the chart corresponding to $\bar{p}$ and UCL_p.

The final result appears in Fig. 6.5.

■ 6.3.4 Control status

The four rules for interpreting special causes are now applied. The middle third rule needs to be used with some caution. Because the lower limit is often negative, this means that there is not an equal distance between UCL and the central line, and the central line and the time axis. The middle third, as previously understood, is now not so clearly defined. One approach is to use only the top of the 'middle third', but it is probably best to restrict the use of this rule only to instances where it is clear that there is an unusual grouping of points.

The process represented in Fig. 6.5 is seen to be 'in-control'. Lines corresponding to $\bar{p}$ and UCL_p should now be projected to monitor the system. Improvement can only follow by management action in the main and will result in reducing the value of $\bar{p}$ and, by definition, the value of UCL_p.

Table 6.4 Values for number of incorrect forms (typical sample from authors work in applying techniques in administrative areas).

No. of incorrect documents	5	4	8	9	3	3	0	4	6	7
Month no.	1	2	3	4	5	6	7	8	9	10
No. of incorrect documents	2	1	3	5	12	4	2	1	4	6
Month no.	11	12	13	14	15	16	17	18	19	20

■ 6.4 The np Chart

■ 6.4.1 Data collection

Each type of attribute chart will be introduced in this chapter, but it should not necessarily be assumed that an immediate example of each chart will be forthcoming in software development.

In applications of SPC in general, the np chart would seem to be the least used of all the charts. In preparing this book, no obvious application of the np chart in software development was available. However, the potential is there for its use.

As the working example, therefore, we have used figures which could relate to the time management form completed for each separate phase of a project. We assume that there are a large number of forms to be vetted, so many that it is not possible to check them all. As a result, a fixed sample of 160 documents is chosen every month, the sample size being chosen in line with the comments made in section 6.2.3. The results for 20 successive months are collected, and are as shown in Table 6.4. The 20 values corresponding to the number of incorrect documents are now transferred into the data boxes on the appropriate control chart.

▨ 6.4.2 Calculation of central line and control limits

The mean value, $\overline{np}$, is obtained directly from:

$$\overline{np} = \frac{\sum np}{20}$$

$$\therefore \quad \overline{np} = \frac{89}{20} = 4.45$$

The upper control limit is given by:

$$UCL_{np} = \overline{np} + 3\sqrt{\overline{np}\left(1 - \frac{\overline{np}}{n}\right)}$$

$$= 4.45 + 3\sqrt{4.45\left(1 - \frac{4.45}{160}\right)}$$

$$= 4.45 + 6.24$$

$$= 1069$$

Similarly,

$$LCL_{np} = 4.45 - 6.24$$
$$= 0$$

In the usual way, these results are recorded in the reference boxes and an appropriate scale chosen for plotting using the value of UCL_{np}.

The result appears in Fig. 6.6.

▨ 6.4.3 Control status

When the four rules for special causes were applied, an out-of-control signal was seen corresponding to month no. 15. Further investigation showed that this excessive error rate of 12 was due to the fact that the forms were being completed at a time when new procedures were being introduced into the company. As a result, this value was eliminated from the data set and the results recalculated using the remaining 19 readings.

The final version of the control chart now appears in Fig. 6.7. The control limits and central line now more adequately represent the 19 readings used, and as the process is stable, the lines have been drawn ahead in order to monitor the level of unacceptable forms and to aid in reducing the reject rate.

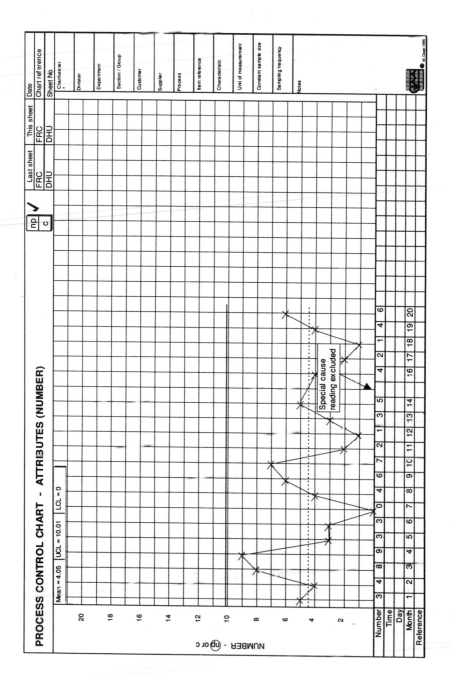

Fig. 6.6 Control chart for number of incorrect forms.

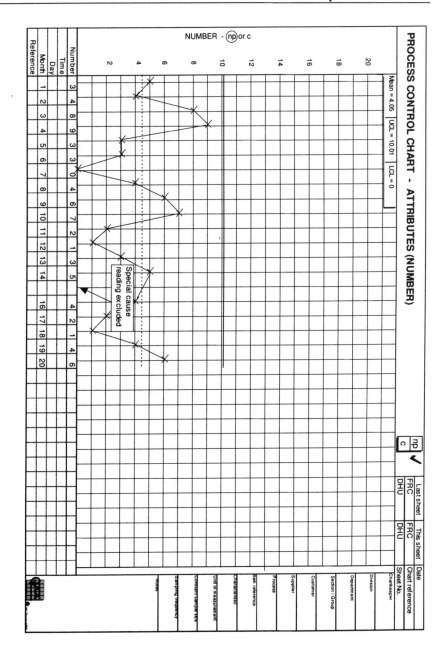

Fig. 6.7 Final control chart for number of incorrect forms.

■ 6.5 The u Chart

■ 6.5.1 Comparison of p and u values

The u chart, and also the c chart described later, both take the level of analysis to a further level of detail. Fig. 6.8 illustrates the point with symbols used to represent different types of errors in the document, for example, an incorrect value, a missed record.

Instead of looking at the number of unacceptable documents in a varying sample size, where the document is a time management form, an invoice, etc., we now concentrate on the number of errors in the document, irrespective of the type of error. Six reject documents out of the 185 under analysis gives a p value of $\frac{6}{185}$. Within the 6 reject documents, there are 15 errors of different types. Hence as a u value for the sample we have $\frac{15}{185}$. The u value must always be greater than or equal to the p value because a document can be rejected carrying one or more faults.

At this stage we are not concerned about the type of fault, or reason for unacceptability. We are only interested in the number, irrespective of type. Clearly we do need to analyse the different types at some stage, and the multiple characteristics chart, covered in section 6.7, enables us to deal with this.

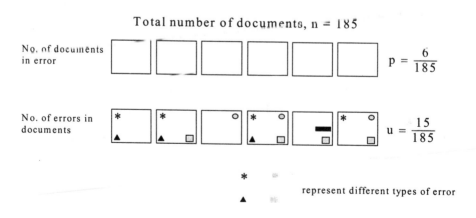

Fig. 6.8 Diagrammatic representation of a p value and a u value.

Table 6.5 Number of errors found in inspection.

No. of errors	4	6	3	6	4	2	3	5	3	2
No. of pages inspected	14	13	12	15	12	10	15	15	16	14
Ref. no.	1	2	3	4	5	6	7	8	9	10

No. of errors	1	2	3	5	2	5	2	4	3	2
No. of pages inspected	11	13	15	15	13	12	15	15	13	11
Ref. no.	11	12	13	14	15	16	17	18	19	20

■ 6.5.2 Data collection

Since there is a very close relationship between a p chart and a u chart, it makes sense to base our working example on that used in section 6.3.1. This time, however, instead of analysing the number of pages in error, we shall analyse the total number of errors distributed across the 20 samples used to set up the chart.

Using a similar set of 20 documents, therefore, the results for the number of errors detected in the pages are shown in Table 6.5.

These readings are transferred to the appropriate section of the control chart and the corresponding proportions are calculated and recorded.

■ 6.5.3 Calculation of central line and control limits

In the same way as with the p chart, the mean value $\bar{u}$ is obtained from:

$$\bar{u} = \frac{\sum u}{\sum n}$$

Hence

$$\bar{u} = \frac{\sum u}{\sum n} = \frac{67}{269} = 0.249$$

This value is recorded in the information box.

We will need the mean sample size obtained from:

$$\bar{n} = \frac{\sum n}{20} = \frac{269}{20} = 13.45$$

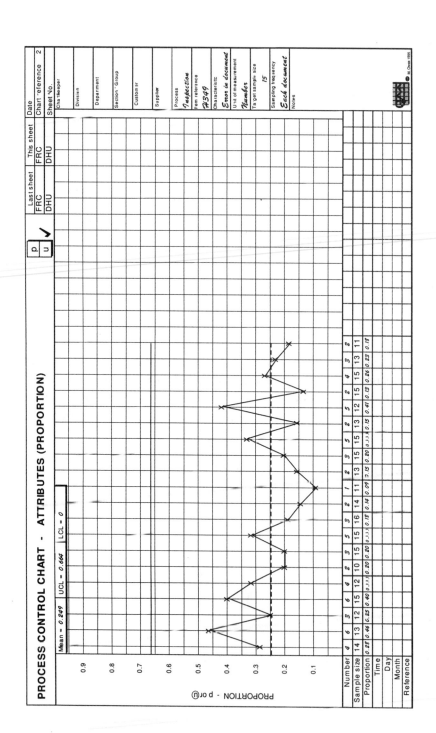

Fig. 6.9 Control chart for number of errors found in software inspection.

It is normal practice to round this figure to the nearest digital value.
The upper control limit is now given by:

$$UCL_u = \overline{u} + 3\sqrt{\frac{\overline{u}}{n}}$$

$$= 0.249 + 3\sqrt{\frac{0.249}{13}}$$

$$= 0.249 + 0.415$$

$$= 0.664$$

Similarly,

$$LCL_u = \overline{u} - 3\sqrt{\frac{\overline{u}}{n}}$$

$$= 0.249 - 0.415$$

$$= 0$$

The results are recorded, a suitable scale chosen, u values plotted and lines drawn on the chart, giving the final form shown in Fig. 6.9.

▧ 6.5.4 Control status

Applying the four rules in the usual way shows the process to be under control. It is therefore in order to project the lines ahead.

The fact that the process is under control is not necessarily a cause for satisfaction. The process may well be predictable, but it is operating at a level of error which is unacceptable. We need to work further on the system in order to reduce this level of $\overline{u}$ towards zero.

▧ 6.6 The c Chart

▧ 6.6.1 Comparison of np and c values

In the same way that there is a relationship between the p chart and the u chart, then similarly there is one between the np chart and the c chart.

Fig. 6.10 shows how a np value based on a constant sample size becomes a c value when it is errors that are being analysed rather than documents. So a np value of 5 becomes a c value of 7.

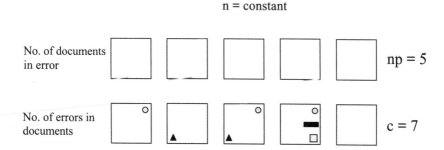

Fig. 6.10 Diagrammatic representation of an np value and a c value

For a given fixed sample size, the c value must be greater than or equal to the np value.

■ 6.6.2 Data collection

For this example we shall again make use of figures relating to the inspection of pages, and for the c chart to be valid the error rate should be in single figures. In other words, the sample size is large and the chance of an error occurring is small. In practice, in software inspection, the sample size will vary, and as with the np chart, a direct application of the c chart in software development might not be obvious. Even so, the chart has applications in related areas, such as analysing complaints.

Results for the first 20 inspections are shown in Table 6.6.

Table 6.6 Values for number of errors in documents.

No. of errors	2	0	4	2	3	3	1	2	3	2
Job no.	1	2	3	4	5	6	7	8	9	10

No. of errors	3	6	2	3	0	4	3	1	2	4
Job no.	11	12	13	14	15	16	17	18	19	20

■ 6.6.3 Calculation of central line and control limit

The mean value, $\bar{c}$, is obtained from $\bar{c} = \dfrac{\sum c}{20}$

$$\therefore \quad \bar{c} = \frac{50}{20} = 2.5$$

The upper control limit is given by:

$$UCL_c = \bar{c} + 3\sqrt{\bar{c}}$$
$$= 2.5 + 3\sqrt{2.5}$$
$$= 2.5 + 4.74$$
$$= 7.24$$

Similarly,

$$LCL_c = \bar{c} - 3\sqrt{\bar{c}}$$
$$= 2.5 - 4.74$$
$$= 0$$

The final control chart is as shown in Fig. 6.11.

■ 6.6.4 Control status

The four rules are applied in the usual way. No special causes are present, and hence the process is stable and predictable but not necessarily satisfactory. More work is required on the system to further reduce the error level towards zero.

■ 6.7 The Multiple Characteristics Chart

■ 6.7.1 Expanding on the detail

The u chart provided more detail on an error rate within a document. However, it did not enlarge on the type of error involved. Similarly for a c chart in comparison with a np chart.

The multiple characteristic chart opens up the analysis to a further level of detail.

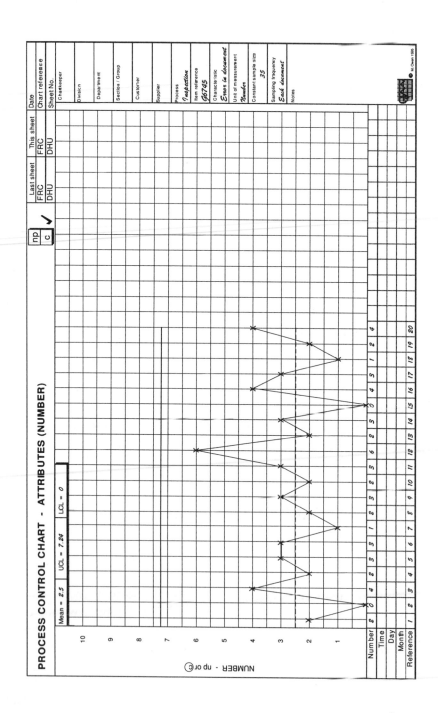

Fig. 6.11 Control chart for number of errors found in software inspection.

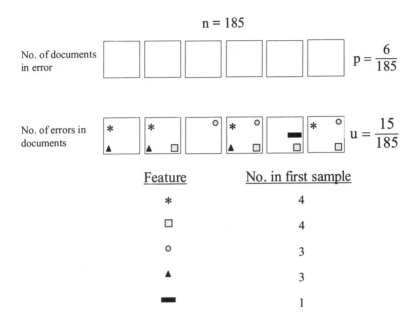

Fig. 6.12 Comparison of a p, u and multiple characteristics analysis.

Instead of counting the total number of errors, we now count the total number of errors in different categories.

Fig. 6.12 shows how a p value becomes a u value which in turn leads on to several multiple characteristic values.

In theory, therefore, we can finish up with as many separate multiple characteristic charts as we had categories of errors. The rules for calculating the sample size from the number of errors found still apply. Consequently, we now need a sample size which is the number of categories selected times bigger than that used for the p chart.

■ 6.7.2 Data collection

For the example to be used in this section, we will revert to the data sheet used in Chapter 4 and reproduced again in Fig. 6.13. The data collection sheet is really part of a multiple characteristics control chart which is shown in Fig. 6.14.

The data is based on the inspection of software for defects of various types. Six categories of error are noted and the number of errors of a particular type for the first 20 inspections carried out are recorded in

CHARACTERISTIC	NO. OF ERRORS														
Typing	1		3		1		1	1		1	1	2		1	1
Spelling	3	2		1	2	7	1	3	4		2	5	3	2	
Grammar	3				2			1	2	2	3	1	1		2
Function		5	2	1		2		3	1	1	4	3	2	1	
User				1			1					1		1	
Consistency	2		1				1	1	2		1	2			2
TOTAL	9	7	6	3	5	10	3	9	9	4	11	14	6	5	5

Fig. 6.13 Section from data collection sheet for software defects.

sequence. The total number of errors for each category can then be determined and these are appropriately recorded in Fig. 6.14.

■ 6.7.3 Calculation of central line and control limits

The central line is based on the mean of the 20 totals, i.e. $\dfrac{141}{20} = 7.0$

What type of chart does this central line relate to?

In the early stages of getting to grips with attribute charts, there is often some uncertainty as to which type of chart to use.

In this case we use a c chart. This is because we have a large sample size, which can be assumed sufficiently constant as to not make it worthwhile using a u chart, and the incidence of error is low in comparison to sample size.

The flow chart shown in Fig. 6.15 may be of help in deciding which chart to use.

With the knowledge that we are to use a c chart, then 7.05 is $\bar{c}$ then the control limits are given by:

$$UCL_c = \bar{c} + 3\sqrt{\bar{c}}$$
$$= 7.05 + 3\sqrt{7.05}$$
$$= 7.05 + 7.97$$
$$= 15.02$$

LCL_c must be 0.

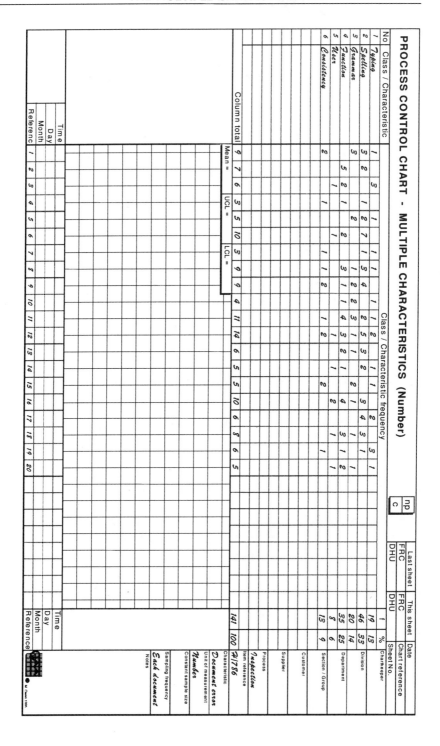

Fig. 6.14 Control chart for different types of software defects.

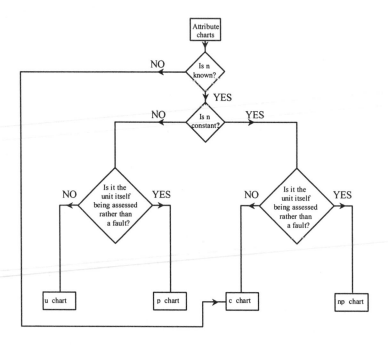

Fig. 6.15 Flow chart for deciding on the appropriate attribute chart to use.

The control chart can now be drawn in the usual way, and the final chart appears in Fig. 6.16.

■ 6.7.4 Control status

The process is assumed to be under control. Sample no. 6 does indicate a possible special cause, but further investigation showed nothing unusual and hence the value was taken to be part of the system. As with other charts we have looked at, the defect level may be unacceptably high. This has to be reduced and the multiple characteristics chart is found to be extremely useful in directing attention to those areas which need to be concentrated on first.

■ 6.7.5 Assessing priorities

As well as allowing for the total for each inspection to be recorded, the chart also allows for the total for each type of error to be recorded.

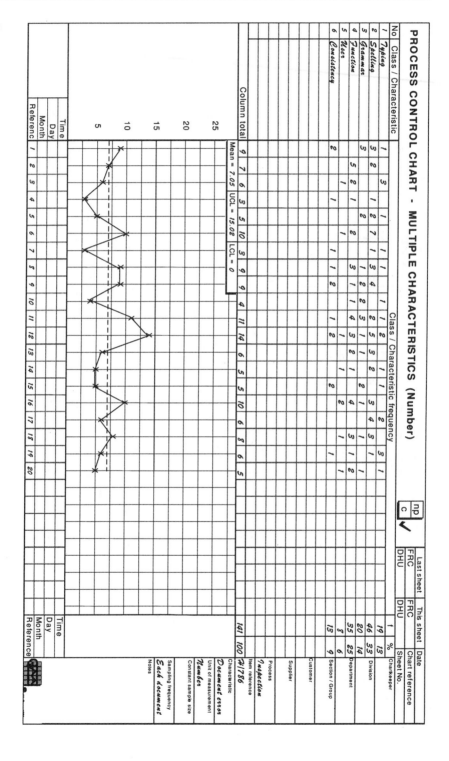

Fig. 6.16 Completed control chart for different types of software defects.

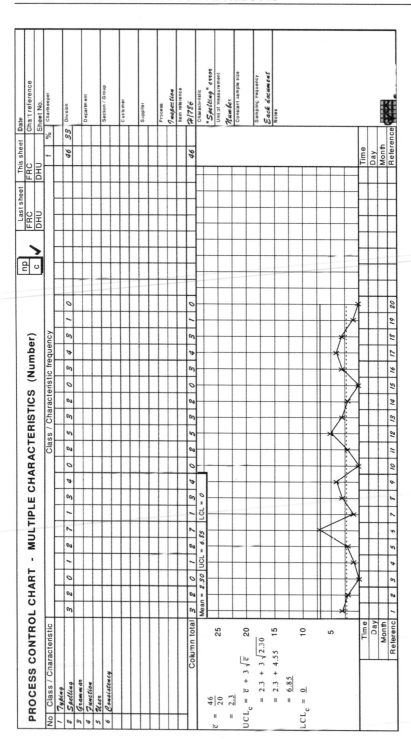

Fig. 6.17 Completed control chart for 'spelling' defects.

The data boxes for these have already been completed on the chart, as have the results for the percentage contribution based on a total number of errors of 141. The usefulness of the chart can now be seen in that by completing these last two columns, the Pareto principle can be applied. It is seen that 46% of the problem is caused by 'spelling'. The 'spelling' figures are now used to develop a second control chart, shown in Fig. 6.17.

The central lines and control limits for this chart have again been calculated on the basis of a c chart.

The process is assumed to be under control. Sample no. 6 does suggest the presence of a special cause, but further investigation showed nothing unusual associated with that point. The value was therefore taken to be part of the system and hence it would be in order to extend the lines. Further analysis is now an option in that secondary charts can be developed for the other features in order of priority, i.e. function (35%), grammar (20%), typing (19%), consistency (13%) and user (8%).

This ability to allow for various charting options based on applying the Pareto principle is an important feature of the multiple characteristics chart. Some organisations have developed impressive software packages to provide excellent miniature summary charts along these lines.

■ 6.8 Capability for Attributes

The capability of an organisation to manage its defect rate for any of its activities can be measured by using attribute data. With attribute charts there are no specification limits involved. Hence a measure of capability has to be defined in a different way. A slightly different approach is adopted, depending on whether we are analysing a whole unit, as in a p or np chart, or faults within the unit, as in a u or a c chart.

■ 6.8.1 Capability for the p and the np charts

For these two charts, the capability is generally defined as first run capability (FRC) and obtained from:

$$\text{FRC} = \left(1 - \bar{p}\right) \times 100\%$$

For the data used, for the p chart used in section 6.3.2, we know that $\bar{p}$ is 0.136. Therefore, FRC = 86.4%.

■ 6.8.2 Capability for the u and the c charts

For these charts, capability is defined in terms of defects per hundred units (DHU).

Hence, for the u chart used in section 6.5.3, we know that $\bar{u}$ is 0.249.
Therefore, DHU $= 0.249 \times 100$
$$= 24.9$$

■ 6.9 Other Aspects

■ 6.9.1 Allowing for sample size

By definition, the sample size will vary for both the p and u chart. This variation is to be expected and both charts can accommodate this, providing the variation is not excessive. What do we mean by excessive?

The statistical guideline is that a sample size change within the limits of $\pm 25\%$ of the mean sample size is acceptable. For samples outside this range, then we should recalculate individual control limits based on the more correct formulae which use n rather than $\bar{n}$ in the appropriate calculations.

Fig. 6.18 illustrates the point. It shows a section from a p chart where the chart has been set up with $\bar{p} = 0.037$ and $\bar{n} = 255$. These values enable UCL_p to be determined as 0.0725. The particular sample in question has a value of p of 0.0727, which is outside the UCL_p value based on the mean sample size. Twenty-five per cent of $\bar{n}$ is 64 and this gives limits on n of 255 ± 64, i.e. 319 and 191. The sample size in question (165) is outside this band and hence a new control limit is calculated, specific to this sample, and based on the formula:

$$UCL_p = \bar{p} + 3\sqrt{\frac{\bar{p}(1-\bar{p})}{n}}$$

This gives a new control limit of 0.081 which means that the point is actually under control, after allowing for the unusually small sample size.

It is worth noting that recalculating control limits based on variation in sample size is really only worthwhile if, in so doing, the status of the point in question is changed.

■ 6.9.2 Allowing for unstable processes

When plotting attribute charts, and particularly for the p and u charts, it sometimes seems that there are more points outside the control limits than there are inside. There then could be a danger of tracking down what appear to be special causes, when in fact it is the chart itself which is at fault. Generally, if the numbers, or proportions, come from a process which is not stable, for example, the proportions vary widely and are not reasonably constant from sample to sample, then the advice is to treat the readings as individuals and plot the results on an (X, Moving R) chart.

This can be seen when comparing Fig. 6.19 and Fig. 6.20.

Fig. 6.19 shows a p chart for a set of readings relating to document inspection. The process is unstable in that there are large variations in the sample sizes as well as in the proportions themselves. The control limits are very tight with the result that half the points are outside the control limits.

Fig. 6.20 provides a more helpful picture. Here the p values are treated as individuals and plotted on an (X, Moving R) chart. The control limits are wider apart and are more appropriate for the figures being charted. As

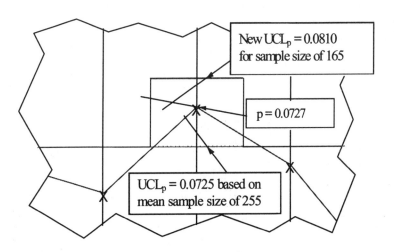

New UCL$_p$ = 0.0810 for sample size of 165

p = 0.0727

UCL$_p$ = 0.0725 based on mean sample size of 255

Fig. 6.18 Diagram showing the effect of an excessive sample on the UCL value.

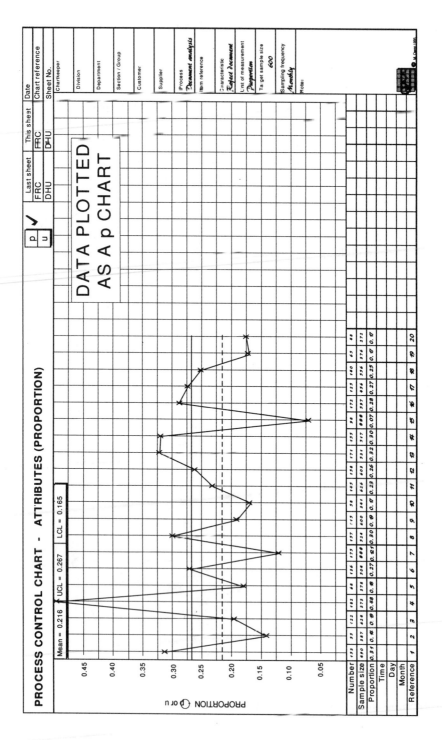

Fig. 6.19 Reject document figures plotted as a p chart.

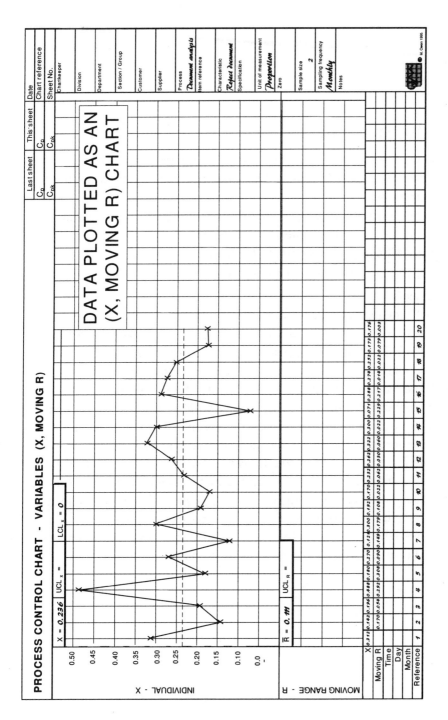

Fig. 6.20 Reject document figures plotted as an (X, Moving R) chart.

a rough rule you would not be too far out in using an (X, Moving R) approach for all attributes, although this is not to be adopted as a general principle. It is always best to go through the attribute approach first, and if it is clear that it will not give a sensible result, then use the alternative approach.

■ 6.10 Summary

- Attribute charts allow for varying or constant sample sizes.
- Charts also allow for the analysis of nonconforming units and faults within the units.
- Sample sizes for attributes are much larger than those for variables.
- Clear definitions of faults/errors are required.
- Four different types of attribute charts are available.
- All charts are based on limits using the mean $\pm 3 \times$ standard deviations.
- Both the p and u charts make use of a mean sample size.
- Use specific control limits for those sample sizes outside these limits.
- Use FRC as the capability index for nonconforming units.
- Use DHU as the capability index for nonconformities.
- If the readings are unstable, use the (X, Moving R) chart.

The attribute charting methods together with the selection process for choosing the chart most appropriate to the task in hand has been described and, together with the variable charting methods described in Chapter 5 the tools for process control have been completed. However the control model described in Chapter 2 requires methods for displaying data for supervisory and process improvement purposes. There are also more sophisticated techniques available for process control that cater for conditions where the variable and attribute charts will not be adequate. The next chapter provides these charting techniques.

7 Other Control Charts

7.1 Introduction

We said at the start of this book that the control chart was the most significant tool for the control of processes. However the control charts so far outlined cannot provide the answers in all circumstances. This chapter provides some of the other techniques that are available to overcome the shortcomings of the ($\overline{X}$, R) or (X, Moving R) control charts, to be referred to as variables charts in this chapter.

7.1.1 Limitations of the control chart

Powerful as it is, there are some limitations and difficulties associated with the control chart. The main limitations come from its concentration on time, ability to detect change, and single process orientation.

Time related data

The control chart is fundamentally designed to collect and display sequential data. This may be directly time related where each measurement or count is followed by another, or may be sequential in the manner in which the information is treated, such as the count of lines of code in a module which may be developed in any order. Many of the benefits of using the control chart will only be gained by using the information as a prevention measure and consequently it is best used in time sequence rather than off-line.

The chart cannot be used in the classical statistics sense of relating a sample to a batch or population. Its prime purpose is to relate a current event to the last events that result from the same process.

Techniques are required to relate data over periods of time greater than can normally be achieved with the control chart. This is particularly true of the management charts required for process improvement monitoring and general management decision making. Particular formats of control chart are available for this purpose.

■ Process limitations

The control chart is a method of analysing and interpreting information from a single process and a single variable which must be clearly defined. Multiple attribute charts are one of the standard charting methods but variables require special techniques to provide comparative information. Often there is confusion between handling varying data, which inherently comes from a common process for which one chart is required, and handling data from changing processes where there is a direct cause. A method of establishing the difference is required and the cusum chart can provide an indication of the trends of data much more quickly.

The single process, single variable problem is handled by multiple process or multiple variable charts.

■ Data limitations

The control chart is limited to data that is expected to remain stable over time. The data is expected to be reliable and complete – a problem that many charts suffer from. However if data is expected to vary over time then a different type of chart is required that can cope with the change and the angled control charts provide examples of achieving this.

A second limitation is related to the number of variables that are required to characterise a process. This type of control chart provides a mechanism of charting one variable. However, if many variables are to be compared then mechanisms for using the same statistical control mechanisms are required to ensure that out-of-control situations are still detected. Star or Kiveat diagrams provide one solution to this problem.

■ 7.1.2 Alternative charts

To overcome the limitations of the charting techniques other methods of displaying statistical information for the purposes of controlling a process are available.

In order to control a small but continuing trend in the mean of a process, a technique is required that looks at differences in the values. The cusum chart cumulates the sum of the differences from the mean between readings so that for a normal variables chart we would get a very small reading centred about zero. A small deviation in the mean from the target causes the plotted values to drift away from the zero line and provides an early signal that the process, which although on an ($\overline{X}$, R) chart may look satisfactory, is actually operating at a level different from the target mean.

In the software industry, where there may be a wide dispersion of results, this chart can be very useful at detecting the small differences in the error rates. This is particularly true of the cusum chart when it is used to find differences between teams and projects due to its increased sensitivity to small shifts in the mean value over time.

For many of the metrics gathered in the development process, we are looking for a continual change in the characteristic. This may be a growth of completeness or confidence, or a reduction in errors. The variables charts have been modified to meet this need by providing angled control lines which provide a changing mean and range throughout the development lifecycle. This is a time based control and consequently provides both project management information and process control.

In most software projects, a single measurement is not appropriate to characterise the quality of either the product or the process. We have already seen the multi-characteristic chart in Chapter 6, which is suited to characterisation of a single process. However most projects consist of several teams working in parallel effectively creating similar, but not identical, processes. For this type of development a chart that provides comparison of the mean and variance is provided. The chart is a multiple process chart.

The SPC control loops described in Chapter 2 expect the managers and supervisors to make use of the data in order to establish methods of improving the processes. In order for them to make sense of the data, control information is required and this chapter describes the presentation of the different types of charts for management use.

Finally, time charts can provide most of the control required, but for software there is a second statistical requirement. This is to reveal differences between areas of code, parts of documents or project teams. To achieve this the information is presented using statistical mapping which can better reveal significant differences. Managers and developers can then use this to support their decisions about where best to target their efforts in order to achieve maximum benefit.

■ 7.2 Selecting Process Charts

These charts are all derived from the data used to produce the variables charts. The collection methods follow the rules outlined in Chapter 4. A guide to which chart to use in specific circumstances is provided in Table 7.1.

■ 7.3 Angled Control Chart

The angled control chart is used when the expected results for the project are either increasing or declining. This means that the target level and the calculated control limits will be continually changing through the project.

There are two types of chart in this category as shown in Fig. 7.1:

(1) angled mean with constant level of expected variance
(2) angled mean with reducing variance.

The first of these is used where the variation in the process is not expected to change with time, but the process values are expected to change. This is represented by factors relating to the learning processes within a project or project team. The overall effectiveness of a team might be expected to improve with time, but the variance is a measure of the ability of the

Table 7.1 Which chart type to use.

Chart type	When to use
Variable chart	Single variables for process or product
Attribute charts	Single or multiple attributes for process or product
Angled chart	Either of the above but where the value is expected to trend toward a finite value in a finite time
Cusum chart	Single variables or attributes where small changes in mean are expected
Multiple process	Either variables or attributes where parallel processes are occurring

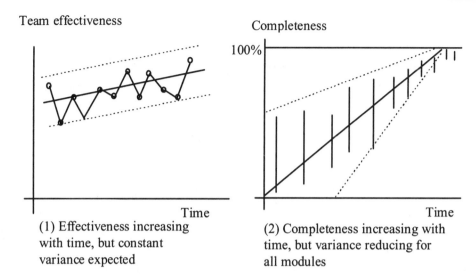

Team effectiveness

Completeness

Time

(1) Effectiveness increasing
with time, but constant
variance expected

(2) Completeness increasing with
time, but variance reducing for
all modules

Fig. 7.1 Parallel and convergent control lines examples.

individuals and can only be expected to change with positive input of training and personnel development. Consequently it is reasonable to expect a continual rise in effectiveness as the team become more familiar with the tools, the project, the product and the input documents. It is not reasonable to expect the team variance to improve unless there has been training and development input. The distribution spread will therefore remain constant and the control lines will remain parallel to the mean lines (and to the target if the expected improvement is achieved).

The situation for project completeness demonstrates the second phenomena. The target line is expected to start at zero and take a path through to 100%. However the variance on this for all modules will also be expected to change – from 100% when the first module is completed and there are still modules not started, to a theoretical zero when all modules are 100% complete. The mean completeness of the system is measured during the inspections when the system is compared with requirements, specifications, standards and other input materials. The variance is determined from the distribution of completeness at any stage through a project. While this distribution can be expected to reduce in width at the outset, it will come to a point when the small amount of variance left cannot be reduced. This is when the product is accepted to be as complete as expected.

▮ 7.3.1 Control limits

For these angled charts the control limits are calculated using the variable control line formulae as described in Chapter 5. For the parallel control lines the calculation is based on the values for each individual or sub-group readings but with the historic trend subtracted before the calculations are completed. This means that the calculations cannot be initiated until a trend has been established, usually defined as being after seven sampled results have been collected (see the second rule for variable trend detection in Chapter 4). Note that the control limits are calculated from the ranges of the readings and not the from individual's actual values and consequently the control limits are placed either side of the rising or falling trend in the mean.

For a typical set of nine readings for project team effectiveness (measured as the improvement in the difference between estimated and actual project times), shown in Table 7.2, the trend is calculated from the straight line fit through the mean values for the grouped data. The values of m and c in the straight line formula:

$$y = mx + c$$

are calculated from the values of x where y = 1 to 8 (these could be in actual period times but this is not of any benefit to the result). The starting control limits are then calculated from:

$$UCL = c + A_2R$$

where c is the value at which x would cross the start line and

$$LCL = c - A_2R$$

The value of these limits anywhere in the chart is given by:

$$CL = mx + c \pm A_2R$$

Table 7.2 The calculation of mean and control lines for project effectiveness

Team no	Estimate/actual								
	Aug 91	Nov	Feb 92	May	Aug	Dec	Mar 93	Jun	Sep
1	85	83	90	79	86	85	92	79	84
2	75	92	74	74	85	82	79	84	85
3	83	76	76	85	94	92	86	78	93
4	68	84	81	73	76	79	82	96	88
5	73	79	86	92	72	84	79	92	86
Sum	384	414	407	403	413	422	418	429	436
Mean	76.8	82.8	81.4	80.6	82.6	84.4	83.6	85.8	87.2
Range	17	16	16	18	22	13	13	18	9
R	15.78	X	82.8	m	0.77	c	-58	X_0	75.5

The actual values of m and c will depend on the method used for determining the fit of the line. This can be approximated by taking the end point and the mean value of x at the mid value of time. This has the benefit of ignoring start-up variation and concentrates on values once the project teams are used to the idea of being monitored in this way.

The same general rules apply as for standard charts regarding out-of-control situations. From this example management have no cause for exceptional concern until the difference between estimate and actual falls outside the control limits, e.g.

$$UCL = 87.2 + 0.58 \times 15.78$$
$$= 96.35$$

and similarly

$$LCL = 79.05.$$

However the range is of concern and action should be taken to reduce the variance of estimating.

■ 7.4 Cusum Chart

The cusum technique was developed in the 1950s as an alternative to the Shewhart approach to be used when a small change in process level needs to be detected as quickly as possible. Its early application was in the textile industry, but there have been developments in other fields. It is rather more technical than the Shewhart chart, but in its basic form could well have applications in software development.

■ 7.4.1 Definition of cusum

One of the drawbacks of the method is the name. The word cusum does not immediately suggest what it means. In fact cusum is just an abbreviation for **cu**mulative **sum**. An example will help in explaining the definition and the initial calculations involved.

We have a series of readings as follows:

5   6   3   8   4

The figures could relate to a variety of situations. The only requirement is that there is an associated target figure. This can, in some circumstances, be calculated from the mean of the data. We are told that the target, normally denoted by T, is 5 for this particular process. We can now generate a cusum

Table 7.3 Calculation of cusum values from collected data.

	Target (T) = 5	
Value X	(X–T)	Σ(X–T)
5	0	0
6	1	1
3	–?	–1
8	3	2
4	–1	1

table as shown in Table 7.3. The cusum values are obtained by accumulating the successive differences between each value and the target.

■ 7.4.2 Properties of a cusum graph

These can be explained by comparing a cusum graph with a conventional variable chart. Fig. 7.2 shows a variable chart for a set of 30 individual readings taken in time sequence. No obvious irregularity is seen. The values seem to show a natural pattern indicative of a process under statistical control.

The process has a target of 4 units, and this value is used to generate a cusum graph, shown in Fig. 7.3. A trend is now visible. Somewhere about sample 15, a change seems to have occurred in that the slope of the cusum graph has changed. At this stage we cannot be specific about the exact time and the degree of change. We need some guidance to help discriminate between the random changes in slope expected of a naturally varying process, and genuine changes due to special causes.

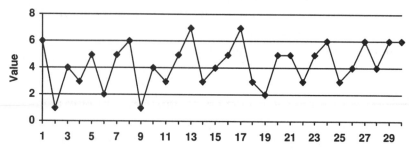

Fig. 7.2 Control chart for a sequence of 30 individual readings.

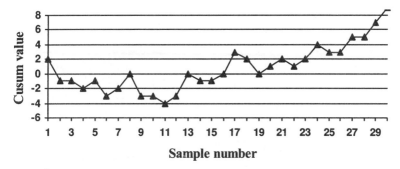

Fig. 7.3 Cusum chart for the 30 readings in Fig. 7.2.

Interpreting a cusum chart is quite different to interpreting a conventional variable chart. It is the slope of the cusum that is important in that the slope represents that level at which the process is running. It therefore follows that a change in slope on the cusum chart corresponds to a change in performance level as represented on the conventional chart. It also suggests that there must be a way of measuring the slope on the cusum graph in such a way as to directly provide the performance level. This is done by means of a slope protractor.

■ 7.4.3 The slope protractor

Fig. 7.4 shows how a protractor can be designed to measure the changes in the slope of a given process.

Angled lines are drawn corresponding to fixed intervals on the vertical scale. In our case the interval is 0.2 units. The horizontal line on the protractor corresponds to the target value of 5 units. The gradient of the first line above horizontal on the protractor is –0.2/10. This is added to the target value to give a value of 5.02 on the cusum graph. A line inclined at the same angle as this line on the protractor indicates that the process is running at a level of 5.02 units.

The protractor is drawn to scale and positioned in the top right-hand corner of the cusum graph. Fig. 7.5 shows a completed cusum graph and a relevant protractor designed on the basis of a target sales figure of 25 units. For the first 20 or so points the process appears to be running on target. Over the next 5 or 6 points a change has occurred with the process now running at a level of 29. A further change then occurs with the process now running at a level of 39.

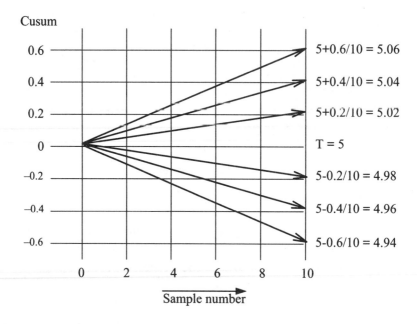

Fig. 7.4 Construction of a cusum protractor using a target value of 5 units.

This example has shown the three key features of a cusum graph, i.e.
(1) If a process is remaining on target then the cusum graph remains horizontal.
(2) A change in the process level on a run chart corresponds to a change in the slope on the corresponding cusum graph.
(3) The numerical value of the slope on the cusum graph corresponds to the performance mean as indicated on a run chart.

■ 7.4.4 Choice of cusum scale

It is important to choose an appropriate scale for the cusum axis on the graph. Too large a scale over-emphasises the natural changes in the process. Too small a scale makes it difficult to detect genuine changes in the process. Experience will suggest an appropriate scale to use, although the BSI standard (54) on the cusum method provides more detailed information.

One method of selecting the scale is to use the upper control limit calculation to predict the maximum slope expected. The chart should allow the process to run with a maximum slope of 1/3 (equivalent to the one standard deviation) for a period of seven consecutive points.

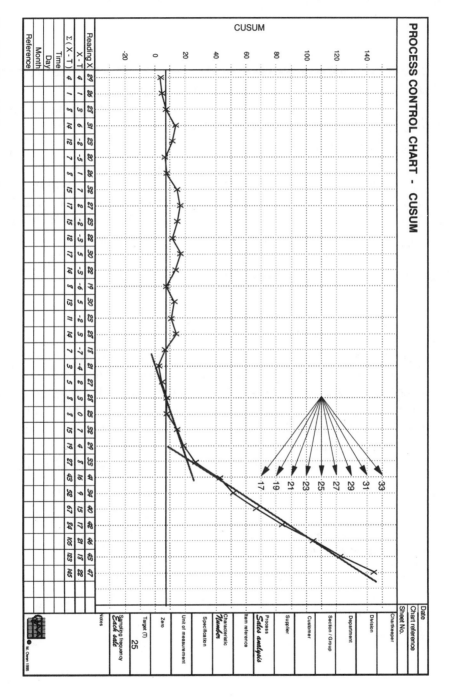

Fig. 7.5 Completed cusum graph.

■ 7.4.5 Detecting changes

More sophisticated methods are available for detecting process change than the purely visual estimate based on the protractor. One of these makes use of a truncated V mask, such as that shown in Fig. 7.6.

Only a brief description is provided here. The reader is referred to the four-part British Standard, BS 5703, on cusum methods (54) for a more comprehensive description.

The mask is placed with the axis parallel to the time axis of the cusum graph, and the notch placed on the most recent point on the graph. If all the previous points on the graph fall within the actual (or extended) arms of the V mask, then the process is under control. It is possible to alter the shape of the mask by redefining some of the parameters, e.g. the angle of the slope and the width of the narrow end of the mask, in order to detect smaller changes in the process more quickly.

■ 7.5 Multiple Process Charts

These charts present a few snapshots of several similar processes side by side and are applicable to software development in areas such as where several teams are developing code in parallel. This is because we cannot expect the processes, which are different perhaps because of the team members, to have identical control limits. This is equally true of one team changing some other parameter in the development cycle such as the language used, the development computers or the development method.

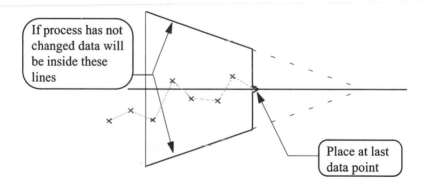

Fig. 7.6 Outline of truncated V mask.

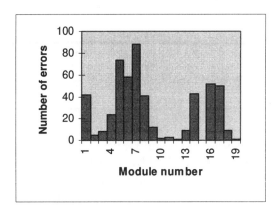

Fig. 7.7 Snapshot of errors left in code from a graphical interface project.

A snapshot of a project that consists of several different teams producing several different types of code is shown in Fig. 7.7.

The software under consideration is part way through the phase of measuring and finding the errors, and is several stages before the error levels have been reduced to an acceptance level. These error levels show several distinct groupings which suggest similarity in the development methods within these groups. The groups selected for analysis are for error levels as shown in Table 7.4

After a 20 cycles of measurement for all groupings the control lines can be calculated from the standard formula (using the rule of 20 values as indicated in Chapter 4). At one moment in time the data collected is shown in Table 7.5. For this particular set of groupings the control line for each group can now be added as the current mean and range values as shown in Fig. 7.8.

Table 7.4 Error level grouping.

Group number	Error levels
1	0–25
2	26–50
3	51–75
4	76–100

Table 7.5 Data for one grouping.

Group number	No. of modules	Mean error level	Error range
0–25	10	6.77	0–24
26–50	5	44	42 50
51–75	2	58.6	52–74
76–100	2	88	88

If we add the data for each of the groupings the result is a comparative snapshot for the process as shown in Fig. 7.9. The control lines are representative of the overall process, but each of the lines represents a particular group of processes. Fig. 7.9 shows three snapshots of the same product as it progressed through development. The improvement of the product is evidenced by the reducing values and ranges, but the comparative capability of the groupings remains constant.

This charting method can be used to compare the performance of different development teams, across different projects and utilising different development environments.

The chart can be used also for non-continuous developments. An example is found in software houses where the first project, using a particular team and development environment, may not be repeated for several months or even years. The chart can be preserved and restarted when a new project using similar methods is started. This effectively

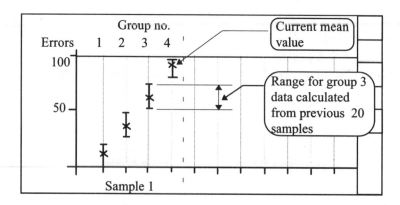

Fig 7.8 The multiple process chart.

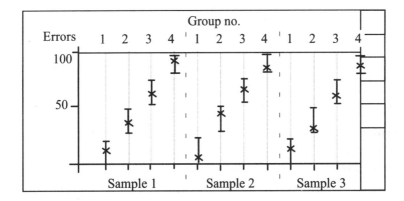

Fig. 7.9 The multiple process chart for three snapshots (monthly samples).

provides a benchmark for the new development team so that a measure of performance is available. In the intervening time the changes to equipment tools and software should have increased the performance of the team. The measure will then need recalculating when the 20 new readings have been collected, although the existing chart is used until the recalculation can take place.

The time intervals of the snapshots can be as short as a few days for projects that are only going to last a few weeks. When setting up the charts for a process metric that may vary with time, it is important to consider the effect of the sample period on the data. An instance of this is the weekday effect, which, because of administrative activities, may reduce the amount of effort on a project on Mondays and Fridays. A chart set up for a three-day period would cyclically include both Monday and Friday, only Monday or Friday, and then neither of these days, and would inevitably display a cyclic characteristic, but this would not be easily observed on this type of chart. On a standard variables charts the cycle would be evident. The sample period for this particular metric would probably ensure that at least one Monday and Friday pair was included. A sample period of 10 or 12 days would be appropriate.

■ 7.6 Management Charts

From the SPC loops described in Chapter 2 the managers and supervisors of projects have a responsibility to look at data collected and use this data to initiate both real-time corrective actions and long-term process improvement.

■ 7.6.1 Project statistics

In most software development companies the only measurements that may be available are time and a feel for the progress of the developers. If completeness, confidence and error statistics are gathered then the project progress can be monitored in terms of the state of control being achieved. Any significant differences can be observed and action taken to ensure that the process remains in control. The effect of changes to the process, such as new tools, machines, or extra staff can be monitored for the expected process improvement.

This prevents a manager from reacting to one single reading which seems unusual. An example of the type of problems that occur can be seen from an individual's chart for one project team within a software company that produces many different types of product (Fig. 7.10).

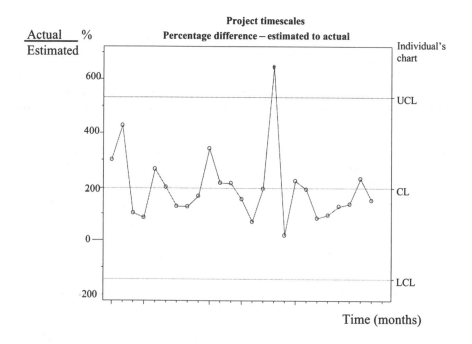

Fig. 7.10 Individual's chart for project delivery.

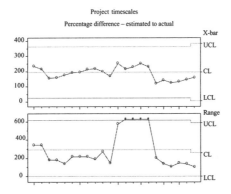

Fig. 7.11 Control charts for delivery performance.

The managers react to the out-of-control events on the chart as indicated by the return to a controlled status, but the overall effect on the company cannot be seen. In particular the effect on the projects in the long term is not provided by the data.

The alternative statistical view of the same data (Fig. 7.11) shows that the exceptions are now far fewer, and these events are explained by causes in the process. The target of removing these causes has a profound effect on the organisation since the company has a mechanism for detecting them and consequently re-aligning the expected time for projects that require this extra input. In financial terms this means that the company now has a means of getting customers to pay for changes to specifications when they occur. Individual progress charts are also used to detect when causes have occurred since progress in these periods is usually (statistically) significantly different, i.e. an out-of-control condition occurs on the progress charts.

▓ 7.6.2 Summary charts

If a project manager has many different areas of responsibility then the individual project summary chart looking at only one variable may give a misleading view of the project. The combination of charts as shown in Fig. 7.12 provides one way of presenting management information that will enable a whole process to be considered.

More frequently managers require a summary of current position compared with a previous position. There are two ways of providing this information, both derived from a current snapshot of the process and product.

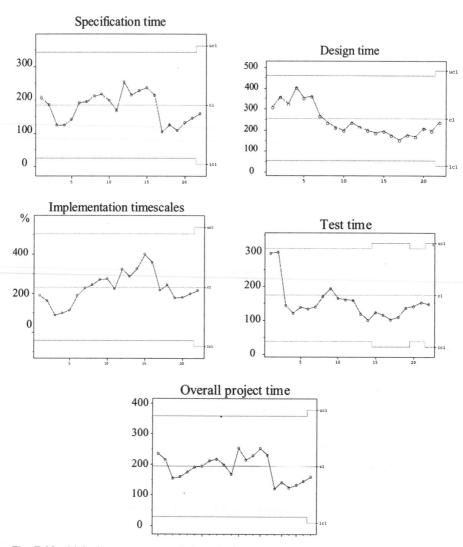

Fig. 7.12 Multiple process control chart display.

■ 7.6.3 The management individual summary chart

This type of chart is derived directly from the previous charts and provides the current value together with the target, upper and lower control values. These are scaled to be the same length for all variables being plotted. The chart for the last reading of the above set of results (Fig. 7.12) is shown in Fig. 7.13 as a series of single horizontal lines representing the y axis of each of the charts.

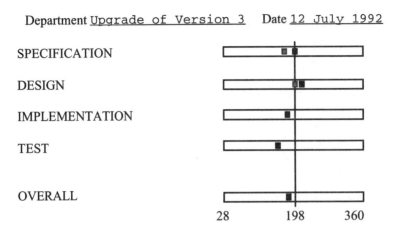

Fig. 7.13   Management summary charts.

The black squares in this diagram are the current mean value and the gray squares are the previous immediate value. If a value is well outside of the range of the graph then the square is placed to the high or low side with the value showing how far outside the control lines this is.

The ends of the box represent the upper and lower control lines and the line through the centre is the mean of the historic data.

■ 7.6.4 Star charts

The combination of each of the management bar charts can provide a quick picture both of the current state of a process and an indication of whether the process is improving. The management summary bars are arranged so that the origin (or LCL) is at the centre of a star with each of the lines radiating out so that the furthest point is the UCL. Then by joining the mean values for each characteristic we can describe a polygon for the particular snapshot. Fig. 7.14 shows the polygon for the snapshot used throughout this section.

In addition to the polygon for the mean values, the outside points can be joined to describe the upper control limit line. The centre point can be either a scaled origin or the lower control limit, depending on whether any of the characteristics has a value lower than this limit. Finally, marks on

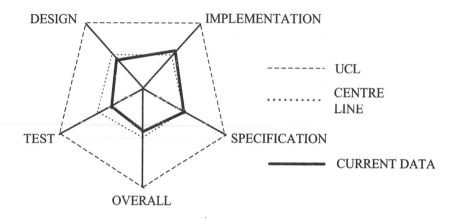

Fig. 7.14 The snapshot star chart.

the axis can be used to define the range of the characteristic over the period under consideration as shown in Fig. 7.15.

The final addition to the star chart is the historical comparison which can either be made by placing monthly charts close to one another, or by plotting the information on the same chart, as shown in Fig. 7.16. An ever improving chart should reveal more and more of the older polygons as time progresses. This is valid until the control limits are recalculated.

The star chart can also be arranged such that the areas within the chart

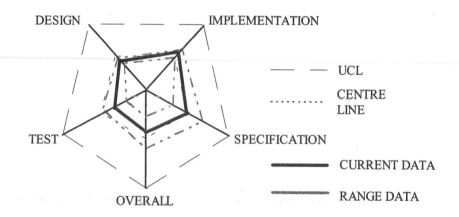

Fig. 7.15 The completed star chart.

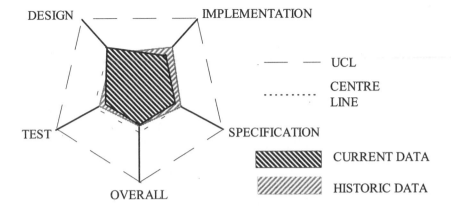

Fig. 7.16 A star chart with historic data.

have significance. Two main axis can be identified – one for product and process improvement and one for measuring the product and the process. There are three characteristics on each axis representing the progress and quality of the product and the process. These are drawn so that all product metrics are above the horizontal and all process metrics are below. The vertical split has all metrics to the right representing the improvement progress for both the product and the process and the metrics to the left representing the project progress. In this way the management have a complete picture of a process and product statistically represented for each of the prime characteristics (Fig. 7.17). The targets for these metrics are as follows:

progress metrics

(1) Conformance – starts at 0 and aims to achieve 100% (may exceed this if requirements change).

(2) Completeness – has a target of 100% and starts at 0.

(3) Confidence – again a metric that changes from 0 to close to 100% as the project progresses.

process improvement metrics

(1) Size – has an optimum for the company and the project – this chart is for size variance which should be maintained at a target level.

(2) Complexity – has an optimum level. The variance is used here to identify exceptional differences between modules within a project.

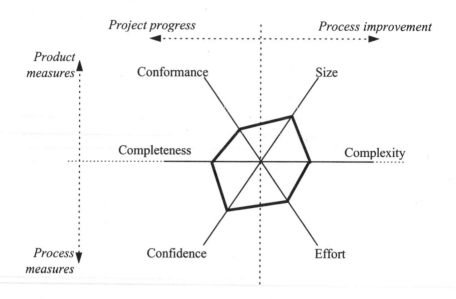

Fig. 7.17 The management star.

(3) Effort – the normalised effort metric that measures work days per Kbytes of code. It has a target level, but the variance is the metric required on this chart.

Note that size is considered a process improvement metric because of the relationship between defects and module size indicating that an optimum for any organisation is appropriate as discussed in section 3.8. The completeness and complexity metrics can be considered either as process or product metrics. They indicate the effectiveness of the process as well as measure the product.

As a project progresses the metrics star charts can be expected to fill out as shown in Fig. 7.18.

■ 7.7 Other Statistical Charts

Charting is the basis for establishing the variance and control status of a process, but the use of mapping techniques provides extra detection ability. The map can be used to analyse the capability of some of the tools, methods and machines used in the software development process.

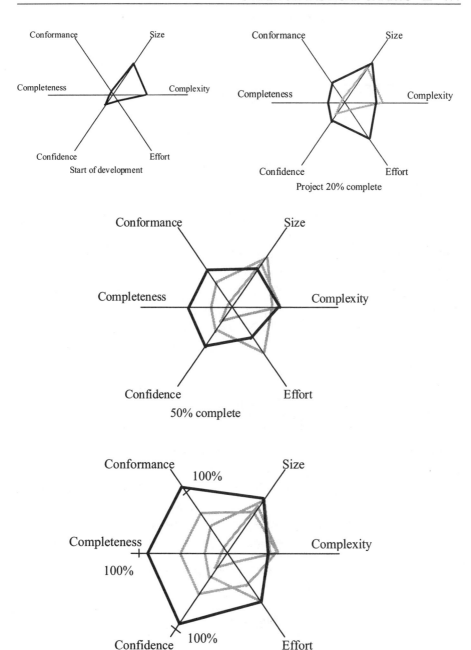

Fig. 7.18 The star chart through a project.

Table 7.6 Types of errors in the module of a particular product.

Module	Error types	1	2	3	4
Main control prog		24	12	11	19
Graphics		4	2	1	5
Draw		17	7	26	16
Comms		45	5	38	7

There are two main areas of error mapping resulting from any testing or inspection results. The first of these is to establish where different types of errors are within the code or documents. The part of a table shown in Table 7.6 is for a system under development and shows several high values which are related to different types of errors.

However the significance of these values is greatly enhanced by looking at the values in the categories of $> 1\sigma < 2\sigma$, $>2\sigma < 3\sigma$ and $> 3\sigma$. The values are calculated for each of the error types based on the formula for standard deviation.

$$\text{Standard deviation } \sigma = \sqrt{\frac{\sum(x - \bar{x})^2}{n-1}}$$

Values below 1σ are not evaluated, and the table is filled with either 1, 2 or 3 respectively. Table 7.7 is the new map for the product which shows that the error levels are only significant for a few of the values. The rest are considered to be within the normal capability of the company.

One of the purposes of testing is to find, and help developers eliminate, errors. These maps show where effort should be placed in terms of the

Table 7.7 Error map with only significant areas highlighted by their range.

Module	Error types	1	2	3	4
Main control prog		1	3		2
Graphics					
Draw			2	2	1
Comms		3		3	

most significant numbers. However the numbers found also depend on the effectiveness of the testing.

The same types of chart can be used to establish the relationship between errors found and the test method used. This mapping provides some indication of the effectiveness of a test method on a particular function. A '-' is used to indicate where no tests have been completed of this type. The map serves two purposes:

- to find the effectiveness of test methods by comparing the errors of particular types found by a particular test method
- to find the areas where error densities of significant types of error occur so that test and correction effort can be targeted at these areas.

Another application of mapping is in the coverage achieved by test methods. In this instance the test method, the modules being tested and the coverage figures provide a three-dimensional map of the system as shown in Fig. 7.19.

A contour map provides the same type of information revealing which modules require attention and which are not of concern. Fig. 7.20 shows this map for the same data.

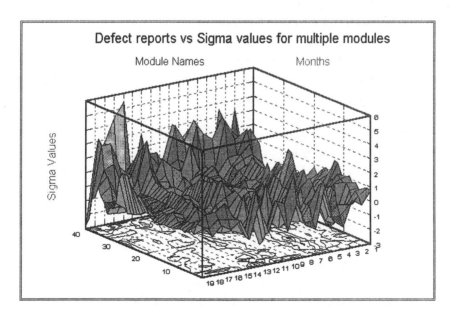

Fig. 7.19 The control surface for modules tested on a system based on the errors detected and not fixed at each monthly period.

Height = Sigma values

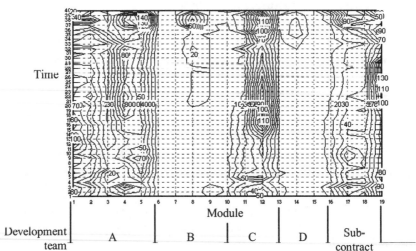

Fig. 7.20   The contour map for the data of Fig. 7.19.

■ 7.8 Summary

- These extra charting methods provide useful information that the standard Shewhart control charts cannot provide.
- The angled control lines chart provides a tool essential to software development where progress, confidence and error rates are expected to change over time.
- The cusum chart is used for detecting slowly changing and small changes in the mean for a process. It is used for either variables or attributes and as the output for multi-variate data.
- The multiple process chart provides a means of summarising the results from several teams and several processes. It is not commonly used except as a management tool.
- Management summaries can be derived from variables charts, but the single line summary chart provides a simple mechanism for comparative management.
- The star chart provides a profile for software development that can be used to assist with process improvement. One progress and one quality metric can be calculated which may be charted to ensure

that the company is always achieving the same, or better, objectives as stated in statistical terms.

- Mapping techniques, usually used for error mapping, reveal the significant defect levels within code, and provide analysis tools for establishing the effectiveness of tests. Maps can be developed as three-dimensional pictures.

This section has outlined other charting tools for statistical control of processes but it is not exhaustive. Most standard texts on statistics will provide details of data decomposition and correlation based on populations. There are other analysis techniques that are not mentioned here such as box-and-whisker analysis. These methods are not considered to be important in the control of processes for software development although they may have their place in the analysis of data to improve overall understanding of processes. It must be emphasised that analysis using population methods can only be carried out on data collected from processes that are stable. In other words the processes must be in statistical control and this book is about getting that control.

8 Process Improvement Methods

8.1 Introduction

Statistical control is at the heart of process improvement. Most software houses with a wide variety of projects to complete claim that every project is different, and there are special causes in each project that cannot be eliminated. However, it is still a fact that the underlying processes for particular project types are common. If the project teams can be trained to follow a consistent process for each of the different activities – however many different activities can be envisaged – then the underlying processes can be controlled. For many types of software development the process is stable and the procedures can readily be identified and then continually improved.

This chapter provides details of the overall strategy for process improvement and the details of the tools required to make statistical process improvement work. There are examples of the use of some of the tools for controlling the supplier/customer interface and for managing computer facilities in the final section of the chapter .

Process improvement is not just about looking inward at the process of software development. It includes techniques for assuring both the customer and the company aims are satisfied by all activities. It also includes methods for measuring the maturity of the company in order for quality to be seen to be improving. These factors are included to make the model relevant for commercial success as well as to provide benefits for marketing and project control. The model also is directly relevant to the engineers and managers working closely with the projects.

A process consists of inputs from many sources and it is important to get these sources under control before embarking on the improvement of the actual development process. An example of this might be the input that a compiler has to a project. If the normal language usage profile does not match the error free regions of the compiler, then work on process improvement within a project will always be clouded by the variance of the compiler introduced errors.

■ 8.2 Process Improvement Strategy

The desire for process improvement may be motivated by either:
- an internal need to improve the effectiveness of the company, characterised by a desire for improved profit, reputation and market share
- external pressures to improve the service and product delivered, characterised by a need to maintain customer relationships and usually motivated by customer dissatisfaction or a customers' drive for supplier quality improvement.

Whichever is the cause of the action, consideration must be given to the whole of the company not just concentrating on product or process improvement. The aim is to improve the maturity of the company by identifying the processes and then making them increasingly repeatable. As described in Chapter 3, improvement is achieved by changing processes from the chaotic condition where a different distribution results from each use of the process, to the repeatable condition that results in the same distribution. The next step is to change the state to ensure that every repeated cycle of the process has a reduced spread or variation. Without knowing what the current variability is, the opportunity for controlling the process and reducing variability can never be achieved, and the benefits will not be gained. Data gathering is essential right from the start of an improvement project. It provides the basis from which improvement opportunities are discovered, grasped and developed. It is also through the analysis of process metrics distributions that processes can be classified, and over time evidence for commonality between processes can be found. This requires a study of special causes that are present in existing systems so that they can be taken into account when justifying the classifications of processes.

The ISO SPICE project (47) is developing a process improvement standard for the software industry which will define the requirements of process improvement in terms of the constituent activities. This will bring together many of the current models for the stages of process improvement. However it is the actions between the stages that are of interest here. These stages of a process improvement project relate directly to the SEI maturity levels (which is based on the Deming process improvement model) of chaotic, identified processes, process control, repeatable processes and optimised processes. The improvement models described concern the actions required to achieve each of these levels.

▓ 8.2.1 Level 1 to 2 – 'chaotic' to 'identified processes'

Most software companies start out at the chaotic level because they have relied on the skills of the individual to produce code without defining a process of producing code. They can quickly move from the chaotic state (level 1) to level 2 or 3 using the following actions.

▓ Actions

Flowcharting and process modelling are used to identify processes and sub-processes. The processes are proceduralised at all levels, possibly with ISO 9000 registration as the target. The commonality between processes is identified using distribution analysis of common metrics and causes for non-common processes are identified using brainstorming and fishbone analysis.

Causes are removed to achieve commonality between processes where possible. However ISO 9000 does not exclude special causes, but provides a mechanism through preventative and corrective actions to deal with them. If a project requires a special task it is included in the quality plan for the project. If a 'special' activity becomes a frequent requirement it is included into the process specification or operating procedure.

■ End status

Projects are completed through a standard set of procedures (may be a selected subset) with few exceptions. Standard sets of process and product metrics are collected and analysed to establish whether processes are common. Sampling is used for measurement in order to minimise initial costs and maximise benefits from the metrics. Quality plans are used to enable process commonality to be identified between different project types.

■ 8.2.2 Level 2 to 3 – 'identified processes' to 'process controlled'

The change from identified to controlled implies an improvement in understanding of the processes, since to control the processes an understanding of the relationships between the product quality and the process inputs is required. The actions are aimed at achieving this understanding of processes.

■ Actions

Metrics for the processes are selected and analysed for variation and continuous monitoring of these metrics using control charts indicates if there are special causes occurring. The charts are managed and issued for every project as part of the standard procedure. The charts are analysed off-line for special and variation causes in order to get improvement in the variance. Metrics are selected and the control status is monitored to establish whether better control is actually beneficial. New metrics and variables are continually being identified and control charts set up. Variables are temporarily discarded if no benefit arises from their measurement.

■ End status

Control charts are part of the process and are reacted to if an out-of-control situation arises. Improvement teams are established to identify and eliminate special causes and to find common causes of variance. Process control improvement is a standard feature of project management.

▮ 8.2.3 Level 3 to 4 – 'process controlled' to 'repeatable process'

A repeatable process is both identified and has a standard control mechanism and so the effort required is to ensure that no special causes exist. Any differences between processes are identified and controlled in the same way as for the standard project. The aim is to enable the same project to be completed by a different team, in a different language and on different hardware but within the same control distribution. This does not mean the same time, cost and performance, but suitably corrected values. An intermediary aim is for the company to have confidence that a repetition of the project will have the same result. This assumes completion by the same team using the same tools. The result is expected to be completion within the same time, performance and cost distributions.

▮ Actions

The stabilised metrics from level 3 can now be used to establish relationships for the individual organisation. The differences between project resources are minimised by ensuring commonality through projects and these are measured using control charts. Exceptions occurring on a control chart are analysed for cause and a standard action plan is set in motion to eliminate, justify or incorporate the cause. Repeatability is measured across different projects using measures for common processes and normalisation relationships for different processes.

▮ End status

At the end of this process the processes are repeatable and measured by the quality of the output (time, cost and performance). A policy for reducing the variance of processes by analysing causes and relationships between process metrics and product quality is in place.

▮ 8.2.4 Level 4 to 5 – 'repeatable process' to 'optimised process'

Once a process is controlled and repeatability is achieved, then the task is to optimise it. Many quality programmes start out with this optimisation as the goal – cost reduction for the process is one of these standard quality achievement metrics. Without process control and repeatability any cost reduction is likely to be at the expense of technical performance or is unlikely to be repeatable.

The aim of the task is to increase customer satisfaction and increase profitability. The actions are taken in line with commercial pressures to keep abreast of the competitors. There are costs associated with being too far ahead and so this stage enables a company to remain a world class organisation, competing with the best on equal terms.

■ Actions

The metrics for control are now known and understood and their relationship to the product quality is studied to optimise the process for efficiency and effectiveness. This should also reduce variance and increase repeatability of the processes. The tasks involve establishing which activities contribute most to the variance and then re-engineering the processes to improve the effectiveness and efficiency. The non-conformance and process control management tasks are reduced as tasks by designing them for maximum efficiency. The aim is to minimise costs while still detecting out-of-control situations. All the procedures for dealing with these situations are in place and are part of the everyday activities of the company.

■ End status

This stage does not have an end status – there are always reasons for improving the process including changing the procedures and the tools. However, whenever a major change is made the effect is to take the company back to the level 2 status. The process is no longer clearly understood and effort will be required to bring the process back into statistical control. By including these actions in the plan for introducing new tools and methods you will ensure that the changes made are aimed at improving the stability, efficiency and effectiveness of the process.

■ 8.3 Process Control

Processes are controlled using statistical control loops as shown in Fig. 8.1 and described in Chapter 2. The preceding sections have concentrated on the tools for gathering data, producing charts and analysing them using statistical control techniques and have shown examples of the charts used

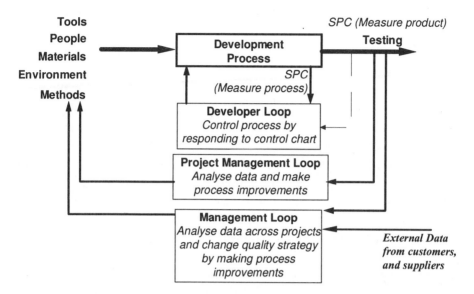

Fig. 8.1 The process control model.

for process control purposes. These charts are used in the developer loop to provide real time control of the development activities. In Chapter 7 the use of the data from the charts to provide information for the management and supervisory loops was discussed and specialised charts were outlined. The real time loop ensures the current development is controlled and disregards (although it will be in line with) the long term strategy and operates on an hour-by-hour time frame.

The middle loops represent time spans of days and weeks, whereas the management loop is concerned about the long-term strategy for the company in months and years.

There is evidence that long-term use of control procedures at the developer level will provide process improvement in terms of stability of the process. The major benefits are obtained through activities which aim at a better understanding and consequent optimisation of the processes used within an individual company. This has to be considered in conjunction with the life cycle of the organisation. There is little point in establishing a long-term improvement plan for a company that is expected to complete one development and then be replaced with a sales and system maintenance organisation. This requires a strategy for process improvement of the maintenance activity rather than the development phase.

■ 8.3.1 Process contribution to product quality

The inherently human aspects of software design and development make it impossible to eliminate the contribution that the individual process stages make to the end product. The human influences introduce variability into the project and consequently are a major cause of differences between individual projects. These differences in project output are measures of the instability of the process.

The variability of a process can be described in terms of the opportunity to improve the product. Fig. 8.2, shows how each individual stage of a traditional sequential process contributes to the overall capability of the product to satisfy the customer needs. Each stage has the opportunity to either improve or reduce this capability and consequently this justifies the need for improved control of this variability. The best projects end up by satisfying the customer, but the worst are disasters, being rejected by the customers and resulting in costly litigation. Both of these results can be obtained from seemingly the same capable process. The point of failure can be at any stage of the cycle. Few can argue against finding the causes and eliminating them so that future projects have a higher probability of success.

A process can be designed to measure the success of smaller, repeated development cycles. This will provide the feedback required to minimise the corrective action loops (test/debug cycles and their consequential costs) in the project, thus ensuring customer satisfaction. The rapid application development (RAD) or simultaneous engineered method of developing software provides such a control. However this method requires a mechanism for measuring the success of each iteration. Otherwise the project will be free to follow a path leading to less than maximum satisfaction for both the customer and the project team (Fig. 8.3).

■ 8.4 Process Improvement

Much of the process improvement activity occurs at management and senior management levels. Only this level of seniority can have the insight to develop a company that understands and continually improves its processes ensuring maximum benefit both for the company itself and for its customers.

Process improvement activity is planned as part of the normal management strategy planning and it relies on factual information. This is

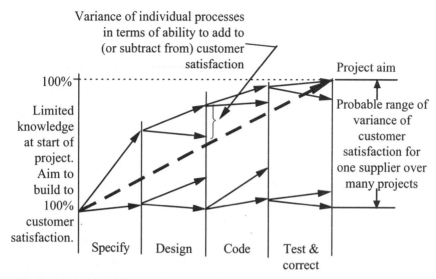

Fig. 8.2 Cumulative variability in a V model project.

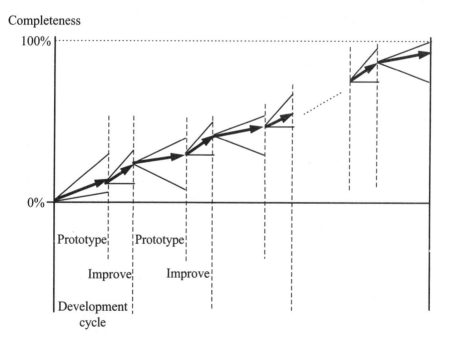

Fig. 8.3 Variability through a RAD project.

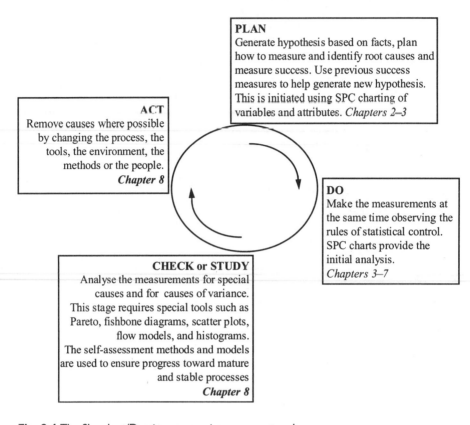

Fig. 8.4 The Shewhart/Deming process improvement cycle.

analysed for improvement opportunities and for making changes to the process to incorporate the benefits from successful projects. Management also require a method of measurement that will tell them whether the improvement strategy implemented has been beneficial. These functions are provided by the basic Shewhart or Deming cycle as shown in Fig. 8.4.

■ 8.4.1 The improvement cycle actions

The process improvement cycle as shown in Fig. 8.4 is broken down into a number of detail stages as shown in Fig. 8.5. These activities are usually allocated to individuals and small teams to investigate and develop. They may resort back to a group responsible for the improvement process, but two factors must always be considered:

Planning

- ◆ Establish improvement aims related to company policy.
- ◆ Use factual information (if available) to identify processes that do not conform to these aims.
- ◆ Identify exceptional causes from the variability measurements of processes.
- ◆ Plan a mechanism for measuring variables and attributes that will detect causes based on a hypothesis of causes produced as a result of brainstorming, Ishikawa, and Pareto analysis.
- ◆ Initiate the Shewhart process improvement loops at the supervisory and technical levels in order to instigate process stability.
- ◆ Establish a mechanism for monitoring the improvements and measuring success and communicate this with the whole team.

Doing

- ◆ Take measurements according to the plan for each process.
- ◆ React to out-of-control situations as they occur and maintain process stability where possible.
- ◆ Mark up exceptional circumstances and changes that occur as the measurements are being taken.
- ◆ Use measurement management to ensure that the history of measurements is available and future charts are based on the current control status.

Checking or Study

- ◆ Use the information to identify causes as they occur, to identify historic trends, to measure capability, and as a source for analysis.
- ◆ Check for measurement causes before process causes.
- ◆ Analyse for relationships only when data is in statistical control.
- ◆ Analyse for process causes and eliminate simple control causes early.
- ◆ Analyse for process causes and work with suppliers, managers and customers to eliminate them.

Act

- ◆ Once the causes have been found, pilot removal methods and use measurement to prove their success.
- ◆ Put successful change into standard practice and train staff to understand and use them.
- ◆ Implement a monitoring procedure to ensure continued success.
- ◆ Initiate the next loop with new commercial goals at a time when it is clearly beneficial in financial and competitive terms to do this.

Fig. 8.5 Detailed processd improvement cycle.

- It is usually those working close to the problem who have answers. They may not realise what the answers are, but can usually be drawn into revealing problems and issues and providing localised solutions.
- These localised solutions rarely solve the whole problem. It is an overall view of the integrated systems together with real data on what is currently happening that can identify where the place for action is and what changes should be made.

■ 8.4.2 Preparing to improve

■ Setting goals

Deming is often misquoted as stating in one of his 14 management points that goals or targets should not be part of the process improvement cycle. The actual statement is that goals should not be part of a process unless management action is taken to provide the means of achieving them. So the first part of any process improvement activity is to identify the goals of the project. This enables management to schedule resources, finances and effort for change to meet the new goals.

This means asking questions about the purpose of the company and the benefits expected from delivering the service or product. For a charitable organisation, quality is defined as delivering the best possible service with zero profit (neither negative nor positive but excluding working capital). For most commercial organisations the balance between maximising profits by minimising costs, while at the same time satisfying customers, is a difficult task. However a successful process improvement activity must have both customer and internal company satisfaction as its goals and these are stated in terms of the policy of the organisation.

In order to establish what sort of goals are reasonable, benchmarks are used that compare a company with a standard model or a set of standards derived from other organisations. By using profiling techniques for benchmarking, processes that are not required in the model can be identified and new benchmark levels can be developed to reflect their reduced importance. The new profile model is us to provide a rating for the status or maturity of the company.

The idea that there is an ideal benchmark for a particular type of company suggests that they should be utilising the same types of staff, equipment and processes, and providing the same service to the same standard. Clearly this is an absurd state of affairs since the customer needs are very different, even within a particular sector. Also it is often the ethos of a company that provides the competitive edge rather than processes themselves. So any profile generated must relate directly to the requirements of the organisation, with financial benefit being the first priority for the improvement. There are types of benchmarking systems that provide a profile for an organisation showing up the weaknesses and strengths, as well as assessing the status against a maturity model. These are described in the later sections of this chapter.

Note that any assessment can only be a snapshot of the organisation based on historical information. Since assessments do not take account of statistical control status they cannot tell whether the company is likely to improve, or whether a reassessment in 6 months or a year will show a worse or better state. The assessments undertaken by suppliers in manufacturing concentrate on the repeatability and reliability of the processes, using statistical control evidence to show whether the process is firstly in control, and secondly, whether it is improving. This is included within ISO 9000 in that the standard requires 'processes to be capable and

Table 8.1 The typical results of an assessment – areas that require improvement.

Process	Rating
Requirements gathering	80%
Requirements control	*20%*
Specification generation	82%
Specification inspection	*25%*
Specification improvement control	*45%*
Design generation	94%
Design inspection	86%
Design improvement control	64%
Code generation	75%
Compilation	88%
Module test	*45%*
Module inspect	65%
Code walkthrough	75%
Integration test	68%
System testing	*27%*

mechanisms for the maintenance of capability to be in place'. As we have seen earlier, capability of a process can only be properly assessed from the control status of an organisation.

For any type of assessment, further analysis is required to discover the importance of the measures in terms of the targets and objectives of the company. An example in software development is testing which is seen as an essential part of the development cycle. From a commercial viewpoint, however, it can be seen as a financial burden that is not benefiting the organisation. Its aim is to detect defects in the product and it has no capability for improving the product and consequently, no opportunity of adding value. Testing is beneficial only in terms of managing customer satisfaction. Note the way that many software organisations get the testing done by customers for the dual benefit of gaining customer commitment and removing the opportunity for complaint about failure.

Post-assessment analysis takes into account the goals of each process and identifies those that are inconsistent or not achieving benefit to the company. Once these have been identified they can be subjected to greater scrutiny. Taking an example, the areas highlighted in Table 8.1 are considered to be costs to the organisation rather than providers of financial benefits, and so these are the sections highlighted for further analysis.

For this particular organisation the areas for immediate attention are control of requirements gathering, specification inspections, specification improvement control, module testing and system testing. If this company is producing shrink-wrapped product for a non-critical application then the profile compared with the commercial requirements of the organisation can probably be accepted. However, if the profile is for critical applications, then an emphasis on requirements and specification management is required, and improvement in system testing is essential.

■ Non-conforming processes

The processes are now subjected to planning for improvement. The aim is to find causes that can be tackled and the measures that can be used during the Deming improvement cycle. The plan should include:

(1) What to measure
(2) What its current status is – this may initially be just the assessment results plus a guess from the planning team. However where metrics exist these should be assessed for special causes.

(3) How to measure – the measurement tools to be used and the resolution and accuracy required

(4) What resources and commitments are required for the improvement process

(5) What should happen to the measurements once they have been taken

(6) Allocation of responsibility for the measurement activity and for taking appropriate actions to particular individuals.

If a history of measurements is available, then the starting point for accuracy and resolution is taken from the statistical analysis of charts based on this data. This is true even if the measurements were taken without statistical analysis on mind. This gives some idea of the type of action to be taken later, and the method of measurement to be included in the planning phase. Examples of this, based on the assumption that the process is not providing the benefits expected, are shown in Table 8.2.

▓ Identify exceptional causes from variability

Historic data can provide immediate indicators of out-of-control situations. The first stage of planning may be to use this information to establish a preventative programme so that these particular types of exceptions cannot re-occur. This will provide benefits to the project at the earliest possible stage (before data gathering has actually begun). The improvement tools used include cause analysis using brainstorming, categorisation and solution development techniques.

Table 8.2 Effects of patterns on the next data collection activity.

Mean fluctuations and patterns	Range fluctuations and patterns	New method of measurement
Trend	Consistent within control limits	Use the same and control the trend
Within middle third	Varying out of control	Increase sample rate
Within middle third	Within middle third	Increase resolution and sample rate
Outside middle 2/3rds	Random within control limits	Decrease resolution
Outside control lines	Outside control lines	Restart control chart
Outside control lines	Inside control lines	Re-centre control Chart

■ **Supervisory and technical process improvement loops**

Once a mechanism for data gathering has been planned the staff involved must be prepared so that actions required when out-of-control conditions arise do not cause changes that will not benefit the company. The information collected should be expected by all staff and improvement comes not from blaming staff, but from gaining their assistance and respect for producing solutions for the out-of-control situations that occur.

The charts should be used by the technical staff (those directly involved with specifying, designing and developing the product) to prevent out-of-control situations arising. If, for instance, lines of code is to be used as a control metric for code quality, then the developers will be expected to produce the code in the normal way. When an out-of-control case occurs (i.e. a measurement is outside of the control limits), the developer will be expected either to be able to justify that case or to assist in the analysis to find a cause. This cause analysis will be used to find appropriate corrective actions for the individual case. This example is based on the relationship between defects and lines of code. The developer is provided with a chart with the control limits defined from historical data using the minimum defect region (see Fig. 2.7).

To get commitment to statistical methods throughout the organisation, the information collected is summarised for supervisory management, and company-wide metrics are produced for senior and board level managers. The mechanisms and training required for all levels of staff must be available for this to be successful.

■ **Monitoring the improvements**

Once the process of producing charts is in place, then the whole project requires justification. If charting the process has not caused any process improvement, perhaps because there are few commercial reasons for making the changes, then the company is justified in reducing the charting activity so that it is used only when testing detects an out-of-control situation. However a background level is required to trap any occurrences even at this level. Also the whole process can be re-established quickly in response to changed commercial situations, and in order to stay one step ahead of competitors.

▪ 8.4.3 Gathering evidence

The doing activity takes the plans developed and provides the raw collected data in form of charts for off-line analysis. It consists of continual use of charts, chart management to ensure that correct control lines are used, and the daily use of charts to maintain control of the development process.

▪ Measurement and response to control charts

All staff who have responsibility for development should be trained in the use of variance as a control mechanism. This can be used for self-control – the engineer or developer responding interactively to the charts, or management control – the analysis of charts takes place off-line and the responses are rework of products.

The off-line analysis brings with it the danger or resentment and de-motivation that rework always causes. The more on-line the charts can be made the better, then the better the result for all involved. In many situations, there is little need for the data to be provided outside of an individuals' own work area. The charts require summarising for management, but the actual daily readings can be subjected to a regular audit and rewards provided for recognition of process improvement opportunities.

▪ Records management

Charts must be based on historic data. Consequently a mechanism for releasing new versions only when the changes to the process have been both successful and beneficial, must be put into place. A history of charts can provide evidence that the organisation is attempting to continually improve, but this history must be seen to be useful and not just an archive.

ISO 9000 dictates how charts are used and managed since they represent quality records for the company. Consequently, the issue of a chart to a project, with specific control lines and targets, must be version controlled and changes made only through formal checking and release procedures. This may seem a burden, but electronic methods of holding the information and managing the process of releasing new charts, can reduce the effort required. The task of changing a procedure, as a result of cause analysis and in response to a control chart, can also be managed using software solutions. There are now many quality management systems on the market (56) as well as tools for automating the SPC processes (57).

■ 8.4.4 Checking the evidence

■ Post collection analysis

The checking activity provides the opportunity to establish relationships between variables and attributes from the process and the product. It also is the opportunity to analyse multiple charts and discover whether relationships exist between the out-of-control situations and the values on other charts.

The tools for this purpose are the rules governing charts, the use of scatter plots and correlation methods, and the use of error maps which can provide the dependency relationships as shown in Chapter 7.

■ Cause and effect analysis

Once the out-of-control situations have been identified and dealt with the second level of information that can be gathered from the chart is the variance data. This data is dealt with in the same way as an out-of-control signal. It is analysed for causes and then process improvements are initiated in order to provide the continual reduction in variance that Deming has stated will provide the quality benefits.

The main tools for this are cause and effect (Ishikawa) or fishbone diagrams and error maps. These two tools, coupled with the use of the knowledge of the developers gained from the brainstorming sessions, indicate the likely cause of individual events and the variance of the process. Methods of eliminating these are then developed.

■ Pareto analysis and finding what to tackle first

The results of the cause and effect analysis are ranked for importance and Pareto analysis for the number of occurrences of a cause, the cost of change and the expected financial benefits are produced. These charts are used to decide what to change first. The Pareto diagram of the cost of change is drawn reversed in order to find the cheapest, easiest and most cost effective first.

■ 8.4.5 Making improvement changes

The final stage of the process improvement cycle is to act on the findings of the previous stages to eliminate special causes and develop improvements for the new understanding of the process.

▓ Removal of causes

The actions that follow Pareto analysis are the allocation of the removal tasks to individuals or groups within the organisation. The monitoring task is also initiated to ensure that the removal task is successfully completed. The removal task often involves monitoring the use of control charts. This activity enables any re-occurrence of a cause to be highlighted so that the people doing the work can be trained to avoid them. This is particularly the case in the early stages of the software development activity. In the automated activities of the development cycle the causes may be due to the development tools used. Consequently the charts provide an input to the task of producing quality plans, tool specifications and the procedures for their use.

▓ Who is responsible?

The most senior person in the company! Mainly for initiating the activity and providing the resources for it. Blame for any cause should not be apportioned. This is destructive. The aim must be to reward the success and provide encouragement to make the rest of the organisation more reactive to the needs of both the organisation and its customers. Each and every member of staff is responsible for the improvement in their own field of influence. It is not possible to allocate responsibility without suggesting that there is someone, somewhere with no responsibility. The emphasis should be on responsibility for all.

▓ 8.4.6 Integrating the improvement actions into the development cycle

All the previous actions seem to be added activities to the development cycle, however process improvement has two essential functions:
- the short term objective of controlling the current project and improving the current product
- the longer term objective of improving the process regardless of individual projects.

The improvement cycle for each is the same. The analysis of the long-term cycle provides input to each individual project for process changes. Each individual project provides capability measurements and information for off-line cause analysis and removal.

Identifying the quality aims and the causes of failure at the company level requires sophisticated analysis, but two main strategies are applied:

- Variance in a process adds to costs and should be reduced wherever possible.
- The customer/profit balance is the main quality metric for measuring the success of the organisation.

With this in mind the organisation requires some mechanism for establishing the current capability of the organisation for its main activities. The relationship to be explored is between the customer and the development process.

Quality Function Deployment (QFD) is designed to take the requirements, concerns and issues of the customer and incorporate these into the design. The method provides an indicator for where effort should be put in the development process in order to maximise customer satisfaction. Failure Mode Effect Analysis (FMEA) provides a way of analysing the process and the product in order to prevent failure by determining where it is likely to happen and then using prevention as the cure. For ongoing customer care, interactive confidence measurement indicates whether satisfaction is being delivered. Sampling and questionnaires are used to determine what the customer thinks of a delivered system. Each of these actions is designed to ensure that the product and process will deliver a satisfactory result both for the company and the customer.

The second part of these operational or level 1 activities is process improvement. This takes observed problems from either the customer-based analysis or from the internal process and analyses this data to find causes. It then attempts to eliminate these causes or change the process to improve one of the inputs or development events.

This improvement cycle for the process provides input to a second strategic level that is used to decide which improvements best match the requirements of the organisation as a whole. The resultant integrated improvement cycle, Fig. 8.6, for the three cycles and two levels of activity, embed improvement into the daily management tasks of producing a product for a customer.

Planning in the outer loop establishes what is required of the process in order to provide customer, owner and employee satisfaction. This is then realised by defining the process in terms of what there is to do and how it is to be done. It is the responsibility of management to define what there is

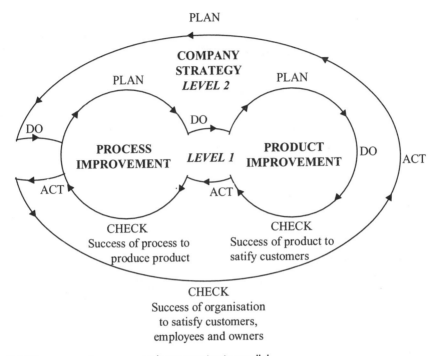

Fig. 8.6 The process improvement loops running in parallel.

to be achieved as well as to provide the tools for achieving this.

Once a process has been defined with inputs and outputs then it can be used to plan the requirements of the product. The product improvement loop is by its nature a loop that will iterate many times in order to build a product from nothing to a salable item. Each time round the loop the process can be improved by checking on how effective it was in producing the product. This information is then provided to the strategic level in order to change the process.

Once a process is improving it is important to know whether the improvement rate is being achieved throughout the company – or at least where it can be seen to be effective. Maturity measurement has been a significant activity over the last few years. It has driven companies to consider methods for changing from the chaotic state to the development of repeatable processes for producing software. However all companies are not the same. The maturity that is striven for should be different depending on the type of company involved. A company that is developing a line of similar products using common processes may aim for mature and repeatable development processes. A project oriented company that continually develops new products using new processes and tools will develop a mature project management and development method selection process.

Whichever type of company is being considered the place to start analysis is with the customer. The adage of 'no customer – no work' will remain true as long as democratic and market driven economies exist and so satisfying the customer is the first aim.

■ 8.5 Tools for Process Improvement

The standard tools for process improvement include Pareto analysis, brainstorming and Ishikawa or cause and effect analysis, process modelling, questionnaires, FMEA and QFD, and design of measurement. Charting and distribution analysis has been described in the previous chapters and these methods provide the input to the cause and effect analysis and process modelling activities.

Once control has been achieved then the relationships between variables and defectiveness can be used to reduce the variance of the process. These techniques include correlation methods, scatter plots and experimental analysis.

■ 8.5.1 Pareto analysis

Pareto analysis is the task of ranking the events in order of frequency of occurrence, importance, or cost. The improvement tasks to prevent defects in a software development process have been identified (Table 8.3) for one particular company. The ranking for occurrence is provided in the Pareto diagram (Fig. 8.7).

This is a simple ranking based on the number of observed errors that were likely to have been caused by any one of the newly controlled activities. However there are two other factors to consider. If one of the improvements is likely to prevent the failure of critical parts of the software, then this should be considered as more important than the others, regardless of its position in the occurrence frequency table.

Secondly, if one of the controls will prevent an error that is likely to be costly to fix, and in itself is not as expensive as others to implement, then

Table 8.3 Improvement tasks and the frequency of the errors they are designed to prevent.

Improvement tasks	Error causes	Number of errors
Improve use of tools	Compiler	1737
	Editor	1605
	Keyboard	275
Improve effectiveness of processes	Designer	217
	Specifier	763
Improve conformance of inspection process	Spec inspection	114
	Design inspection	305
	Code inspection	1293
Improve hardware conformance and compatibility	Equipment selection	56

Table 8.4 The completed Pareto analisys table.

Error causes	Number of errors	Criticality weight	Weighted data	Cost weight	Cost data
Compiler	1737	1.0	1738.00	300	521100
Editor	1605	0.5	802.50	280	449400
Keyboard	275	0.7	192.50	500	137500
Designer	217	1.2	260.40	1200	260400
Specifier	763	1.5	1144.50	1500	1144500
Spec inspection	114	1.5	171.00	2000	228000
Design inspection	305	1.2	366.00	1800	549000
Code inspection	1293	1.0	1293.00	1000	1293000
Equipment selection	56	1.0	56.00	5000	280000

Table 8.5 Standard input categories for the software industry.

Standard category	Software category	Software inputs included
Methods	Processes	Tasks such as inspections, editing sessions, design process, requirements gathering, test methods, etc.
People	People	The influence of different people on the task and particularly the relationship between knowledge, skill, effectiveness and personality
Tools	Systems	Computers, editors, spelling checkers, logic checkers, etc.
Materials	Consumables	Language (words, grammar and syntax), compiler, and any other consumables used for the project (disks etc.)
Environment	Environment	The working environment, pressure of work, political environment

again this has a higher level of priority. These two weightings can be used to provide Pareto diagrams that will ensure those actions that are critical get completed first. Table 8.4 shows the weighted data and the three Pareto diagrams are shown in Fig. 8.8.

■ 8.5.2 Ishikawa and brainstorming

The Ishikawa or fishbone diagram is coupled with brainstorming to obtain conformation about processes that are based on the experience and knowledge of the people involved with them. The diagram divides the process into its constituent parts which, in a software development activity, may be re-labelled as shown in Table 8.5.

■ A brainstorming session

The brainstorming session should involve all staff who have a knowledge of the effect that is being analysed as well as those with a vested interest. Someone with no personal interest in the effect is required as a moderator for the meeting.

The target of the method is to get down as many ideas in each of the categories as possible in a reasonably short time, without discussion and without ruling out any ideas. There are no hard and fast rules, but usually these sessions start slowly and move into a state where ideas are being

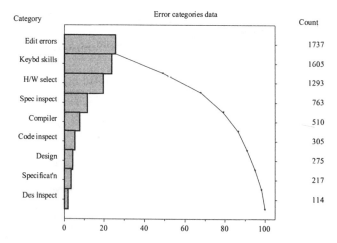

Fig. 8.7 Pareto diagram based on frequency of occurrence.

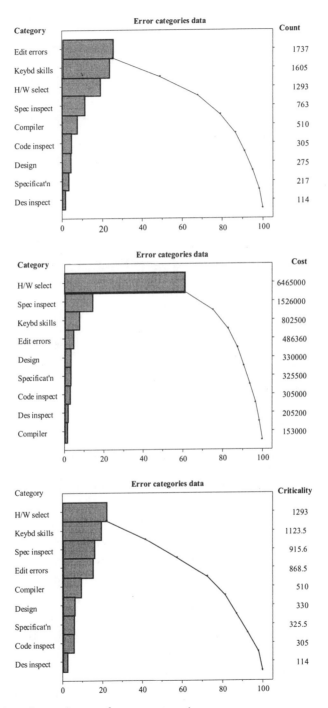

Fig. 8.8 The three Pareto diagrams for error prevention.

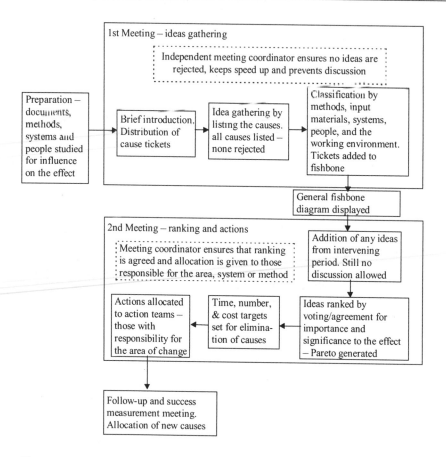

Fig. 8.9 Action required to set up a cause and effect meeting.

brought forward at a rate of 5–10 per minute. These ideas are then transferred onto the Fishbone diagram in order to categorise the information. This transfer should happen as part of the meeting in order to ensure that the interested parties provide input to the transfer process.

Preparation before the logging meeting allowing the effect to be analysed for causes by each of the attendees can help to make the meeting more productive. The methods used for an inspection are also useful in making sure that all possible avenues are covered during the meeting. A guideline document is provided to the attendees outlining the scope of the problem to be investigated and highlighting the areas to be studied for causes. During the meeting these can be broken down into smaller areas of consideration. Fig. 8.9 shows the flow diagram for actions for setting up a cause and effect meeting in order to maximise its effectiveness.

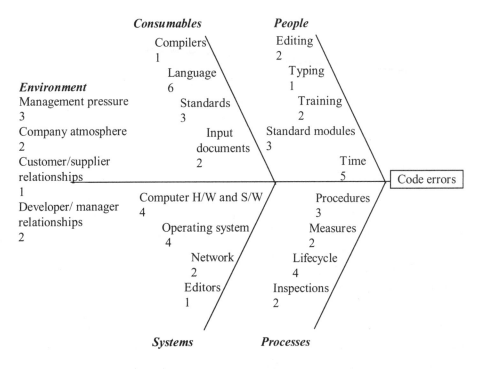

Fig. 8.10 The ranked Ishikawa or cause and effect diagram.

Once the ideas are available, they are again quickly ranked for importance and interest. This can be completed interactively with people in the meeting shouting out results. A second method can be used which involves each individual prioritising the list and then the average of all of these being used as the weighting. The ranked fishbone is shown in Fig. 8.10.

▨ Using the fishbone information

The highest rankings are then assigned to individuals or small groups for reconsideration. They require analysis and costing before implementation. The resulting plans are then added to a Pareto diagram that is used to analyse this round of the process improvement activity. As each entry is eliminated, then the next priorities are initiated for analysis and they are then applied until there are few items left on the fishbone – it has been picked clean. It is rare for this condition to be achieved. If the brainstorming session was really working, there will be low priority ideas which are either too expensive or too ineffective to implement, or even just too difficult.

Once the process has been completed or is in progress and new ideas are required a new effect is used and this is brainstormed in the same way. Frequently a company will have effects being researched by a number of small teams which are concentrating on particular areas of the development process. This may be effects such as compiler generated errors, a particular type of software component, or a training requirement.

■ 8.5.3 Process modelling

In general the development process in each individual company has evolved over the life of the company. However, models are now available for different types of development including the traditional waterfall and V models. The latest simultaneous engineered and RAD models have provided a number of methods that can be chosen as suitable for particular development projects.

The alternative is to model the process that exists within the organisation as a flow model for the activities, control model for quality, and a cost model for improving quality. These three parallel models will provide input for the process improvement activity.

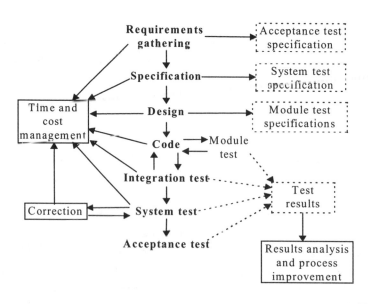

Fig. 8.11   Flow model for ideal and actual V model organisation.

The relationship between the process control parameters and the product quality provides a fourth model of the development process. This model requires the tools of correlation and Taguchi analysis and is reliant on variance for its success. The model can only be completed when the metrics being used are statistically controlled and all special causes have been eliminated.

▓ Flow, control and cost modelling

Much of this book has been about providing models for these factors. To formally model a system using the three parameters is a matter of studying not what should happen, but what actually does happen. A typical organisation using the V model claims to have a flow model as shown in Fig. 8.11. The actual model is shown alongside and the differences are clear. Testing is an ad hoc activity that is occurring within the coding activity, module testing never happens and integration testing is the main test activity. On the development arm the requirements specification and system specification are usually one document developed at the start of the project and there is an iterative process between the design and code stages.

The metrics to control this process are global in extent – time for completion and cost, and do not measure any of the stages. The ideal for a

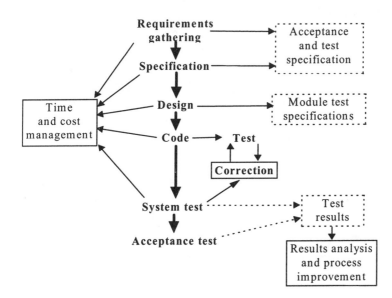

Fig. 8.12 Control and cost models for the V model organisations

V model is shown in Fig. 8.12 and provides metrics for the stages and for quality costs.

These models tend not to have a control model with them. Management is by asking for completeness without factual evidence. Great emphasis is on trust between the staff and the developers.

A different type of model is provided by organisations using formalised processes, of which PRINCE (58) is one, where metrics are a requirement of the process and the costs are measured for each stage of the process (Fig. 8.13). However quality costing is still not an essential feature of the process.

▓ Metrics relationship models, scatter and correlation

The control of a process is reliant on continual action to ensure that no part of the process is allowed to regress to an out-of-control situation. Once this state of control is achieved and all special causes have been removed, then the task of learning more about the influences of different control parameters on the process can be investigated.

The parameters that have most effect will be different for each and every company simply because the influences on the company are different. This means that for one company pressure of work will produce the highest quality solution as specified by the customers. For another, the control will be an ability to plan in detail and work meticulously to that plan.

There is no 'right solution' for choosing the control parameters, it is a question of finding what works and then sticking by this and developing by slowly improving the stability of the process.

The following sections describe a few tools that can be used to understand the process better in terms of the relationship between the control parameters and the quality of the product (its timelines, cost effectiveness and performance).

▓ Scatter plots

As the name suggests these plots are used to identify whether the relationship between two variables results in random scatter or whether strong correlation exists. The technique is the first stage of correlating the data and finding relationships that will either provide new control parameters for the process, provide the bounds of existing relationships, or show that no relationships exist.

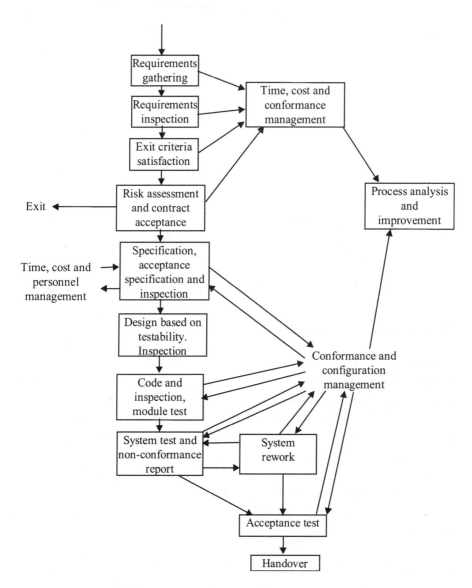

Fig. 8.13 A formalised development process model.

McCabes complexity (X) vs. Predicted errors/1000 lines

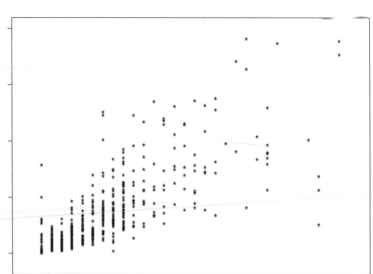

Fig. 8.14 Defects vs. complexity for 6 companies and 900 programmes.

Analysis to identify relationships between product defectiveness and the process metrics has been going on throughout the 1980s with little real success. Attempts to create relationships based on several organisations who use different development processes show little indication of correlation. Fig. 8.14 shows a particular relationship for complexity against defects found within a group of large companies. It is evident that there is a relationship in this chart but it is not well defined, and this is evidence that several different processes are included on the model.

By separating the information for the individual development languages and the individual types of organisation, the X – R charts for complexity (Fig. 8.15) show that there are still a few out-of-control situations occurring. Generally the data is better distributed and control charts could be used to control the modules (detect out-of-control) as they are produced.

Scatter diagrams can be used between variables, Fig. 8.14, multiple variables, Fig. 8.16, or between variables and qualitative measures, as shown in Fig. 8.17.

The danger with this type of plot is that the relationships are taken out

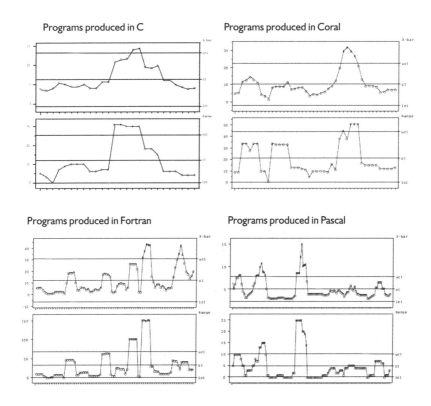

Fig. 8.15 Complexity control charts for each of the individual companies.

of context. The significance of the quality system vs. error levels plot is not that quality systems have no effect (there is no correlation), but that the processes were not in control, and were not the same processes. Consequently the probability of achieving the same error levels for each of the different companies was very unlikely.

The two variable plots show several possible different correlations. The plot can be interpreted as showing at least three different processes each with a strong correlation between the two variables. However there may be more hidden in the data and so we can only surmise that at least three may exist.

The original data source for this is eight different companies using different languages and development methods and consequently we could expect to see more than just the three correlations.

The multiple scatter graph technique is useful for identifying multiple relationships between data. It can mislead but is useful for providing the

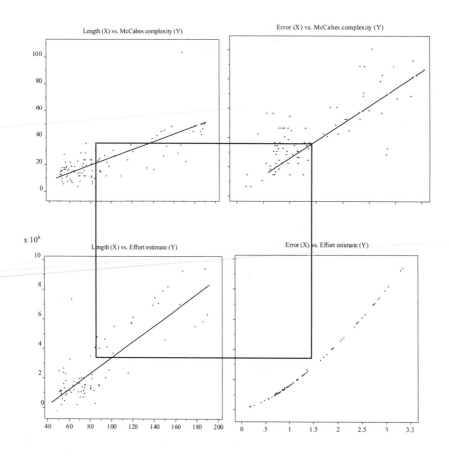

Fig. 8.16 Several variables related on scatter plots.

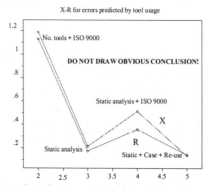

Fig. 8.17 Use of quality system vs. error levels for various different organisations.

first view of the whole process, and for providing some input into the next activity. This next activity is to identify the relationship so that targets can be set for the control variable.

■ Correlation

The relationship can be characterised by a statistical analysis of the mathematical best fit equation for the points. The result of this is to analyse the variance and establish what the differences are between the predicted values and the actual data sets. This can be completed on both independent variables and dependent variables, where a relationship can be expected to exist. For dependent variables the correlation is proving that the relationship for dependency is as expected and the variation seen in results is caused by other factors on the development process. The variables may each be dependent on other variables that do not have the same relationship.

In analysing variance in this way we establish a relationship that might be true for a particular organisation and for a particular project team. The relationship is unlikely to be useful outside of this particular working environment.

The most useful way to use this analysis is in developing relationships between process and product variables in order to establish the causes of high defect levels, poor structure of code or other non-desirable quality metrics. The reader is left to find mathematical texts on correlation in order to understand these principles. It is the view of the authors that these correlations rarely lead to better process control, but may indicate which variables to use to control a process. An example of this is the scatter plots of lines of code per module vs. product defectiveness, which shows that there is an optimum level. The mathematical relationships would not provide any useful extra information.

The standard methods of correlation of metrics include simple linear regression, multiple regression and modelling, and a number of tests can be used to establish the significance of relationships.

The simplest of the correlation techniques is to take a mean squared fit of the data and calculate the differences between the actual data and the calculated curve or line. If these residuals are within an area that could be predicted from a normal distribution, then the correlation has a reasonable probability of being valid. Fig. 8.18 shows the relationship between the two variables and the least squares fit of a power curve. The residuals plot shows that the data is all within $\pm 3\sigma$ of the curve and consequently has a

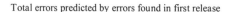

Total errors predicted by errors found in first release

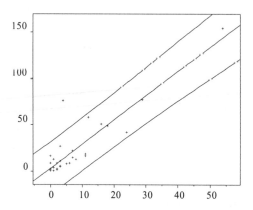

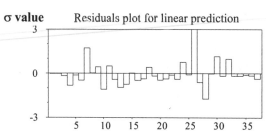

σ value   Residuals plot for linear prediction

Fig. 8.18   Number of defects after 10 releases predicted by defects found in the first release.

reasonable chance of being predicted by it.

If we look at the distribution for the data at any value of error (within the bounds of the resolution of the measurement (± 1)), then the distribution is for all purposes normal. This can be carried out in both directions and plotted. Any point falling outside these areas cannot be expected to provide a correlation. However if there are less than 0.3% of these then the correlation can be expected to work in future since the probability of a variance outside the 3σ lines is predicted 0.3% of the time.

If the figure is greater than this then there are two possible causes:
- the correlation is invalid
- the correlation is valid but the process had special causes causing the variance to change.

This is why data to be correlated must come from sources where special causes have previously been eliminated.

There are many texts on correlation on the statistical bookshelves (59,60) which include technical details of multi-variate correlation beyond the scope of this book. You are recommended to read those that have an engineering bias (rather than being mathematical in background), to gain an understanding of the basic principles.

This is still only a relationship between two metrics in what we know to be a multi-parameter process.

■ Multiple metrics analysis

The main method of analysing multiple sets of metrics for correlation based on the variance that is occurring is to use analysis of controlled experiments that have been designed to minimise the data sets required. Taguchi established a methodology for this which allows sets of data to be analysed for correlation based on finding sets of data where a process has been controlled at one or another extreme of the process. The experiment requires that the process is in control throughout, which means that historical data can only be used if there is supporting evidence for control of the metrics to be used. The basis of the experiment is that only a few of the parameters need be correlated because not all metrics have relationships. Finding the few that have significance is the target of this type of experiment. This book does not aim to provide the details of this type of experiment and detailed explanations are covered in (40).

■ Experimental analysis

Traditionally an experiment on a process using multivariate analysis would require a large number of working conditions to be studied in order to characterise the process. The aims of the experiment are to find what causes higher defect rates, to find the optimum control parameters to minimise defects and maximise process efficiency. Through the experiment, data must be gathered to establish that all except the parameter of interest are continually being kept in control. For instance let us consider lines of code per module as a control parameter. An experiment would require a project where developers of the same technical capability were given the same project and asked to produce the code with specified target lines of code per module levels. Testing of each solution using a standard test set and test method can then be used to establish the defectiveness of the code. The results can then be correlated and any relationship identified.

In a process where the control variables can number tens or hundreds, then the sets of tests become impractical, assuming that the limited experiment on one variable is even practical.

What is required is a method taking metrics from current projects, identifying sets of data that can be used to establish the significance of any group of variables when correlated against the product attributes of defectiveness, costliness and timeliness. Methods are available for doing this but they are of limited success unless the process is basically kept in control. Genichi Taguchi has provided a method of designing experiments of this nature using minimum numbers of data sets in order to establish the significance of relationships found. The basic principles allow the data collected from existing projects to be sifted for extremes (say combinations of low number of lines, low cost, low time scale, and high levels for these three parameters). These extremes are used to generate 5–10 sets of data (depending on the number of variables used), each with its own measure of the defectiveness of the code.

The Taguchi method has been designed to take into account the probability of a single set being related to the whole and is designed to establish the relationships using minimum sets of data. The method is described in detail in the book by Taguchi (40).

■ 8.5.4 Questionnaires

The use of questionnaires for gathering information about relationships can be powerful and is the basis of such actions as inspections, structured walkthroughs and other methods of identifying errors and defects. The basis of any questionnaire is ranking based on numerical values. However there are psychological restraints to the design of such data collection methods which include the design of the questions and the number of values to be provided. Problems associated with the variability of the way the forms are filled will also make the data less reliable.

A few rules for the design of successful questionnaires are:

- Ensure that the questions are not ambiguous to the readers of the questionnaire.
- Ensure that each question and its associated answer has relevance to the policy of the organisation.
- Provide an even number of answer boxes so that the middle is not an option. This helps to force a decision.
- Break down the questions into logical steps leading the thoughts

of the answerer.

- Occasionally supply a question out of sequence to gather some knowledge of the respondent's understanding of the questions.
- Repeat a question reworded at a later stage at a strategic point to establish whether a decision made earlier has changed due to the thoughts provoked by the questionnaire.

For more detail Appendix D lists a few specialist books that can be found on the subject of questionnaires.

▓ 8.5.5 FMEA and quality function deployment (QFD)

This technique, which is not widely used in the software industry currently, is a method of analysis that takes the prime inputs and outputs of an organisation and compares them in terms of their importance to 'quality'. The relationships between these quality functions and their costs are graphically displayed and then the graphs are used to minimise costs and concentrate improvement effort.

The first stage of this is to analyse how the item under scrutiny might fail. This is carried out using a technique that analyses and weights the modes of failure that can occur and then relates these to the effects of the failure. The technique is known as failure mode and effects analysis (FMEA) (36) and can be put to good use for both product failures and for analysis of a project. The example shown in Fig. 8.19 is a sample for a real time data collection project. The items that are critical to the success of the project are shown in the table, their effects are analysed and the criticality of the quality function is enumerated.

This is then used to generate a QFD diagram (39). The items critical to the success of the product – the WHATs – are listed down the side and the methods to be used to produce this success – the HOWs – are generated along the top. The relationship between these two factors is then logged as either weak, medium or strong. The top of the diagram is used to determine the relationship between the HOW factors. They may have strongly positive, positive, null, negative or strongly negative influences and the result of this analysis is an analysis of the importance of each of the factors to the overall success of the project in terms of the WHAT factors identified.

An example of this type of diagram, Fig. 8.20, shows the important functions for the real time control project from both the internal project and the customers viewpoints. The diagram costs out the effects of the different

SOFTWARE DEVELOPMENT FMEA

Date: 10/4/1992   **Produced by:**   AB

Document No: tMSc   **FMEA For:**   Production of Software
                         FMEA1_15/1.00   Design Specification

HISTORY

Version	Update	Updated by	Date
1	New Issue	AB	10/4/95

<u>PROCESS FMEA FORM</u>
S = Severity, O = Number of occurrences, D = occurrences detected

Proce-dure	Failure Mode	Potential Effect(s)	Possible Cause	S	O	D	RPN
Design brief	Interrupted meeting	Design of incorrect or incomplete product	Failure to understand importance of meeting	20	5	5	500
		Project time scale failure	Schedule planning	15	2	1	30
	Inputs failure	Incorrect or incomplete product	Schedule failure	22	7	2	308
	Attendance failure	Incorrect or incomplete product	Schedule failure	40	1	1	40
	Input preparation	Meeting time failure	Project schedule failure	20	10	8	1600

and this can be continued for ...

Design outline,

Outline review,

Outline inspection,

Review for re-use,

Design detail,

Design review,

Design inspection,

Design re-use review,

Library store,

Design process review,

Process metric.

Fig. 8.19 Sample of FMEA for generic design process.

requirements and provides the relationships between those for internal quality control and those for customer satisfaction. Note that this diagram is for the project and not just for the product.

Once this level of analysis is complete the technique can be applied at lower levels of analysis by using the HOW factors as the input to the next level. An example may be the use of a high-level language which becomes the target WHAT factor for the next level. The HOW factors then become items such as selection of the compiler based on the speed of the compiler and the speed of the compiled code. This analysis can be continued until a relationship is built between the customer requirements and the functional methods. The diagram – known as the 'house of quality' – provides assistance with rating the importance of each of the factors that influence the success of the project. This guides effort to those areas that will ensure that success is based on those things that the customer sees as important and that the company identifies as a measure of success. This can include making a profit!

▨ 8.6 Summary

- Process improvement is divided into four main areas of activity: customer satisfaction management, process analysis and improvement, process modelling and success measurement using maturity methods.
- The process improvement tools include: brainstorming, cause and effect analysis, Pareto analysis, flow graphing, scatter plots, correlation, Taguchi and quality function deployment.
- Customer satisfaction measurement can be a driving force for process improvement. Equally, keeping one step ahead of the competition can be used to drive the improvement process forward at a realistic rate.
- Process analysis is used to find opportunities for improving the process – to find root causes and eliminate them, and to find control mechanisms that will improve process stability.
- Process modelling is normally only used when a process is becoming stable and consequently the variation is due to causes that are inherent in the process. The model assists in finding new controls and improving understanding of the process.

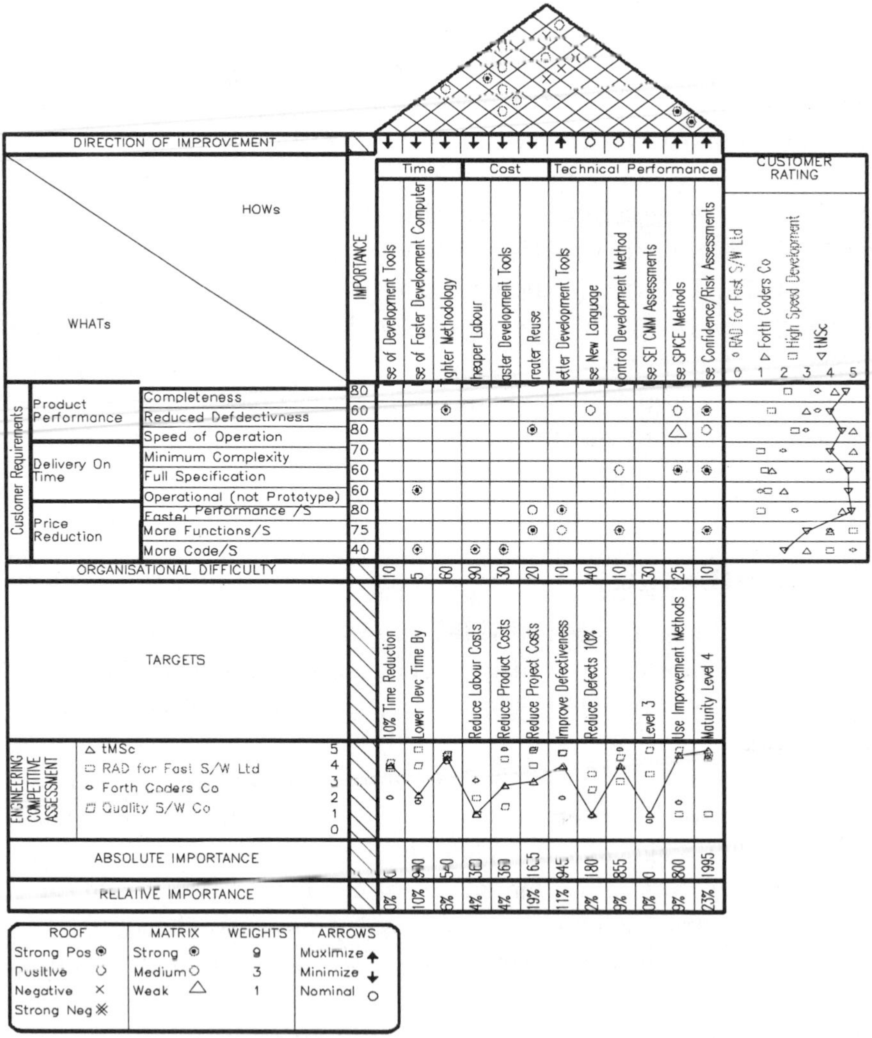

Fig. 8.20 QFD for a real time control project – process improvement.

- Maturity measurement can be used as a benchmarking activity to establish a company's position with reference to its competitors. However it can also be used as an internal control mechanism to ensure that some long-term goal is being achieved. It must not be used to replace the management task of monitoring the long-term goal. This monitoring task should also be updated with new ideas and methods and methods of increasing capability.

Process improvement is the final step in a statistical methodology that gives metrics purpose and meaning. The following chapters provide examples of the use of these techniques in the software development environment.

■ 8.7 An Example

This example is from a company that provides facilities management services to a large number of UK businesses. The complaints and problems reporting system for this company was based around a help desk as the first line support. Utilisation management provides the opportunity for service optimisation dependent on how the systems are being used and improvement based on how the facilities are set up.

For the help desk response a typical graph (Fig. 8.21) charts the times between departments from the point of receipt of a problem to the time of resolution of the problem. This shows that the response achieved is 0.9 hours and no exceptions have been recorded over the period observed.

This chart is used to reduce the time between receipt and response, not by finding special causes, but by tackling the process variance. If the 0.5 hour interval can be achieved why can it not be met on all occasions? What prevents a quicker response? These and similar questions allowed the company to change the way the answer desk information was fed to the solution providers. The chart was monitored and new control lines established for grouped data ($\overline{X}$,R). While more exceptions are expected, the reasons can be defined and better cover obtained at critical times.

Two other aspects of quality performance from the viewpoint of the customer can be used in this facilities management example:

(1) the need to maximise computer resource utilisation
(2) the need to take preventive action from either intrusion or from failure.

A chart for utilisation shown in Fig. 8.22 shows how the goal of increasing utilisation provided extra capacity on the system (the actual utilisation was

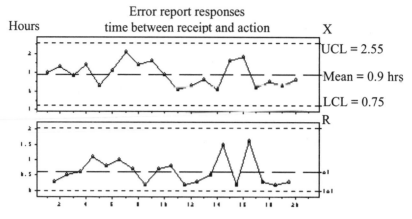

Fig. 8.21 Problem timing through a help desk system.

reduced) creating the opportunity for new sales at no extra hardware costs and consequently increasing the profitability of the system. In this business utilisation is achieved by balancing the allocation of resources on the multi-tasking computers to each of the users and programs. These resources (memory, disk buffer space, priority level) depend on what other programs are likely to be running at any one time.

The $(\overline{X}, R)$ chart shows that the balance of utilisation before optimisation was averaging a high level but with only a small range. By reducing the limitation on the range (allowing allocation of memory to fluctuate more), the level of utilisation dropped dramatically leaving space for new programs to be run for new customers.

Intrusions into multi-user wide area networks such as the systems used by this company are always a problem, but the profile of log-on accesses and activities while logged on can quickly spot differences, particularly if the difference between activities on particular days are used as the basis of the charts. This means that for, say, a Friday, a particular log-on and activity profile is being used. The profile for last Friday is compared with the current activities and the information is sampled at 6 minute intervals. Every 5 samples (30 minutes) the mean level and range values are calculated and plotted and, if an out-of-control point results, an investigation into the system with the exception is initiated. This should find the cause of the exception, but one of the programs run was a log-tracking system, enabling any intruder to be traced.

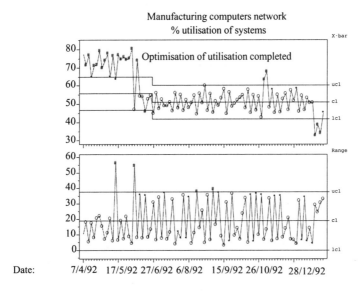

Fig. 8.22 Computer utilisation control chart.

These types of process improvement show how, on a complex multi-user system where every activity could be different every day, the control process can provide unforeseen benefits.

9 Measuring Success

■ 9.1 Improvement and Success Measures

We said at the start of the last chapter that improvement is an activity that must become endemic within a company. One way of achieving this is to provide a measure of success for the company that must be seen to be continually improving.

There are three ways to obtain this measure of success:
- internal measurements based on customer satisfaction
- external models used as a benchmark of success
- external benchmark comparisons with competitive organisations.

The first of these uses the statistics gathered within individual projects to guide the future development. The most important of these statistics is the measure of what is happening at the customer interface. We have already seen many of the other measures in previous chapters and so this chapter concentrates on this customer interface measurement.

Comparing your company with a similar organisation is one way of ensuring that the balance between improvement and competitiveness is at the right level. The external models of quality systems provide a mechanism for reaching a particular level.

■ 9.2 Success Measurement at the Customer Interface

■ 9.2.1 Customer-based analysis

A project-oriented software house uses both in-house and contract staff to complete a project for its clients. The issue is that they enjoy producing solutions to their own problems interpreted from the customer requirements. The net result is that projects are delivered late and with little profit. There is usually no difficulty in selling the concept to the customer since it is well in excess of expectation.

This scenario was not unusual in the software industry in the early and mid 1980s. It is tackled by training on supplier/customer relationships and by putting in place mechanisms for measuring the effectiveness of the interface between the staff involved.

Table 9.1 The supplier–customer chain with a project.

Person in chain	Receives	Supplies	Payback incentive
Purchaser	Idea, concept, etc.	Requirement, outline specification, contract	Based on purchase decision. Use of delivered product is prime motivation
Company management including sales managers	Specification, and development contract	Company objectives through contract review quality policy	Survival and development of company reputation, financial reward, experience
Designer	Specification, company objectives, quality policy	System specification and design	Pay, experience, skills, new knowledge, satisfaction
Developer	Design specification	Detail design, code	Pay, experience, skills, knowledge, satisfaction
Test designer	Specification	Test specification and test sets	Pay, experience skills, satisfaction
Test engineer	Test specification and code	Code measures and defects reports	Pay, skills experience, satisfaction
Project manager	Time and cost requirements	Product within budget and time	Pay, skills, experience, satisfaction

■ The supplier/customer concept

The 'supplier' and 'customer' for most people within the development chain is someone within the same organisation and the consequence of this is clear. Ask the question: Would you buy a second-hand car from the person giving you a specification? – or in critical environments, would you buy a heart transplant from them!

The concept of the supplier–customer relationship within a software development activity is demonstrated in Table 9.1.

From this table it is clear that all staff involved within a project have an identified incentive to complete the task of providing a specified output from a given input. It is also evident that the quality of each output is dependent on the quality of input. This means that the nearer completion the project is, the more difficult it will be to detect and correct errors made in the early stages of the development. So quality is more critical at the early stages of a project than at the end.

Analysis of the variance of each of the processes shows that each new process builds on the errors of the past, i.e. it will add its own probability of introducing new errors. Fig. 9.1, shows how the probability accumulates through internal customers that make up a typical V model process.

This is a simplified view since many of the processes overlap and are not sequential events. However the principle that errors generated in one

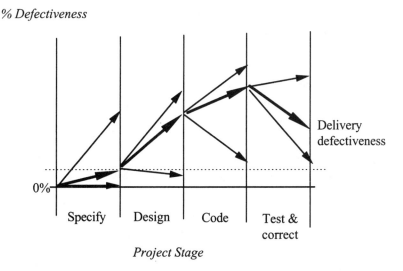

Fig. 9.1 Additive process variance.

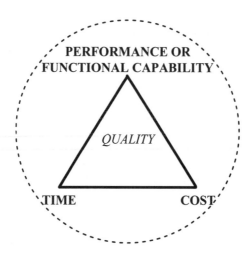

Fig. 9.2 The three aspects of quality.

stage can increase the probability of errors in the following stages highlights the importance of detecting and removing errors as early as possible through the development cycle.

▨ Quality from a customer viewpoint

This example concentrated on customer satisfaction as the process measure of quality, but this includes several elements described in the standard quality triangle shown in Fig. 9.2.

Note that the third corner of the triangle is not 'quality' as defined in several texts, but the technical capability of the product being supplied. This technical capability is defined as performance, reliability, defectiveness, conformance, and overall ability to satisfy the requirements of the customer. From an internal company viewpoint this corner represents the ability of the project, service or product to satisfy the customer with minimum maintenance or correction (i.e. at minimum cost). This is only achieved by minimising the defectiveness of the deliverables.

Time and cost are the familiar metrics for any project, and these are two measures that can be compared project to project. They are used to measure whether the company is achieving goals of delivery (cost or profit and time) commensurate with achieving customer satisfaction.

The charts for project cost and timeliness are measured for project-oriented software companies and a typical graph is shown in Fig. 9.3.

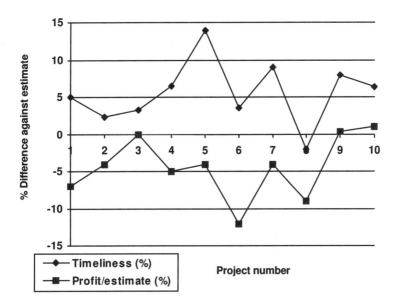

Fig. 9.3 Time to delivery and profit calculations as a percentage of estimated values.

This chart shows the results for 10 projects where only one was delivered before estimated completion date and only the last two exceeded the profit expectation. However the charts do not indicate that there are any exceptional causes. By recalculating and redrawing the graphs on (X, Moving R) control charts, the comparison with the normal capability of the company is revealed. Exceptions can be handled by using a process that will identify and remove the underlying causes (Fig. 9.4).

These charts show that the situation is in control for the process that is being used. The control charts indicate what is already known – that the process involves engineers over-specifying – and consequently this confirms suspicions that this is normal practice. This process is in fact a level 2 maturity process. It was previously defined and all the steps understood and known. However the definition of a process does not guarantee control or success.

Correction of this situation involves providing control charts for project progress, conformance and customer confidence. The targets for each of these charts are defined by their nature. Acceptance of the project is 100% for every stage of the project and over-specification becomes clear early on since the specification activity is terminated once 100% is achieved for any part of the system.

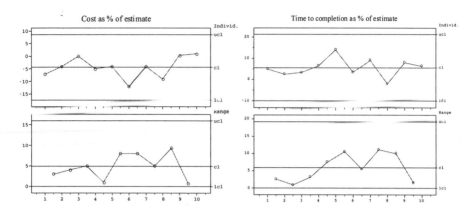

Fig. 9.4 (X, Moving R) charts for time to delivery.

■ 9.2.2 Customer satisfaction sampling

The use of surveys of customers to find problems with the service, or the product being delivered, is well established. Most banks, car manufacturers and household goods producers are continually bombarding us with survey questionnaires. What has changed is the quality of the questioning. Providing questions are effectively selected the questionnaires can provide invaluable information about the service, the market sector, and the changing market environment that is be serviced.

The analysis of this type of data must be rigorous in the sense of only comparing data from sources that have the same attributes. This means that if your company is developing one-off solutions on a project basis, there is little to be gained from this method unless some grounds of commonality can be found within the service being provided.

A typical example, shown in Fig. 9.5 and Table 9.2, is a company working in the financial services sector that provides bespoke solutions for 'dealing room' systems. The questionnaire in this instance reflects the financial services industry needs, the current pressures, the methods of fulfilling projects in the sector, and the satisfaction with the achievement of these particular goals within projects completed. These projects may have a particular interest in the technical implementation of communications systems. The experience and knowledge of the project engineers in these areas may be a factor in both winning business, and satisfying that business once the contracts have been won.

```
Sun Software Inc.
```

Customer Survey Questionnaire

Please answer the following questions by circling the appropriate number. The questions are designed to help us improve our service to you, but please tell us anything else relevant to the service provided in the space allocated.

SECTION 1 – Service provided in past projects

Q1 Was the project completed ?

| 1 | Very satisfactory | 2 | Satisfactory | 3 | OK |
| 4 | Could be improved on | 5 | Poor | 6 | Bad |

Q2 Did the team provide the skills and knowledge required?

| 1 | All and more | 2 | Most |
| 3 | Some but lacked a few | 4 | Some but lacked essentials |

Q3 Timeliness
Was there a deadline for this project?   Yes [1]   No [2]

Q4
If yes did the team express confidence that this could be met?
Yes [1]   No [2]   No comment [3]

Q5 Was the project completed on time?

| 1 | Very early | 2 | Early | 3 | On time |
| 4 | Late | 5 | Very late | 6 | Not completed |

SECTION 2 – Technical requirements over the next 3 years

Q6 Speed of computing.
Do you require response rates of:

| <1ms [1] | ms [2] | s [3] | 5s [4] |
| 30s [5] | 1m [6] | Slower [7] | |

Q7 Data collection.
How many variables do you need to monitor at one time with one system?

| 1–7 [1] | 8–15 [2] | 16–64 [3] | 64–127 [4] |
| 128–255 [5] | 156–1023 [6] | over 1024 [7] | |

Fig. 9.5 Questionnaire.

The survey data is used as a control chart to spot exceptions and find causes. The survey data often remains as tables which do little to reveal information about the differences. By providing just simple management control lines, the data starts to reveal the market information to support management decisions, perhaps to initiate training to obtain new skills to meet these market demands.

Table 9.2 Tabulated results.

No.	Scores																							
Q1	4	5	3	4	4	5	3	6	5	5	5	3	3	4	6	4	5	6	5	2	4
Q2	2	3	2	3	2	1	2	3	4	3	3	3	2	2	1	2	3	2	2	3	4
Q3	1	2	2	2	2	1	1	2	1	2	2	2	1	2	2	2	1	1	2	2	1
Q4	1	2	2	2	1	1	1	1	2	2	2	3	3	2	2	2	1	1	1	2	2
Q5	1	3	3	3	2	4	4	4	4	3	3	2	4	5	2	2	2	3	3	1	4
Q6	2	2	2	3	2	2	4	2	2	3	2	2	4	4	5	1	1	2	2	1	2
Q7	3	4	5	4	4	5	5	6	5	5	4	4	5	5	4	3	3	4	4	5	5

An example of the management control lines from questionnaires is shown in Fig. 9.6. This is for a project-based software house in the real time control industry. It identifies the changing market as newer languages and faster code became a necessity. This was largely driven by the increased customer expectations from the faster and cheaper computing power that became available.

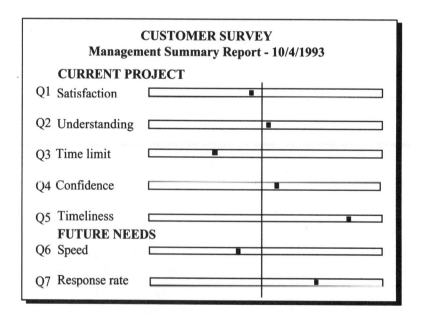

Fig. 9.6 Management control lines for the survey results.

◼ 9.2.3 Customer confidence

The third tool in this process of building relationships with the customer is confidence measurement, arguably the most critical factor for success. It is usually the confidence that the developer and the supplier have in each other and the project that determines the success or failure of the project. Even the most proficient engineers have failed to deliver projects due to the fact that the customer lost confidence before completion. Similarly projects have failed because the supplier has lost confidence in the customers' ability to specify what the requirements are, leaving the supplier guessing at requirements rather than building success together.

There are two ways of measuring confidence: by questionnaire as discussed in the previous section, and by auditing meetings between the developer and the customer. The questionnaire approach provides answers similar to the management control methods and can be useful for finding exceptions. It is unlikely to find a lack of confidence until it is irretrievable since few people will admit to feeling uncertain until they actually have no option.

The audit approach measures not just customer confidence, but also supplier confidence. It is more sensitive since it measures the change in confidence as the project progresses. The expectation is that confidence will be minimum at the start of a project (though it should still be about 80%), and should be expected to build to higher levels as the project develops. A falling off is not a cause for concern unless it is seen to have a special cause, or unless there is no explainable cause that can be tackled.

Confidence measurement is like any audit process – it relies on samples of information which in this case are the affirmative and negative information being passed between the meeting participants. A log of each meeting records information about:

- items reviewed or discussed
- discussion points required
- differences discovered
- the rating of the differences in terms of criticality to the project.

In some instances the criticality can be determined both as technical and expectation based. Projects can fail because of an expectation not being met even though this is totally non-critical to the technical success of the project. Typical examples are when a project fails to operate on-site first time at the acceptance stage. The expectation may have been given that a

MEETING SCORE SHEET

Document Number: tMSc MA1_7/003 Review Date: 14/3/93 Number of Statements: 257
Meeting Between: Supplier: Origin Customer: MA7

Points discussed	Contractual	27
	Technical	84
	Other	23
Major issues	Positive agreements reached	36
	Points still under discussion with dates for resolution	12
	Points unresolved either way	8
Minor issues	Positive agreements reached	40
	Number of responsibilities passed to opposite number	12
	Points still for resolution	15
	Points unresolved	11

Fig. 9.7 Score sheet from project meeting.

failure at this stage is critical, but technically the failure could be minor and not within the scope of the development team at all. The project may still fail.

A score sheet for a project meeting audit is shown in Fig. 9.7. This shows that the meeting provided input to a number of areas of the project and resolved a number of differences. The actual input documents for the meeting are identified and the number of technical, contractual and other sections are counted.

The audit of the meeting has identified that of the 257 statements within the documents reviewed 134 were actually discussed and the results for these are as shown in the table. In addition to these results the rating for the meeting has been added. This is a subjective judgment of body language and atmosphere and determines whether the people involved are likely to bring the project to a positive conclusion.

These results are used to calculate an index for confidence which is calculated as the mean and range of the values entered. If more than one table is produced for a single meeting then the confidence index is the mean range of each chart and the grand mean of the chart means. The value should be specified as being either a single reading confidence index, C_{is}, or for grouped data, C_{ig}.

■ 9.3 Success Measures using External Models

Maturity is usually measured in terms of the repeatability of individual processes, particularly when the product and the organisation are undergoing change. The company is mature when these changes can be made without effecting the quality of the product. It can also be recognised by the ability for the process to be cloned readily. Cloning is only possible when the key control attributes are understood and any out-of-control situation is readily identified and corrected before any effects are observable on the end product (cost, time and performance).

Some of the maturity models appropriate to the software industry are:
- the Software Engineering Institute's Capability Maturity Model (CMM) (31),
- the Bootstrap model from a European ESPRIT programme (32),
- the AMI method (55),
- Software Technology Diagnostic,
- the Healthcheck,
- the Lattice model (33) which has been developed from a generic model of engineering.

Also a number of companies have contributed to a new standard for process improvement in the software industry which is to be used to generate a new ISO standard, SPICE (47).

Statistical techniques are not the emphasis of these models since most expect only the higher levels to use the techniques. It is our hope that through this book you will see that whereever process definition, measurement and control are to be used, statistical methods provide the most effective and efficient collection and analysis method.

The SEI model adopted much of the Deming process improvement strategy, using terms such as repeatability and location to determine how process improvement is to occur in terms of specific metrics. This requires an understanding of statistical control in order to prevent decisions being taken to change the process in reaction to a single value, which may only be the 1 in a 100 expected of a stable process anyway.

The Bootstrap method takes the idea that some parts of an organisation can be allowed to develop more slowly. Much the same thinking went into quality systems when they were first developed. The principles behind the Bootstrap method do not take into account the statistical control techniques and consequently the measures can vary on each snapshot taken at the point of a benchmark audit. The effect is that some areas will improve, while others will appear to have degraded. Having read this far you will understand that this may not be the case at all – this may only be the single reading that can be expected to be low.

The Lattice method uses a common model for all industries – a model that defines expectations of a mature process in terms of commercial benefit, stability and control. It uses statistical measurement techniques to establish control, and uses variance and location of particular metrics to measure maturity. This model also expects different levels of maturity to exist across an organisation and consequently expects different levels to be used for each activity within an industry sector.

This model also defines the activities required to develop from one level of maturity to the next. The activities are not defined in terms of the measures to be achieved, but in terms of what must be done during the intervening time between achieving each of the levels.

The following paragraphs describe three of the methods in outline only. This book is about statistical techniques and as such only the link between the methods and the statistics can be defined here. For more details there are references to the appropriate books in the bibliography.

■ 9.3.1 The SEI method

The SEI's Capability Maturity Model (CMM) (31) provides five levels of development in line with the Deming ideas of the stages of process improvement. The five stages are:
   (1) undefined and chaotic
   (2) project control
   (3) process control
   (4) efficiency management
   (5) process optimisation.

When these are related to the process control models mentioned in Chapter 3 they can be restated in terms of the actions to get from one level to the next:
   1–2 Defining the process of software development and then generating and observing the procedures (ISO 9000-3).
   2–3 Deciding which variables to use as controls for the process in order to understand the process.

3–4 Measuring the variability of the process using the identified variables and then controlling these to remove special causes to get the process under control.

4–5 Measuring the process variance and tackling this to minimise variance.

You will note that the core of these actions is using statistical methods – even from level 1 to level 2. Defining the process and ensuring the procedures are properly used can be superficially completed in order to satisfy the requirements of ISO 9000. However the standard states that processes must be capable and this can only be achieved by putting in place a mechanism for measuring capability. If the standard is applied rigorously then only companies with level 3 and above can hope to achieve ISO 9000 – they are the only companies who know what the capability of their organisation is. However the standard is usually interpreted somewhat less rigorously than this and capability is proven by an organisation showing a history of successful projects rather than showing measured capability of the processes.

The CMM assesses an organisation and the company is graded according to the level that is in overall use throughout the company.

▓ 9.3.2 The Bootstrap method

This method takes a slightly different line to SEI in that the assessment is carried out on particular tasks and activities of the organisation and a grade is attached to each of these. This is a strengths and weaknesses type of assessment that provides a profile enabling the company to identify where to put improvement effort. The model, shown in Fig. 9.8, assesses the organisation for:

- its use of quality systems and for resource management,
- the technology for innovation, tools for the life cycle, and tools for management, and the integration of the tools set,
- the methodology for project, risk, change, quality and subcontractor management, use of design and development methodologies, and use of process definition, measurement and control.

'Quality' is seen as a separate function in all of this and not the all-embracing term for technical performance of process, products and methods that is more normally associated with a company managed through quality.

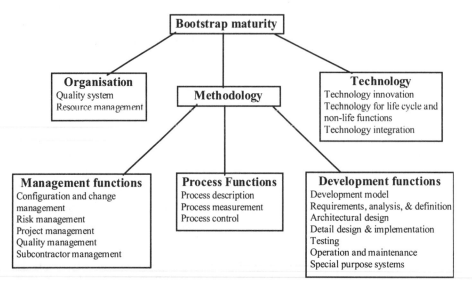

Fig. 9.8 The Bootstrap assessment process.

The assessment however provides a rating between 1 and 5 for each of the global levels (overall, organisation, methodology, technology) calculated as the mean of the levels below. The lowest levels are assessed individually and contribute to the rating of each higher level. They are plotted as a profile for the area under consideration.

The assessment is provided then as a series of bar charts for each of the areas, and for each of the global and intermediary levels. It shows where the company is weak and where there are requirements for improvement effort.

■ 9.3.3 The Lattice method

This assessment method takes the inputs and expectations of an organisation and provides the mechanism for controlling the three main elements of activity for completion – planning, activity and validation. The four main inputs are modelled according to the industry sector that they are being applied in, but for software are shown in Fig. 9.9.

The third axis of the model is a maturity measure, which provides the ability to profile the organisation in three dimensions. This profile provides two pieces of information:

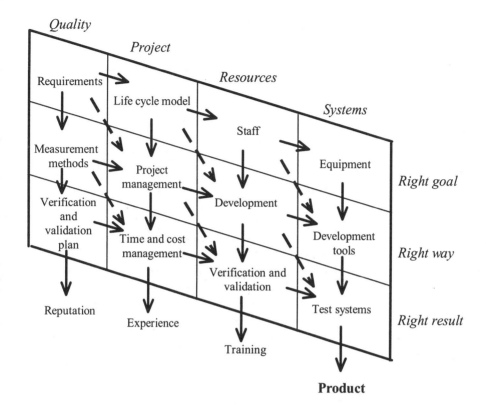

Fig. 9.9 The Lattice for a software company.

- where the company strengths and weaknesses are
- a match to the expected profile for the type of organisation that is being assessed.

The model takes as its basis the expectation that some types of organisation require strong market presence. For these companies activities at the validation end of the company must be strong, but requirements are loosely defined and so must be handled within the development process. Other companies are entirely the opposite. The requirements need to be firm at the outset in order to tackle and achieve in the market place, but the product validation very much takes place as it arrives in that market. Fig. 9.10 shows the lattice profile for a number of different types of organisations.

Statistical process control is embedded in this model for the purposes of providing the measures of capability as well as controlling each of the individual processes themselves. The use of statistical methods for

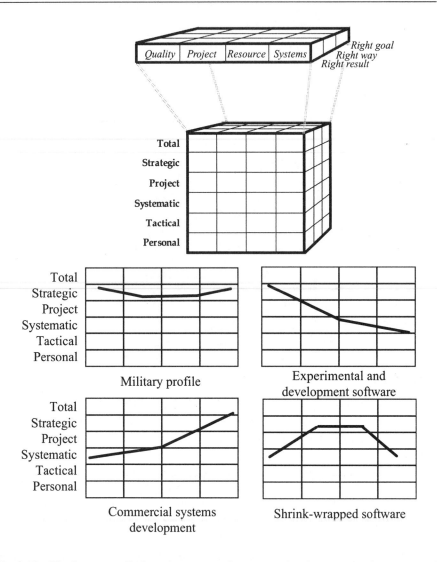

Fig. 9.10 The Lattice profile for military, general commercial and experimental systems, and shrink-wrapped software product companies.

controlling the project management, resource and materials allocation, product development, and product validation is essential to the success of an organisation. The methods are used in the processes at any one of the stages as shown in Fig. 9.11. Note the similarity of this to the SPC loops model described earlier in this chapter.

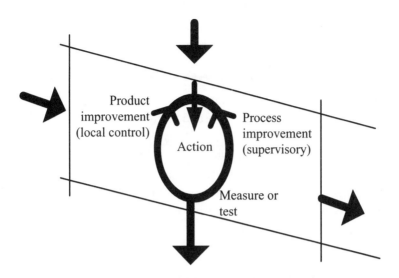

Fig. 9.11 The individual process in the Lattice.

▓ 9.4 Using Models for Benchmarking

The SEI CMM model provides a single measure for the success of a project and this can be used to compare all companies who have been through the assessment process. It should be used with some caution though comparing only companies that are using similar processes and tools, and producing similar products. This is because maturity in different types of company is likely to relate to different activities and consequently the measure may not be comparing what is important to your organisation.

The Bootstrap and Lattice models can also provide a single figure for maturity, but these models recognise the differences and consequently the benchmark is provided as a profile. This provides a much better mechanism for comparing what you are doing with what competitive companies might be doing.

At the time of writing few companies have achieved level 5 of the SEI maturity model. This has been the reserve of companies producing critical software rather than the more general applications. In fact in 1995 the level of maturity of the majority of UK industry was level 1 with a few companies achieving levels 2 and 3. However this does not mean that all these companies are chaotic in nature. The nature of the measurement is that all parts of the organisation must be controlled in a similar way and this leads to overall figures that are much lower than expected because most companies have areas where experimentation takes place. It is inefficient to control this activity using all the requirements of a repeatable and controlled development process – indeed it defeats the purpose of the experimentation which is to find new ideas and methods. What should be recognised is that the process here is different. It is not a development activity, but a research activity. The consequence of this will be for grading levels to dramatically change, or profiling techniques to be used where the experimental activities are treated as requiring low development process maturity, but high maturity in the areas of producing new ideas and managing the realisation and use of those ideas. These are clearly outlined in both the Bootstrap and the Lattice models where the profile takes this activity into account.

■ 9.5 Using Models for Improvement Management

The second use of the models is to develop the internal operation of the company. Here the model is not used to gain competitive edge directly, although this will indirectly occur as we will see later. The aim is to use the profile generated to drive improvements where they are seen to be directly beneficial to the company.

This means that the mechanism for measuring individual success for each area within the organisation will contribute to driving the improvement process within that area. The effectiveness can be gathered from the resulting profile which in turn can be compared with a profile that is produced using the company policy as its source.

These types of system are interactive in nature and require support and there are now many software systems that can automate the gathering of the data and the presentation of both local and company-wide profiles (56).

The company now has a mechanism for completing the last loop of the statistical control process – that is generating a measure that will identify where change is appropriate to the success of the company.

▓ 9.6 Summary

- Success measurement can be measured using internal measurements, external models or comparative methods.
- Internal measures include customer satisfaction management and confidence indices.
- External models include the SEI CMM, Bootstrap and Lattice.
- Customer satisfaction measurement can be a driving force for process improvement. Equally, keeping one step ahead of the competition can be used to drive the improvement process forward at a realistic rate.
- Maturity measurement can be used as a benchmarking activity to establish a company's position with reference to its competitors.
- Maturity measurement provides the final loop of the control system to ensure that some long-term goal is being achieved. It is in addition to the management task of monitoring the long-term goal. This monitoring task should also be updated with new ideas and methods and methods of increasing capability.

Success measurement is the final step in a statistical methodology that provides the feedback at management and corporate level for success measurement. It is, of course, a never ending process and requires continuous monitoring to ensure the company does not slide back.

The following chapters provide examples of the use of these techniques in the software development environment.

Part III
Statistical Methods used in Software Development

Part III of this book outlines the use of the techniques seen in the previous sections in the various software development activities. It starts where all projects start, at the management of the project.

Getting the statistical metrics right for **project management** at the start of a project is critical to its success. These metrics provide the comparators that will indicate whether the customer will be happy with the delivered product, and the company satisfaction with the profits achieved. Chapter 10 provides the methods for developing appropriate metrics for successful management of a project to meet the quality goals set at the start of the book.

The second application is in control and management of the **development process**. Chapter 11 provides methods for selecting statistical methods and metrics for each stage of the development process. Consideration of the requirements for the different types of lifecycle, particularly for the V model and RAD or simultaneous development principles, is provided.

The detection of defects early in the development cycle is one way of preventing quality costs and one established method of achieving this is using **inspections**. The methods described in Chapter 12 are used to detect defects in almost any of the project outputs as well as some of the input sources. They provide analysis of the results from testing compilers and other development tools.

Finally, when the development is complete the product requires **testing**. Small selections of tests from vast possible test suites can be effective if used properly. Chapter 13 covers the selection of what to test, interpretation of results from product tests, and the optimisation of testing to minimise the time taken to detect defects.

10 Project Management Techniques

10.1 Introduction

Software projects are late, very late, or just never arrive. So quoted the IT manager of a large industrial company that relied on the delivery of software for the successful development of total quality management within the company.

This is a reputation that we in the software development industry have become used to, and certainly a reputation that manufacturing and construction industries had in the 1960s, but statistical control has changed this. Delivery of products to a just-in-time schedule using a statistical approach to production planning ensures that late delivery is the exception rather than the normal state of affairs. In the construction industry, the use of historic data to improve estimation, followed by the use of Monte Carlo planning to calculate worst case and best case completion dates, means that the majority of projects are completed before the worst case date.

10.1.1 Software time management

Manager: 'How's it going?'
Development Team Leader: 'Well, we're about 80% complete now.'

How often is this conversation repeated throughout the software industry? It seems that this response is the main metric for completion – the developers' guesstimate.

There are a number of statistical methods for deciding when a project is considered to be complete that all rely on defining complete in a way that is understood by both the developer and the customer. This understanding is essential whether or not the definition has been unambiguously stated at any stage during the project.

This lack of understanding between the customer and the developers is the biggest cause of variance in projects. Many papers and discussions are available (64) based on the principle of establishing the risk at each stage of a project to control this difference in understanding. In financial and major construction projects it is usual to use the Monte Carlo method (61) to analyse the probability of completion on time and to budget. This is just one technique for producing an estimate for a project that consists of many concurrent paths, but it does not address the problem of tracking progress through a project. We need a solution related specifically to the software industry, where progress has a specific meaning for delivering code that meets a requirement.

■ 10.1.2 What to measure

The analysis and tracking of risk through a project is analysed in more detail by the RISKMAN project (7), the Eureka project based on eight of Europe's top companies. This project aimed to bring together best practices of risk management. It contains a critique of the use of statistical techniques pointing out that 'as methods mature so the input data will improve and the statistics will become more reliable'. This is an important fact for any statistical approach and was considered in detail in Chapter 4. As the RISKMAN report suggests, many of the Monte Carlo based project modelling systems which are currently available rely on entering data based on far from reliable estimates. Typically they rely on estimates such as the number of lines of code to be produced, which of course cannot be known until the project is complete.

Most project-based software development companies are aware that time estimating is usually less than reliable. Often these estimates are based on an engineers first cost analysis. This is often doubled so that sales, management and customers can cut the time budget without causing too many problems when the project is delivered at the time originally specified.

Many software project managers will find it difficult to understand that risk may be measured and used as a yardstick to control the project. For software development projects the amount of time required to reach a completion point is deterministic. This is because we know that effort or elapsed time is related to the number of lines of code or the number of functions. However, how many projects consider the effort required to test and re-test the software after bug fixing? If these figures are included then the real difficulty can be seen to be the model for the way that the project is expected to be completed, i.e. the development process. If the development cycle model is incomplete, or is not repeatable, then estimates of time, risk or cost will inevitably be incorrect at the start of a project, and will vary for every project completed.

The analysis of risk is one element to project management and the other is the purely administrative task of monitoring progress. This activity is one where we should be able to obtain continuous metrics compared with the specification. When specifications are formally produced using the mathematical language 'Z', then the comparison can be simple and direct (65). More generally for text based specifications various techniques have been attempted including function points analysis (66), but the most frequently used method is the developer's guess. Whatever method is to be used the resulting information is useful to both risk management and to the improvement cycle that is at the heart of any quality initiative.

▨ 10.1.3 Statistical time management

The statistical approach explained in this chapter requires the project to be broken down into small parts each of which is measured for progress. This data is compared with the total project plan to measure conformance to the final product delivery time, confidence in the product and the risk of delivery.

If a project is 80% complete at the time of asking, then common wisdom suggests that there is 80% of the time required to complete the final 20%. This is borne out by plotting the estimated times against the completion dates for various projects (Fig. 10.1). This often leads to the software development continuing until the delivery date is reached, and then the product being rushed out without proper completion. This is often achieved by reducing the testing and not carrying out any form of audit of the product defectiveness.

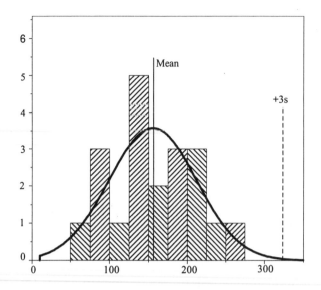

Fig. 10.1 Frequency plot for time taken to complete a module as a percentage of the estimated times (Source: Chemical Analysis Software Systems Company).

This represents a development process that is uncontrolled. Progress is not measured, but the chart is based on the guesstimates of completeness. The estimation process suggested that linear progress would be achieved and no account was taken for iterations round the test debug cycle.

To realistically model the project from the start, factors such as the learning process, the preparation time, and the ideas phase, all represented by the slow progress at the start of the project, are to be included. The data in Table 10.1 is for the completeness of individual modules for the same project. The project S-curve, which is based on measurement of completeness of modules, (section 10.4), is shown in Fig. 10.2. The target value on the data chart is for seven modules all aiming to achieve 100%. This is only a target because some modules may only ever achieve 97% (having a low level of defectiveness rate left at delivery) and others will achieve more than 100% of the target level because of changes in functionality required. These changes are reflected as increases in the amount of work required for completion, but when compared with the original estimate will result in greater than 100% completeness. This technique ensures effective management by adding extra time to the project estimates for every additional function.

Table 10.1 Data collected for project completeness.

	Completeness Chart									
	Target		**User**	**MH**			**Date**		7/5/93	
Months	**Start**	**Final**	**1**	**2**	**3**	**4**	**5**	**6**	**7**	**8**
Initialise	100	105	2	5	9	12	20	40	70	80
Main	100	100	1	3	7	25	55	79	92	95
Control	100	99.2	-	-	-	3	9	15	25	48
Graphics	98	98.6	-	-	-	-	-	5	7	12
Key Entry	100	100	-	-	-	-	-	-	-	2
Maths	100	98.6	-	-	-	-	-	-	-	-
Dbase	100	108	-	-	2	5	24	55	64	78
TOTAL	**698**	**709.4**	**3**	**8**	**16**	**40**	**84**	**194**	**258**	**315**
%		**99.7**	**101.3**	**0.4**	**1.1**	**2.3**	**5.7**	**12**	**27.7**	**36.9**	**45**

When approaching completion of a project, the resolution of the S-curve graph becomes too small to allow decisions about delivery to be made. The last few defects may not be a very large percentage of the total product, and consequently a new view is required. The higher resolution required is achieved by plotting the defectiveness rate of modules. This defectiveness level is used as the delivery criteria for the product and provides a test/ debug cycle control metric. Fig. 10.3 shows the defectiveness curve

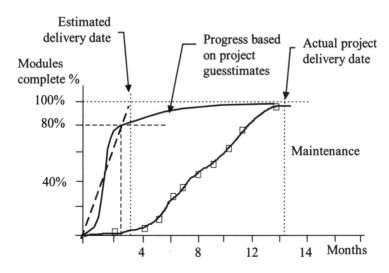

Fig. 10.2 S-curve for actual project based on completeness measurement.

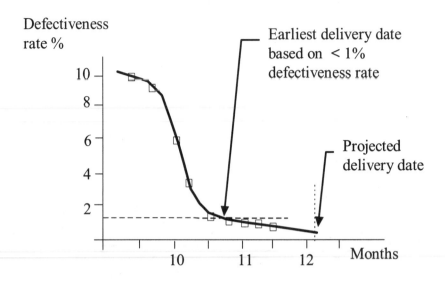

Fig. 10.3 Defectiveness curve for delivery acceptance.

associated with the project described above.

So, why are simple models still used?

The real metrics, such as modules completed as a percentage of total modules to be developed, or defect detection rates for an individual module, are available. Using these metrics, together with statistical limits generated from historical data, the plot can be used to detect when the project is going out of control as well as the capability of a company to achieve a target time. Statisticians will argue that the complexity of the problem is much greater than indicated by this simple statement. However, in real life it is the daily variation of the development team that, when measured, will provide the metrics to enable project time control.

Estimates for the project are best obtained from a model based on the experiences of several of the project team. This provides a realistic project time scale for the purposes of initial monitoring. In addition this can be refined by using a historical normalised capability chart for projects that have similar characteristics. The similarity required is in factors such as people from one company, team or group, using one methodology, producing a product or upgrade of a similar type, and with similar client and management pressures for completion. By comparing the current task and the normalised historical data for the company, the estimate for the

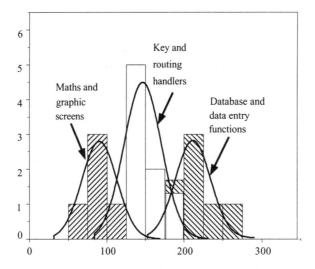

Fig. 10.4 The relationship between the actual completion times, estimated times and the functionality being produced.

current project can be refined. This improvement in estimation capability will enable both the accuracy and the resolution of project time estimates to be improved.

The comparison of the current project with historical data is usually based on common criteria such as the type of modules to be produced. The results are dependent on the skills and experience of the project team and the maturity of the company in terms of the control exercised on the project. However, for any one team a pattern will appear that reflects the common features of software modules. Fig. 10.4 shows a typical pattern for one company whose skills are mainly in the field of mathematics and whose programmers are used to producing graphical software.

The actual times as a percentage of estimated time for these functions appear at the lower end of the distribution, closer to unity or 100%, whereas the functions relating to databases and data gathering tend to be in the higher percentage ratio areas. For project management this immediately enables estimators to suspect the times estimated for these functions, and, depending on how many there are in the system, to make allowance when estimating costs and delivery dates. However the project team is expected to work to its original estimates.

■ 10.1.4 The metrics

Metrics for the completion of a software product are based on an empirical measure, physical measures, and counts or product attributes. The following examples of these measures are used in different organisations for different purposes. Typical empirical measures are confidence and risk, a physical measure is time or rate (lines of code per hour or day), and the counts are lines of code, function points, modules and error counts.

Each of these measures can provide part of the picture of the completeness of a project, and these figures can be relied upon for different development methods without having to make major changes. However, in order to decide on completeness for delivery, a definition of the criteria for completion is required. This definition is a risk-based metric, which is obtained by combining the measure of confidence in the product and a measure of commercial risk of delivery.

The case studies in section 10.8 show the different definitions of delivery completeness required for the major types of product development. Fig. 10.5 provides a guide for selecting the mix of product confidence and delivery risk required for each of these.

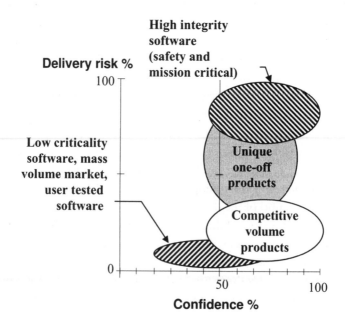

Fig. 10.5 Relationship between delivery risk and product confidence.

This chart is based on experience in one particular type of company and has to be re-calibrated for different companies, teams, processes and methods. The principle is that the high-risk product requires more confidence in its defectiveness, completeness, reliability and conformance in order to be accepted. A low-risk project can often be delivered without the need for high product confidence. This confidence is gained over the first months of defect reporting from the users.

However, low risk must take into account the product competitors and more often the risk factor of delivering low-confidence software is higher than the risk of delivering a higher cost product with a higher product confidence. An example of this is seen in the difference between companies delivering word-processing packages to the market. A small amount of defectiveness soon gets a very bad reputation, whereas a company supplying a unique product can operate with few quality management procedures despite a higher product risk. However a unique product being supplied to a high-risk industry such as the nuclear or aerospace industries, requires a software quality management system that will guarantee low defectiveness (even this software is not guaranteed to be totally defect free).

To understand the detail of this a few metrics can be studied to see how they are produced and what they can tell us about the product.

■ Empirical metrics

Risk and confidence are the two empirical measures considered here. There are others that can be used. However, they can be relied upon only if the method of gathering the information is based on scientific methods. Risk measurement is usually based on the 'many experts' theory, i.e. several experts are called to provide grades or marks for the risk in the product. These marks are combined to provide a mean and range figure for the product. The mean is the risk and the range is a measure of the confidence in the measurement.

For example, 30 software modules were measured by 10 assessors to establish the risk of delivery with marks being awarded between 0 and 10. The results of answering the questions are given in Table 10.2.

Up to 15 standard questions may be usefully used for this process, with some improvement in the quality of the result. The acceptance of values for release of a product are dependent on the history and success of the first attempts. The first five trials are used to calibrate the process and consequently make the process somewhat long and drawn out. However,

Table 10.2 Questionnaire results.

Assessor	1	2	3	4	5	6	7	8	9	10	Mean	Range
Probability of acceptance	5	9	4	6	3	6	5	7	7	5	6.7	6
Market share estimation	4	5	7	4	4	6	4	5	5	7	5.1	3
Price acceptance	8	9	7	8	7	6	7	8	8	9	7.7	3
											Average 6.5	Mean range 4

an internal customer can provide this form of estimation in order to accept the product into the next stage of development and this then provides quicker calibration results, particularly if the product is a small part of any overall product. The questions asked in this case could relate to:

- number of errors
- % conformance with specification
- % conformance with interface conformance
- probability of test success based on the structure, size and conformance of the product to the relevant procedures and standards.

All these questions measure not the risk of delivery, but the confidence of the internal customer in the product. This method takes a statistical selection from the input documents and uses test methods to establish answers to questions about error levels, conformance to requirement, conformance to standard, and conformance to language usage guidelines. These measures are based on statistical testing (see Chapter 13).

Physical measures

The use of physical measures is very dependent on conformance to standards within an organisation. A look at the use of different languages in different projects in different companies provides some indication of the lines of code per module and the complexity per module that the company typically uses. Several researchers have correlated these metrics against defectiveness (1,2) and established that there is a reasonable probability of a relationship existing. However this relationship is somewhat masked by the fact that different companies producing different types of code will produce at their own level of defectiveness, length and complexity. This dependence on company styles means that early calibration and then continued control of the development process is required. This can be achieved if calibration is based on the information gathered from the individual company. These historical facts will help to make sense of individual project time scale and cost management information.

■ 10.1.5 The measurements

If progress data such as lines of code per day or completeness compared with specification are collected, how do you differentiate between the variation that naturally occurs and the special variations that will cause a project to be late? Variation measurement provides a way of gaining confidence in the estimation process and producing a target delivery date that is based on facts, both historical and from the project under development.

The concept of finishing a project to a fixed completion date based on an estimate does not allow changes in the required resources to be detected until the project is well out of control.

The normal estimate of completeness made by the software developers is usually optimistic. Managers do not have adequate information to compare the progress of the project against the time scale and consequently are unable to react to changes in resource requirements until the project is far too close to the delivery date. For this reason the collection and analysis of data can be justified. Extra (or fewer) resources at the right time during the software development cycle, have the biggest influence on the successful delivery of the software on time.

■ 10.2 Setting Targets

Target delivery date is different from the sum of the estimated times for each of the individual modules or functions. This target delivery date is:

> The earliest date that you can have confidence of delivering the product.

The earliest date is the target date plus the variance in the estimation and coding processes and as such is much later than expected. This is shown diagramatically in Fig. 10.6 as the time after all natural variance in the estimating process has been taken into account. It is not the addition or multiplication of the estimation figures in order to arrive at a realistic completion date.

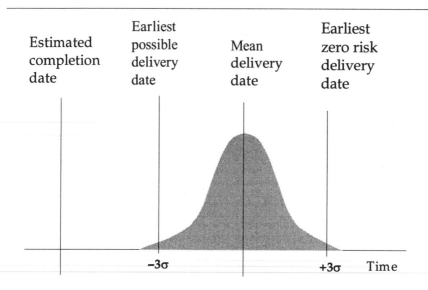

Fig. 10.6 Target date and process variance to obtain delivery date.

Most estimates are based on only the coding time and do not include the removal of errors introduced during coding or design, or the changes of the specification that may occur. This rework effort is an increase in quality costs and should be measured as such. It is the main source of estimation error. Other sources include:

(1) Inexperience (lack of historical data, or lack of process maturity).
(2) Incomplete specification.
(3) New or changed process, often with no indication of the expected improvement in productivity. Software tools, machines and languages are some of the factors which produce a different process.

When planning a project, the first stage is to set up a target time. This is the duration that the project is expected to take for a normally controlled process. The estimate is taken from either historical records of the time taken to produce similar products or the estimation process of the production team. It is not expected to be the period after which the product can be delivered, but it should include all the time necessary for rework, removal of defects and assessing the risk in terms of the likely changes in specification or requirements.

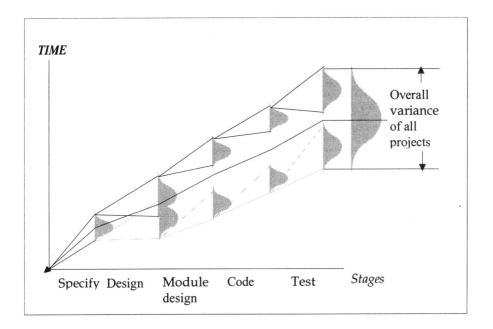

Fig. 10.7 Additive variance through the development process.

The delivery time is generated by adding the variance of each of the development processes to the target time. The process variances to be added include those for all the stages of development (see Chapter 2). The variance for producing a specification, for designing the system, for designing each of the components, and for finally integrating the system are all additive. The final variance shown in Fig. 10.7 is the sum of the variances for each of the stages. That is:

Total Process Variance $\sigma^2 = \sum \sigma^2$ for each of the processes.

From this definition the process variance can be seen to be longer than the estimated time.

It is this variance that can be managed by suitable allocation of resources for oversight, training or improved productivity tools in order to control the final delivery date. To get the earliest and latest delivery date the value of the variance for the whole process is calculated (σ^2_t) to obtain the standard deviation of the whole process (σ_t). Three times this standard deviation is then added to the target date, as shown in Fig. 10.8, giving the latest delivery date, i.e.

$$\text{target date} + \sigma_t$$

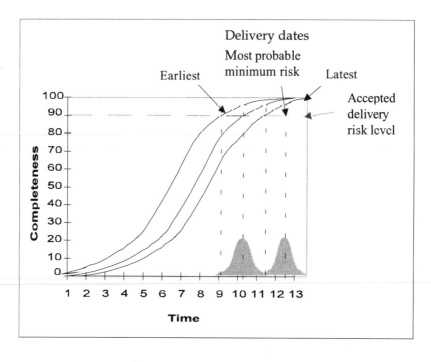

Fig. 10.8 Addition of variance to target time.

Note that this is the expected distribution of the delivery. The date for the developers to use as a target is the earliest possible delivery date (T_{early}). This is calculated from:

$$T_{early} = T_{target} - 3\sigma$$

since this is the earliest possible date that they can be expected to achieve.

During the development process each variance is measured and the sources are analysed for causes. These causes can then be concentrated on to improve the delivery times.

In order to find the variances the progress of a project must be measured and compared against the expected progress. This variance is not always additional time, it could be a reduction on one occasion and an increase on the next. The reduced values require analysis as much as the increases because they can be the source for future process improvements.

Having obtained a best date (the development target), target date (the expected completion date) and the late date (the expected delivery date), a method is required to measure how the project is progressing toward these dates.

■ 10.3 Progress Measurement

The project is expected to be delivered when the latest part of the project is complete. Confidence in this is obtained by measuring the 'progress' of the project which is defined as:

$$\text{Progress} = \frac{\text{actual hours} * \% \text{ completeness}}{\text{total expected hours} * \% \text{ elapsed time}}$$

The actual hours are the man hours expended (not the elapsed time) and the percentage completeness is measured using one of a number of techniques. The most common technique is to compare the number of functions completed with the total number expected in the solution. More sophisticated algorithms will weight the functions according to expected duration obtained from the original estimation process. A table of collected data is shown in Table 10.3.

Progress measurement is continued while the project is active and the progress is plotted on ($\overline{X}$, R) charts

Each chart plotted is associated with a common process, i.e. the distribution expected from the team, and the methods being used must be the same. However, when a step change occurs, such as the introduction of a new tool, the chart is re-calibrated to measure the effect on the variance, and new limits are calculated for this particular process.

An example of this for the data provided in Table 10.4 is the shown in Fig. 10.9.

The control limits on this graph are calculated using the rules provided in Chapter 4.

Table 10.3 Progress project tracking data.

						Mean						Mean
Actual hours	7	24	32	38	64		84	102	123	145	168	
% Completeness	1.6	2.1	4.8	5.6	7.2		9.9	11.1	12.4	14.8	17.2	
Total expected hours	14	28	36	58	60		88	98	121	137	175	
% Elapsed time	1	3.2	4.2	5.6	8.6		10.2	11.5	12.2	13.8	17.5	
Progress	1.4	1.13	1.01	0.65	.89	1.016	0.93	1.00	1.03	1.14	0.94	1.008
Range						0.75						0.21

Table 10.4 Data for project progress.

Date	14/3/1993	Characteristic	Progress			Entered by	GCS	
$\overline{X}$ Chart	UCL 1.16	CL 1.017	LCL 0.875	R Chart	UCL 0.516	CL 0.24	LCL 0

DATE	14/3	19/3	26/3	28/3	4/4	11/4	18/4	25/4	2/5
X_1	1.10	1.12	0.98	0.94	1.13	1.01	0.93	0.92	1.00
X_2	0.92	0.99	1.01	1.08	1.11	0.93	0.85	0.97	1.23
X_3	1.02	1.11	0.99	0.89	0.96	1.10	1.21	0.94	0.99
X_4	0.92	0.99	1.03	0.98	1.14	0.99	1.03	0.89	0.92
X_5	1.12	0.78	0.98	1.03	1.34	0.88	1.23	0.98	1.11
ΣX	5.08	4.99	4.99	4.92	5.68	4.91	5.25	4.7	5.25
$\overline{X}$	1.016	0.998	0.998	0.984	1.136	0.982	1.05	0.94	1.05
Range	0.2	0.34	0.05	0.19	0.38	0.22	0.38	0.11	0.24

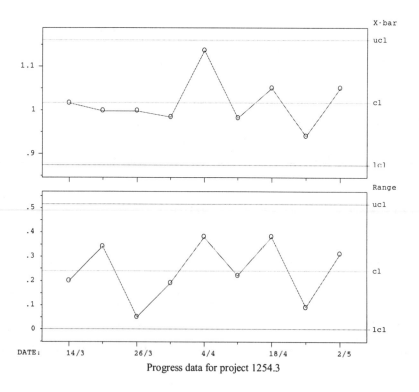

Progress data for project 1254.3

Fig. 10.9 Time management $\overline{X}$, R chart.

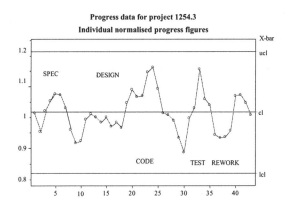

Fig. 10.10 Time management limits and expected delivery date.

A reading that is high on the $\overline{X}$ chart may be cause for correction of the delivery date. An increasing trend on the R chart is showing an increased variance of the process which reflects across that part of the project. It is unlikely to be a one off and should consequently cause a re-calculation of the delivery date based on the increased process variance. It also requires an investigation of the process itself to find out why the variance is increasing.

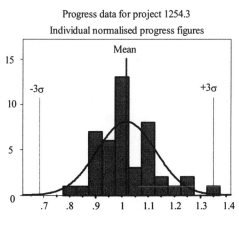

Samples: 45   3s Prob Lim: 0.68, 1.35
Mean: 1.017   Std. Dev.: 0.111

Fig. 10.11 Expected and target dates.

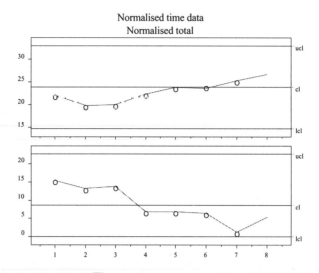

Fig. 10.12 Control points on $\overline{X}$ and R charts.

■ 10.4 Over-estimation of Completeness

Because the graph uses differences in the estimation, it is possible to observe the control situation and the state of control much earlier in the cycle. A response of resource or time plan changes, or with a review of why the out-of-control situation is happening, can be planned.

The estimates for time are taken from weekly time sheets that not only provide the elapsed time and effort expended, but also the estimate for completion, as shown in Fig. 10.13.

This has always been difficult because of the over-optimism of the estimations. It soon loses credibility when engineers are continually estimating between 90 and 100% for the last 80% of the projects life. However this is not significant since two things can provide us with the resolution required for measurement:

- linearisation by using logarithmic scales as shown in Fig. 10.14
- training to improve the estimation.

In time the engineers will be able to differentiate between completed code and working code and the linearisation process can be removed.

Another method of coping with over-estimation and the resistance expected is to divide the process into smaller parts. This will cause the effort required for a debug cycle to be seen and it can then be measured as a separate stage in the development cycle.

Date 14/3/93			
Project Number GRAF1074_246_Upgrade			
Function Module or Program	Estimated Time	Hours Completed	% Completed
Main Control – Module	144	47	35

Fig. 10.13   Weekly time-sheet data.

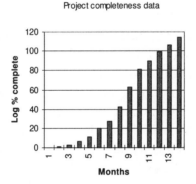

Project completeness data

Fig. 10.14   Linearised data graphs.

This is much more difficult in the generation of specification, system test, design, code test and module test documentation. However even here the task of dividing the work into small manageable parts is to be encouraged. In choosing the size of the elements, increasing integration complexity must be traded against the benefits of the improved metrication.

■ 10.5 Process Control Charts

On completion of each estimation (usually weekly from time sheets), the points are plotted on the graph and the variance is calculated. This may result in a new estimation of both target and delivery date, which can be corrected by resource allocation or process improvement. A few cycles of doing this will reduce the natural variance as staff begin to understand the causes of the variation seen. The underlying pattern will become apparent and will remain static unless the project experiences interruptions or unless modifications are made to the requirements.

The normal variance can reasonably be applied to the first set of data from a project in order to establish internal target dates and the final completion date for the project. This will give greater confidence to management in believing that this is not another project that will run beyond the estimated time scales.

■ 10.6 Completion Measurement

The concept of completeness in the software industry is often 'when the customer wants the product'. Far too often this may be before the product is ready for delivery.

The way completeness is measured is largely dependent on the nature of changes or development. For 'new' code the concept can be conformance to specification and this can be measured by complete and thorough testing. However this is time consuming and impractical for all but the smallest project. The defectiveness observed during the development process provides some indication of the readiness of the code. This approach is very limited in its capability for detecting all but the obvious defects in the product module under test (62,63).

The use of a technique for detecting system defectiveness prior to release will greatly improve the confidence of the company in terms of the reliability and maintenance support required for the product. This is the subject of Chapter 13. The measure obtained is used as a feedback mechanism for the project management cycle. If the product is still too defective to be released, then the development process has not finished. The defective rate of both the modules and the integrated system are used as input for calculation of the completeness of the product before release to system test. The definition of a finished project is therefore 'release to system test' and is defined by a given defectiveness level (preferably a very small number such as 3 defects per million functions or some such figure!). Release levels of between 10 and 500 defects per module for large new systems have been achieved by one company (67). They are aiming for release levels of between 10 and 50 defects per module. A second example is given at the end of this chapter where the release levels are between 5 and 50 errors per module even after 6 months of Beta trial. Where SPC is practised these levels are as low as 10 to 50 defects per million lines of code.

▓ 10.7 Summary

- Project time control involves taking the first estimates as the target times and then adding the variances in order to obtain a realistic delivery date.
- Progress measurement will allow resource requirements to be established early.
- The measurement of progress variance provides the control input necessary to keep a project on target. A trend or a 2σ signal means 'take an early look at the project to establish the significance of the point'. A high point outside the 3σ lines means re-estimate delivery date for the project and investigate the causes of the variance.
- Process improvement comes from the analysis and correction of out-of-control points when they are above the upper control limit and from observation of what went right when the out-of-control point is below the lower control limit.
- The use of cause analysis techniques early in the project will provide corrective actions before the out-of-control situation has serious effects on the delivery date (since normal variation has already been taken into account).
- The use of completion metrics, which should be decided on early in the project, will enable accurate measures of variance that can be used during the setting up of future similar projects.

▓ 10.8 Examples

▓ 10.8.1 Confidence measures used to manage project activities

This example uses confidence measurement and outlines how several measures can be used to select the appropriate development process and to control the success of the project.

A small manufacturing company was in the process of developing a system for measuring process variables on manufacturing machines and required both localised instrumentation and a central data collection, analysis and display system. The measurement system had been in development for several years and had been successfully proven on one of the machines, and as a result required some modification to provide the network facilities and to enhance the functionality. The centralised data collection system that was to collect summary data from over 30 machines was a new idea at the time the project was initiated.

To control the project a mechanism was required for minimising the risk. With four suppliers (hardware, network, measurement software and centralised software systems), the requirement was for a system that would ensure that the relationships between the organisations were satisfactory. The method chosen was to measure confidence as well as measuring the conformance of the products as the project developed.

Conformance measurement is a matter of measuring the products completed against the expectations of the customer. Since a specification had been agreed, this measurement was a case of comparison, associated with some discussion where any ambiguity was identified.

Confidence is a different matter. It is destroyed by a single major defect or increased by the smooth talking of a good salesperson. The success of most projects is based not on its ability to provide conformance, but by meeting the expectations of the customer and inspiring confidence. Consequently a system that may not provide 100% of the features, but actually has 100% operation and 100% reliability provides the confidence that the customer requires for the production measurement system. Consequently our aim in the project was to measure the start confidence of each of the suppliers and the customer, and to improve that confidence through the life of the project.

With the upgrade of the project the confidence was measured by attending the meetings and logging the differences between the supplier and the customer reactions to the requirements and the delivered products. The initial meeting indicated the following profile for the supplier and the customer. These results were measured by counting the occurrences of the following events for both the supplier and the developer:

(1) Requirement not defined – The supplier or the developer had a question of clarification that neither party could define at the meeting.

(2) Requirement unclear – A specified requirement could not be clarified at the meeting.

(3) Requirement not understood – A specified requirement could not be understood by one of the parties at the meeting.

(4) Requirement cleared – The requirement was questioned but

clarified by both parties at the meeting.

(5) Requirement OK – The requirement was reviewed and no outstanding questions arose.

These questions are given values of 1 to 5 and the final percentage for any part of the system is given by:

$$\% \, \text{Confidence} = \frac{\text{the score of the questions} * 100}{\left(\text{number of requirements} + \text{not defined requirements}\right) * 5}$$

The results for this project are given in Table 10.5. At subsequent meetings records were obtained as shown in Table 10.6. A similar table for the customer shows how the confidence in the customer was building through the development process. Another important factor in the process is the confidence achieved as a result of testing the system. This is the release confidence index that determines acceptance of the system. Table 10.7 shows the index achieved at each of the three test stages used for the instrumentation system. While the confidence in the system functions attains nearly the 100% level, the network functions still have lower levels of confidence. This is due to the fact that the system is designed to handle the traffic from 30 instruments, but no testing has been able to provide this

Table 10.5 Confidence metrics collected during project.

Measurement functions					
Calculation	90				
Collect	88				
New variables	86	Mean	88	Range	4
Screen displays					
Display variables	94				
Interactive menus	85				
Colours	60				
Warning lights	80	Mean	79.75	Range	34
Alarm system					
Initiating of alarm	98				
Meaning of lights	85				
Clearing alarm	85	Mean	89.33	Range	13
Network requirements					
Data throughput	75				
Protocols	25	Mean	50	Range	50

Table 10.6 Measurements of confidence through project.

	Supplier data					
Measurement functions calculation	90	95	94	97	95	98
Collect	88	90	93	92	95	98
New variables	86	87	85	84	87	110
Mean	88	90.6	90.6	91	92.3	102
Range	4	8	9	13	8	12
Screen displays						
Display variables	94	98	98	97	99	99
Interactive menus	85	82	86	89	95	99
Colours	60	65	60	75	85	100
Warning lights	80	80	80	85	95	100
Mean	79.75	81.25	81	86.5	93.5	99.5
Range	34	33	38	22	14	1
Alarm system						
Initiating of alarm	98	99	99	100	100	100
Meaning of lights	85	87	89	94	100	100
Clearing alarm	85	85	85	85	87	90
Mean	89.33	90.3	91	93	95.6	97.7
Range	13	14	14	15	13	10
Network requirements						
Data throughput	75	75	78	90	90	90
Protocols	25	25	70	85	85	85
Mean	50	50	74	87.5	87.5	87.5
Range	50	50	8	5	5	5

level of activity due to the lack of hardware. The system was not due to achieve this level of throughput for at least 3 years after the date of the acceptance tests and so the acceptance was designed to be at lower level.

The development method for this part of the project was based on a standard V model. Specifications, designs and then coding stages were planned for each part of the project as a separate entity, with clear interfaces specified between the interdependent parts. The method was selected because the confidence in each of the elements was at a level that indicated that both the developer and the supplier understood the problem that the software was being designed to resolve. The network functions, however, were subjected to a number of extra meetings so that joint design decisions could be made between the network hardware supplier and the two software system suppliers. This functionality was tracked to 80% confidence levels before any code was developed in this area. Test software to show

Table 10.7 The calculated Index.

	Customer confidence in Test results		
	Supplier site acceptance tests	Installation tests	Acceptance tests
Measurement functions calculation	99	99	99
Collect	98	95	99
New variables	95	98	98
Mean	97.3	97.3	98.7
Range	4	4	1
Screen displays			
Display variables	85	95	100
Interactive menus	90	95	100
Colours	80	99	100
Warning lights	95	100	100
Mean	87.5	97.25	100
Range	15	5	0
Alarm system			
Initiating of alarm	98	99	99
Meaning of lights	99	99	99
Clearing alarm	85	95	95
Mean	94	97.7	97.7
Range	15	4	4
Network requirements			
Data throughput	75	85	85
Protocols	70	85	95
Mean	72.5	85	90
Range	5	0	10

the principles was provided by the network hardware supplier and demonstrated to both the customer and the software developer. These tests provided the 90% confidence levels required to decide on the hardware and software solutions.

The network software was developed by a method similar to prototyping – the hardware supplier providing software prototypes to match the interface scenarios required by the software developer.

The central data gathering and analysis system was a true prototyping development as the confidence index at the start of this project was less than 20% overall. Neither the supplier nor the customer knew what functionality was expected of the system at the outset. The developer provided screens of functions for comment in order to draw the requirements from the customer and allow them to develop detail requirements. Once the detail requirements had been agreed (a confidence level for all functions of 90% average had been achieved) the detail code behind the functions was developed. This code went through the same acceptance testing procedure in order to ensure that the code arriving on site was acceptable to the customer.

This measurement it all stages was complemented by conformance measurement once the specifications had been agreed at a level of confidence adequate for progressing the project. This level is dependent on the criticality of the code and the cost implications of changes in specifications. For most of these functions the cost implications are minimal – one graphic costs about the same as another to develop, and so the project could progress without specifying the detail of the graphics. The need to maintain an increasing confidence index then became of prime importance and so effort was put into agreeing the graphics screens prior to committing effort to the code and function development. The supplier and customer confidence indices are provided in Fig. 10.15.

■ 10.8.2 Progress for modification of a real time control system

Project data was collected from an enhancement activity involving two software engineers working remotely. The activities had been planned and estimated in order to provide a completion date and cost for the project. The progress is given as:

$$\text{Progress} = \frac{\text{Actual hours * \% complete}}{\text{Total expected elapsed * \% elapsed time}}$$

The figures collected and the computations of progress are shown in Table 10.5.

When the differences are charted as shown in Fig. 10.16, the variance shows that the company has wide variation in estimating capability. The effect on the project is that overall it was expected to be on target (the mean differences were nearly or slightly less than zero). However the variance indicates that, from the $+3\sigma$ value, the latest delivery date that can be confidently predicted is 20 days after the estimate (barring any extra influences on the project in the meantime). In fact continuing the chart for

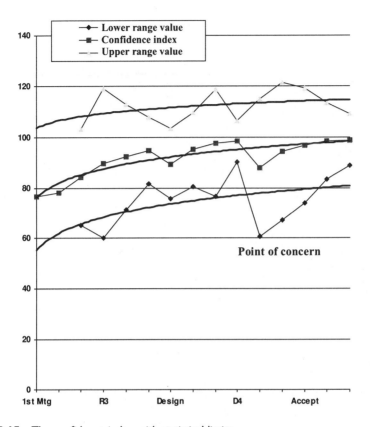

Fig. 10.15 The confidence index with statistical limits.

Table 10.8 Data collected for project time as the project progressed.

Activity	Actual hours	% Complete	Elapsed time %	Total expected hours	Progress	Diff
1	47	65%	50%	96	63.6%	-1.4%
2	138	40%	40%	400	34.5%	-5.5%
3	24	70%	90%	32	51.0%	-19%
4	83	50%	30%	150	92%	42%

the project shows that progress significantly slowed during the latter stages and this was due to delays in other parts of the project. The actual delivery date was 35 days over target and the estimated extra work due to the external inputs was about 25 days. This meant that without external inputs the predicted date of 20 days late was reasonable and would have allowed the company to beat their deadline by 15 days.

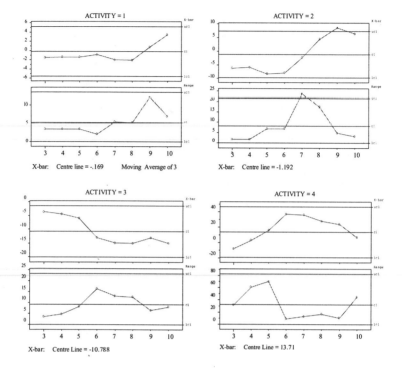

Fig. 10.15 $\overline{X}$,R chart for normalised project time scale differences.

■ 10.8.3 Estimating using means and variance

A company that produces a modelling system for chemical reaction processes which is sold world wide has been developing a new version over a period of months, producing a number of releases. During the project, completion metrics were gathered as shown in Table 10.9. This data was analysed for variance in order to establish how the project team was producing the software compared with a simple categorisation of the complexity and difficulty of the software.

The results are linearised for complexity and difficulty by multiplying the percentage difference value by the corrections factors for the high, medium and low categories. This provides a view of the variation in the difference between the estimated and actual times, removing the effects of the differences in complexity and difficulty. The resulting X, Moving R chart is shown in Fig. 10.17.

Table 10.9   Project completion metrics.

Estimated time	Actual time	% Difference	Complexity	Difficulty	Normalised difference
19.3	21	300	m	m	75
42.8	54	427	h	h	26.7
2	5.5	101.8	l	m	45
2.6	8	83.7	l	l	47.08
5.1	7	264.3	l	m	35.62
12.7	23	197.4	m	m	49.37
24.5	30.9	126.1	m	l	7.25
19.5	24.4	125.1	l	l	70.31
13.5	22.2	164.4	m	l	1.65
24.4	83.4	341.8	h	h	21.36
5.5	11.8	214.5	m	m	53.63
6.5	13.8	212.3	m	m	53.1
22	33.7	153.2	m	l	86.2
6	4.1	68.3	l	l	38.25
4	7.7	192.5	m	m	48.12
7.5	48.2	642.7	h	h	40.17
10	1.8	18	l	l	10.52
34	75.1	220.9	m	m	55
15	28.4	189.3	l	m	41.25
23	18.7	81.3	l	l	45.56
23	21.4	93	l	l	52.31
24	30.1	125.4	l	l	70.53
15	20.2	134.7	m	l	50.51
30	68.8	229.3	m	m	57.33
69	102.2	148.1	m	l	55.53

Key   l = 0.25   m=0.5   h=0.75

The histograms for the different categories of modules are plotted, Fig. 10.18, to provide a mean value for the correction to the estimates for each category of complexity and difficulty for future use. The estimating process will then consist of analysing the code for probable complexity and difficulty and classifying them in one of the three classes. The estimates are then corrected using the best and worst case values from the histogram. This then provides a probable delivery date together with best and worst case estimates.

On completion of a project the time data is entered into the table and the histograms are recalculated. They may also be drawn as control charts (without corrections), showing how the process of estimating is improving.

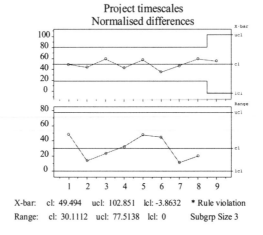

Fig. 10.17 X, Moving R chart estimate to actual project time scale differences.

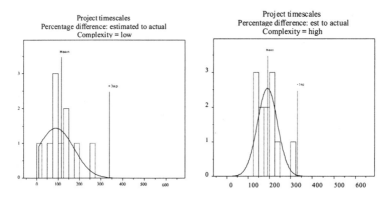

Fig. 10.18 Distribution of project time scales for modules of low and medium complexity.

■ 10.8.4 Defectiveness as a means of deciding on completeness

The same project was analysed for completion based on the defectiveness of the product. The product is regression tested on each release including the extra tests required for the new functionality that may have been added between versions.

One purpose of this testing is to establish what the defectiveness level is and what maintenance can be expected. The result of this is to provide the organisation with a defectiveness measure that can be used to decide whether the product is fit for delivery.

The tests completed on a new product over a set of releases, Table 10.10, shows that defect levels varied according to the release number and that a general trend of reducing numbers of reported defects was achieved. The levels of defects at which it is acceptable to deliver the product is partially determined by financial concerns. However, the data provides the possibility of repeating the fix and test cycle until testing finds defects better than a target number per module. For each release the target number is reduced.

Fig. 10.19 shows the defect level trace over the releases of the product and the sloping control lines provide the targets for each release and for future releases. The achievement of these levels provides a mechanism for deciding on delivery dates.

The data is plotted on the sloping control chart as Moving X data since there would never be an opportunity to calculate the control lines with sub-grouped data. The control limits are calculated from the rate of change of the mean (since it is unrealistic to expect the variance to change over the project). The control lines are established after the first five releases and the control limits calculated from the usual formula

$$ UCL = \overline{X} + \frac{\overline{R}}{d_2} $$

where $\overline{X}$ is used rather than the mean of the subgroup means.

Table 10.10 Errors and calculation of mean and range.

Errors/release	Mean error	Moving range
44		
77		
29		
61		
76	57.4	48
0	48.6	77
34	40	76
2	34.6	76
20	26.4	76
37	18.6	37
4	19.4	35
70	26.6	68
45	35.2	66
0	31.2	70
	Mean	Mean range
	33.8	62.9

Table 10.11 Table for least square fit through means.

Sample number	Mean	Sample number × mean	Release number^2
1	57.4	57.4	1
2	48.6	97.2	4
3	40	120	9
4	34.6	138.4	16
5	26.4	132	25
6	18.6	111.6	36
7	19.4	135.8	49
8	26.6	212.8	64
9	35.2	316.8	81
10	31.2	312	100
55	338	1634	385

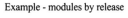

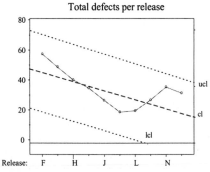

Fig. 10.19 The Moving X chart using sloping control lines.

$$\sum y = a\sum x + nb$$
$$\sum xy = a\sum x^2 + b\sum x$$

$$338 = a \times 55 + 10b$$
$$1634 = a \times 385 + 55b$$

Solving gives a = –2.73 and b = 48.8.

The mean trend line follows the equation y = –2.73x + 48.8.

Consequently the mean starts at 48.8 and crosses the x axis at 17.87.

$$\text{Control lines} = \frac{\overline{R}}{d_2} = \frac{62.9}{2.326} = \pm 27.04 \text{ either side of mean.}$$

The calculations are shown in Table 10.11.

11 SPC in Design and Code Generation

11.1 Introduction

This is the heart of the development process which involves taking the definition, specification and standards documents and generating the design and the code in conformance and to conform with them. Whichever of the various models discussed in Chapter 3 is used, at some stage during the cycle, code is generated from a design. This design has been produced as the result of analysis of the requirements. These two activities may not be designed to produce the deliverable code, but just to provide an initial or subsequent prototype. Alternatively, in the most formal V model situations, they are designed to take all the input documents and generate a working system.

None of the models for software life cycles actually require the use of statistical tools to make them work. However, if the aim is to achieve level 5 on the SEI CMM, which means making the processes repeatable and controlled, then SPC is a requirement for efficiently achieving control.

This is achieved through a few simple steps, which, in practice, may take months or years to both establish and to produce the benefits. The first action is to break down the main phases into the individual activities. Metrics are then selected that can be used to control the timescale, the cost, performance and capability of the product.

The main difficulty in applying statistical techniques at this stage is the confusion between what are 'processes' and what are techniques used within the processes. One of the main techniques in design for instance is 'idea generation', sketching a few ideas and searching for the most effective solution. This by its very nature is an open ended activity. No-one can know what the most effective solution to a particular problem is until a history of solutions has been produced and these have been analysed for effectiveness. If the problem is truly unique then this is made even more difficult. However if this stage is allowed to go on until the designer is satisfied it would probably never end. So an effective end point has to be defined and measured against acceptance criteria such as customer confidence and satisfaction, completeness against the requirements and peer acceptance of the concepts employed. This does not mean that the design is fixed at this point – only that the idea generation stage has been completed.

Many software designs in fact do not use this method at all. They have already formalised the process so that generating a design from a specification is a matter of 'conversion'. This process is much simpler to control because historical information can provide all that is needed to determine the time and cost for a conversion process. Quality is achieved

Table 11.1 Stages for the design of design and code phases.

Stage	Activity
Plan	Break down the phase into activities
	Select metrics to control those activities for time, cost and functionality
	Design the collection, analysis and response systems for the control metrics
	Design a verification system to establish that the control of the metrics is achieving the quality required at any one point in time.
Do	Use the system to gather and analyse the metrics. Detect and note special out-of-control situations, high variability and the effect on the product quality
Check	Find the causes for the special situations and find methods of eliminating them
Act	Initiate plans for changing the system by using new metrics and dropping metrics that provide no special inputs. Initiate a new start of the loop by changing the procedures to include the new methods.

by training in the conversion method and on-line and post-conversion inspection.

The code generation activities are much more a case of converting the design from a specification language to the program language. However, there is usually still an element of innovation and creation since the tools available, i.e. in the development language, are broad in definition and allow scope for multitudes of similar solutions to any one problem.

When the process is to produce code using a GUI, a 4GL or other high-level production interface, then the design element can once again increase. The question of when the design stops and the coding starts then becomes difficult to answer. In fact the question is whether the two phases can be separated at all. The simultaneous or RAD methodology has taken this to the logical conclusion of integrating the activities and controlling them with customer reviews.

The stages for designing a control system for the design and coding phases of the lifecycle are provided in Table 11.1. The resultant system is then subjected to continual review for improvement.

The following sections provide examples of the metrics that can be collected from different stages of a process and from the product. Since all software development is not aimed at mass producing a shrink-wrapped product, this chapter also considers issues of prototyping, development of one off bespoke systems, and the maintenance of large systems.

■ 11.2 The Activities in Design and Coding

Identification of the process within a software development organisation is a function of maturity which means that the more repeatable the process the easier it is to define the actual process activities. Lifecycle models attempt to do this, but at the detail level most companies complain that processes cannot be categorised that easily. Fig. 11.1 shows the relationship between process identification and process maturity using the SEI definition of maturity.

An example of a level 2 company is a process dedicated to designing new bespoke software with well-defined and documented processes. In such a system there are procedures for all the normal actions that must be taken, options to match special cases, and the freedom to add new processes to meet needs that have not been foreseen.

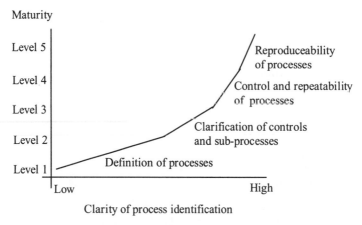

Fig. 11.1 Relationship between maturity and process identification.

■ 11.2.1 Design activities

In a standard V model using a 3GL language the design process starts with collecting requirements for the product and ends at the point where a detail design document is available for the programmers. The implementation or code development stage is then taken as the time until the module testing is completed. Integration is considered as a part of the integration testing phase and not as an integral part of the development stage.

For other development models the differences in the metrics relate more to the resolution and accuracy of measurement achievable at each stage of the project cycle rather than the type of metrics required.

A typical generic design process may be as shown in Table 11.2.

■ 11.2.2 Coding activities

The coding activities are usually much simpler than those required to design and this is reflected in Table 11.3. In many organisations this list will be different and can only be typified here. For instance where RAD is being used, or a GUI type application is being developed then the actual activities will be substantially different. The principle is to break down the activities into small parts with identified start and end metrics that can be used to control the process required to complete the activity. There is obviously a limit to this – flow diagramming a programmers every move would be counter-productive. Just saying 'code', however, is also not productive because this leaves a high a degree of interpretation on the activities.

Table 11.2 Design activities.

Activity stage	Process activity
Preparation for design	Identification and documentation of new requirements
	Inspection of requirements document
	Generation and modification of criticality and innovativeness models
	Acceptance criteria for design
	Estimation of time and cost for complete project
	Design stage planning providing effort, time and inspection effort based on criticality and innovativeness metrics and based on capability of company
Designing	Design activities including interface identification and specification
System acceptance based on design	Test specification modification including criticality and innovativeness models in the test selection model
Documentation of design	Design documentation
Design review	Review preparation
	Review
	Changes to reflect review concerns
Inspection for acceptance	Inspection preparation
	Inspection
	Modification of criticality and innovativeness models based on design
Design release	

Table 11.3 Coding activities.

Phase	Development activity
Preparation for coding	Gather input documents, resources, equipment and tools
Detail	Convert design to detail design
	Inspect detail design
Test specification	Specify module tests
	Inspect module test specification
Code and test	Convert detail design to code
	Test individual modules
	Correct individual modules
Release module for integration	

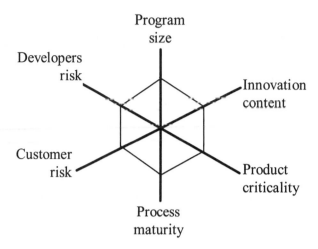

Fig. 11.2 Categories of development characteristics.

■ 11.3 Metrics

In considering the different development processes we can characterise the development environments in terms of the percentage of innovation, development, production (otherwise known as duplication) and maintenance that is occurring. Fig. 11.2 shows these categories in terms of the process and the product metrics.

These metrics provide information about the product being developed and the process being used. Many more product and process measures are available, but these first few provide sufficient activities and enough information to get a control project started. Other metrics can be selected at a later stage once the first set are under statistical control.

■ 11.3.1 Process metrics

The three legs, **developers' risk, customer risk,** and **process maturity** are all process related metrics. They provide a measure of the probable success of any project being completed by the process.

■ Developers' risk

The process used, the skills of the staff and the capability of the organisation all contribute to the developers' risk for the project. One other considerable and often forgotten factor is the capability of the developer to understand the problem that is being placed on the company. Often the real life situation is that the customer will not read the specification in detail, assuming that the supplier understands the problem. Better projects result from a review by supplier and customer that provides a measure of the risk being taken by each party. This is the basis of most RAD developments – the project is initiated on the basis that the specification is ongoing and requires customer agreement throughout the development cycle.Developers' risk is based on measuring the following factors:

The cost of failure – usually defined in terms of the development cost, but also includes the quality costs associated with the legal aspects of not being able to deliver.

The capability risk – taken from the history of the company's ability to develop new products using new processes and methods. The more mature the process the more this risk can be measured and used to determine whether the current project is in control compared with all previous projects. Examples of capability measures are the variance of cost, timescale, conformance and confidence.

▓ Customer risk

This risk measures the knowledge of the customer with respect to the problem being resolved. The risk includes factors such as market and management system risks, but these are not the concern of the software development team. The measures include:

Cost of failure – the cost of not having the system in terms of not receiving the benefits of the functionality of the software.

Supplier confidence – this is what a purchaser buys when a new project is initiated. This is based on knowledge of the suppliers' delivery record. The metrics are based on time and cost ratios for estimates and achievements for previous similar projects.

▓ Metrics for process maturity

The maturity of a process is determined by the stability of the development team and the ability of the process to adapt to change in an orderly way. The measures and issues for maturity relate to the five inputs to any process shown in Table 11.4.

Table 11.4 Maturity measure and issue.

Category	Metrics
People	**Skill rating** – A mechanism for rating skills as appropriate to the project is used. This can be based directly on ISO 9000 or TickIT training records.
	Are the team members changing? If so, are the new team members of the same skill levels and do they have skills in the same disciplines?
Materials	**Language usage metrics** – The Halstead metrics and the language usage metrics from test tools provide direct measures of the number of occurrences of use of operators and operands. They provide counts of the numbers of times operands and operators are used. Compiler testing indicates which parts of a language are most likely to provide error free code. Is the use of language consistent throughout the project and is re-usability a key issue?
	Supplied inputs metrics – Is there a mechanism for ensuring that everything to be used in the project is consistent, of a known defectiveness, and below acceptance thresholds? Is a mechanism for change of these inputs in place? Is there a mechanism for reducing these thresholds?
	Materials include specifications and requirements, standards, the programme language and any other documented inputs to the project. Inspections of documents provide the input metrics for a project.
Machines	**Supplier metrics** – Are the development machines, the software languages, compilers and word processors defect free?
	Are there failures for unknown reasons in any of the tools in use on the project, and are these measured?
Methods	**Project metrics** – Have the development methods been established? What is measured and how? The mean and range for lines of code per day, time per 1000 lines, error rate, time in each stage, corrective action time, developer test time (the time taken by the person producing the code in testing that code).
	Conformance metrics – The non-conformances reported during the project defined as non-conformances to the requirements of the standards and the quality system in use. Is everyone on the team trained to use the methods and is their use measured?
	Are the methods known to produce consistent results for every project and is there a mechanism for measuring improvement?
Environment	**Time and effort non-conformance metrics** – Is the technical and management environment stable both in the method and the application of pressure on the team? Is the physical environment suited to the type of development being undertaken?

■ 11.3.2 Product metrics

The three legs of the star chart, **criticality, innovation content** and **size** are all product metrics that can only be estimated at the start of a project, and then measured on completion. They are used to control the product quality by using input values from the history of the company as process controls.

■ Product criticality

Criticality is a controllable condition that can be minimised by design. The criticality of individual components of the system is assessed and recorded so that effort can be applied according to the criticality at all stages through the project. The most critical component of a system can be duplicated in hardware, may use on-line comparators to assure successful operation, and may be designed to be fail safe with all logical conditions being mapped to prevent failure conditions occurring. The criticality measure is updated throughout the project as a series of re-assessments in order to decide where effort should be applied at the next stage of the project. Criticality is measured using cause and effect charts and assigning criticality criteria to the effects in terms of severity levels. Examples are shown in Table 11.5.

These levels must be set up for each individual project. Cause and effect graphing or FMEA can provide the mechanism for getting a set of severity levels that will ensure that effort in preventing defects is targeted at the most critical areas. Criticality maps may be used to establish whether the

Table 11.5 Criticality grading.

Severity type	Severity levels
Life threatening and catastrophic failure	1
Life threatening but non-catastrophic	2
Catastrophic failure (destroys product) but non-life threatening	3
System failure – causes total failure of system with loss of critical information or control status	4
System failure – causes total failure with loss of non-critical information or control status	5
System crash – no loss of information or control status	6
System error – no loss of control, but loss of data	7
System error – no loss of control and no loss of data	8
System error – error report only and effects computations	9
System error – error report only with no effect on computations	10

particular project has a higher than normal criticality level based on the mean and the range for the project. For a particular organisation producing different code for different types of project, the mean and range control chart for criticality is used. This identifies when there is a higher than normal risk and when extra effort may be required to ensure successful completion of the project.

■ Product innovation

The innovative state of a new product is partially what maintains a product's position in the market place. This is true for both bespoke products and volume market products. There is little point in being many steps ahead when one step will maintain market position, so the innovation must be controlled to maintain the most beneficial position for the company. Again a mapping of the innovativeness of modules is used to direct effort to the parts where the greatest risk exists. Innovativeness is measured by grading the modules and functions. It is dependent on the current knowledge base of an organisation and relates to the amount of change that is to occur in a project.

An example of this is a company initiating a new Windows version of a DOS based product. This company will consider the innovativeness as being greater than for a company adding functionality to an existing Windows based product. This assumes that the project team, the language, the target and development platform and the development tools remain identical for the Windows environment.

An extra input into this equation is the degree of difficulty required for developing the product. The grading mechanism for difficulty may be based on the historical mean effort required per 1000 lines of code for the company, multiplied by a factor based on the changes to the project team, tools, product type and materials. The factor is calculated from experience of the organisation and based on the influence each different change has on the time scales of the project.

■ Product size

The 'size' of the product can be measured in many ways. Examples are the number of lines or functions, the complexity, paths, loops, number of data types, data volumes and function points.

The use of guidelines based on these metrics has been shown to improve

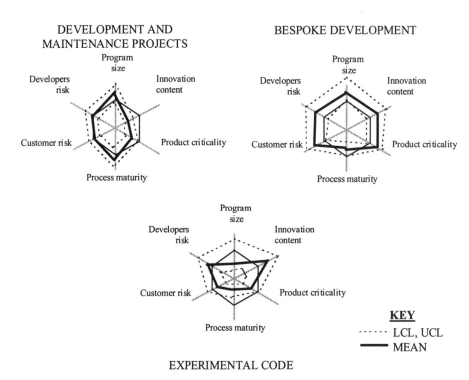

Fig. 11.3   Star charts for different processes.

the quality of the software product if the metrics are kept under statistical control for a particular type of module. The type of module is dependent on three factors:

(1) the program language of the module source
(2) the language usage within the module
(3) the type of operation carried out by the module.

These three factors are used to classify each module and provide the mean and variance expected for future modules of this type. The examples show how this is achieved.

■ 11.4 Designing the Design Phase Control Process

Different star diagrams are obtained for different types of design and development organisation and a few examples are shown in Fig. 11.3. These show that the variability of a purely research organisation using software to prove a point is likely to be far greater than that of a company producing mission critical code.

A common factor to all software development is the innovative stage at the start of the project. Even for the simplest upgrade of existing software this is true, since the starting point is asking questions about what is required, how it can be achieved, and what methods are to be used to achieve it.

The two processes being considered in this section – design and coding – will consequently vary considerably according to the lifecycle, product and management styles adopted and so an example is based on a simple generic process.

■ 11.4.1 Design metrics and control charts

The design metrics are determined for each of the activities identified earlier in the chapter (Table 11.2). Table 11.6 shows the control charts that can be used for each of the different metrics available for each of the activities. These aim to provide control of the activity (the process) and not the methods used within the activity. We will see later that the inspection process benefits from formal specification of its activities and control is used for each of these individually to maximise the benefits of doing each of the individual tasks. So it is with software design. The activity to identify and document new requirements may be further sub-divided into activities such as:

(1) the requirement gathering meeting with the customer
(2) the brainstorming sessions for new requirements, future developments and completeness of requirements (each separate activity)
(3) the selection for inclusion meeting
(4) the document generation
(5) the document inspection
(6) the document correction
(7) the adoption procedure.

The most significant assistance we have in breaking down the development process is the use of flow charts. These should identify not just the flow of the activities, but the metrics required for acceptance, and the acceptance stages, the reject and corrective action flows. By identifying

Table 11.6   The processes in a design activity and the charts used for control.

No.	Process activity	Metrics	Chart types
1	Identification and documentation of new requirements	Number of requirements time and cost/module estimate of complexity and criticality	c chart X, Moving R chart X, Moving R chart
2	Inspection of requirements document	Defects/page, Time and cost Estimate of preparation & inspection hours	c chart X, Moving R chart X, Moving R chart
3	Modification of criticality and innovativeness models	Time and cost	X, Moving R chart
4	Estimation of time and cost for complete project	Time and cost	X, Moving R chart
5	Design stage planning providing effort, time and inspection effort based on criticality and innovativeness metrics and based on capability of company	Effort Difficulty Time Cost	X, Moving R chart X, Moving R chart X, Moving R chart X, Moving R chart
6	Design activities including interface identification and specification	Number of functions/module, effort/module, complexity/module, difficulty/module, Time and cost/module	X, Moving R chart X, Moving R chart X, Moving R chart X, Moving R chart X, Moving R chart
7	Test specification modification including criticality and innovativeness models in the test selection model	Functions/module Cases/module Time and cost	X, Moving R chart X, Moving R chart X, Moving R chart
8	Design documentation	Functions, time and cost	X, Moving R chart
9	Review preparation	Time and cost	X, Moving R chart
10	Review	Errors found, confidence, conformity, time and cost	c chart, X-R chart X, Moving R chart
11	Changes to reflect peer review concerns	Correction cost (quality cost)	X-R chart
12	Inspection preparation	Time/page, errors/page	X, Moving R chart c chart
13	Inspection	Time/page, errors, logging rate	X, Moving R chart c chart, X-R chart
14	Modification of criticality and innovativeness models based on design	Criticality, innovativeness, Time and cost	X, Moving R chart X, Moving R chart
15	Design release	Difference from estimates	X, Moving R chart

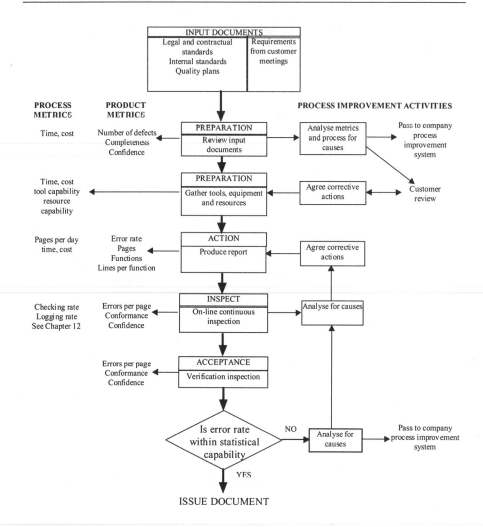

Fig. 11.4 Flow diagram for documentation of new requirements.

each of these stages the appropriate metrics and cost measures can be applied and the effects of control observed. Fig. 11.4 shows the flow diagram for documenting new requirements, which is significantly more complicated than might at first be expected. However this flow diagram ensures that quality control and quality improvement are both built into the process. This matches the process model as described in Chapter 2. Each stage of the process contributes to the management of quality at a local and continuous control level, at the supervisory level and at the company wide level for process improvement management. The quality management system is consequently automatically designed to meet ISO 9000 and TickIT requirements, but will also meet the requirements of the SEI CMM. Statistical control charts are used at each of the different levels of the process.

Applications in different types of design environment will have their own special requirements and the following sections provide details of how these effect the process.

▓ 11.4.2 Repeated design – volume product development

For a company with a single product range based on one environment, a process for designing a new version can be defined, particularly if the innovations to be included are all new functions.

The statistics for these processes are based on the effort used to develop previous versions, because the product, operating systems, and possibly the project team remain constant. The difference is in the requirement, and this can be measured in terms of the expected number, criticality and innovativeness of the functions and modules. The variance from previous projects is used as the basis for the expected variance in the estimates for dates and costs for completion for the current project. Similarly the historical error rate mean and variance is used to estimate the expected error rates for the new design. The design is only deemed to be complete when an inspection provides an error rate result below a threshold value that is within the capability of the organisation. This is a measure of product quality. It is designed to ensure that delivery of the product is always within the capability of the company and to catch probable causes early in the cycle. If this capability is below customer expectations then the company must review its development procedures.

▓ 11.4.3 One off design – bespoke development

A bespoke design may start from a fresh view of the world rather than considering the possibility of upgrade from existing systems. It may be the development of a product that has not been previously experienced. A further complication may be that the product may be developed by a team put together for the purpose of the project, using new tools on a previously unknown platform. This is the worse case scenario which rarely happens. Most companies developing new software solutions use standard sets of tools and base their capability on knowledge of particular platforms and particular market sectors and problem types.

In the worst case scenario the model for the process will inevitably be subject to high levels of variance. For the more normal scenario the company can provide variance estimates of the complexity, difficulty and the time scales and costs. These can then be subjected to the normal calculations based on the variance of a typical project team within the organisation.

This relies on a sophisticated model of the capability of the different project leaders, and the individual team members within the organisation. Statistical methods are used primarily to control the process rather than the product for this type of development. The process is repeated for every new design that is completed, but is scaled up or down to match the estimates of the product metrics such as size, complexity and difficulty. For this type of project critical factors are confidence and conformance.

The main task of statistical process control here is to establish when an individual part of the product is different from other parts. The cause can be found and corrective actions taken on the process before the different part causes problems for the product and the project. Examples are the skills of the individuals, the loss of control of a process metric such as size of a document or code section, or the use of unproven tools and methods.

■ 11.4.4 Upgrade – maintenance of existing systems

In these projects the main effort expended is on the redesign of existing code to improve operation and add enhancements. The new code still has to operate with existing systems. The process here is always of a similar nature and is continually repeated. It may be different in each company visited, but a method across a company can be adopted and is usually dictated by the quality procedures of the company. This type of project uses product metrics from a number of repeated cycles to determine whether the new project is meeting the same capability criteria as the previous development cycles. The process metrics are used as 'scaling' and 'type' factors to determine the target levels of the product metrics.

■ 11.4.5 Experimental – software for proving a point

The prototyping development method quickly provides an example of what a system might look like. The quality requirements are less stringent on the functional side. Instead, emphasis is placed on cost and time, and possibly accuracy of results from the software, rather than robustness of the solution.

The process can again be repeatable although the nature of the company is often such that new languages, tools and methods are tried for each activity. Statistically if the same process is used the metrics of the product can be provided as guidelines from historical data.

■ 11.5 Designing the Metrics for Coding

During development a new set of metrics are used rather than those that were used for desig ning the product. The activities are still largely innovative but using standard sets of solutions to the problems presented by the design. The different development methods may use different metrics but a basic set is provided in Table 11.7. The choice of control charts for

Table 11.7 Coding process metrics.

No.	Development activity	Metrics	Chart type
1	Convert design to detail design	Time, cost, function points, completeness, confidence	Sloping X-R charts
2	Inspect detail design	Time/page errors, errors/page checking/logging time logging rate	X, Moving R chart c chart X, Moving R chart X, Moving R chart
3	Specify module tests	Time, cost number of tests number of paths number of data types data domain size	Sloping X-R chart X, Moving R chart X, Moving R chart X, Moving R chart X-R chart
4	Inspect module test specification	Time/page errors, errors/page checking/logging time logging rate	X, Moving R chart c chart X, Moving R chart X, Moving R chart
5	Convert detail design to code	Time, cost language usage module sise functions/module complexity error rate/module correction loop time	Sloping X-R chart Language map X-R chart X-R chart X-R chart c chart X-R chart
6	Test individual modules	Test time error rates correction time test effectiveness and coverage error rate after correction	X-R chart c chart X-R chart X chart c chart

each of the process metrics is dependent on exactly how the metric is measured. Errors can be measured as errors per module, per line or as a rate of generation. The errors per module or line would be charted on an attribute c chart, whereas the rate would be charted on an (X, Moving R) chart.

The charts are used to monitor the activities of the process. For example lines of code per hour, errors per hour, module size in lines of code, complexity, effort, difficulty, and the usual time and cost metrics which are used for project control are charted. Cost is divided into its constituent parts so that the true quality costs and exceptions can be discovered. Time, and consequently cost, is monitored for the activities shown in Table 11.8.

■ 11.6 Constraints to Improving Quality

Quality improvement in a fast changing environment is constrained by the evolution of the tools, methods and languages. It is much easier to measure and quantify repeatable and unchanging processes rather than processes that are continually developing. The role of process maturity development is to provide a mechanism for ensuring that change occurs to improve the process even if the change can only be observed as a result of completing a development cycle. The only factual evidence that applications can be developed more rapidly now than in the early days of hexadecimal

Table 11.8 Time and cost stages to be measured.

Stage	Sub-sections to be monitored
Design	Preparation – collecting and understanding the input documents
	Detail flow graphing – generating flow graphs for the detail designs
	Detail data graphing – generating data flows
	Criticality analysis – modelling criticality
Test specification	Preparation – collecting design details, test methods specification, test requirements and acceptance criteria
	Test case generation
	Test selection criteria generation
	Test acceptance specification
Code	Preparation – requirements and gathering of hardware and tools according to specified requirements
	Code generation
Code testing	Code test preparation
	Code preliminary test – first test on development machine
	Code modification
	Code re-test

programming, is in the size of programs developed and the time taken in man days or months. There is also evidence that the level of defects per 1000 lines of code in any particular language is decreasing.

One constraint to improving quality is the current maturity of the development process. A second constraint is our ability to measure with an adequate resolution and an example of this is the ability of new test techniques to discover new types of defect. This is an example of increased resolution finding defects that previously were not considered to exist. However even for methods targeted at particular defects there are still limitations as to what can be found.

Further issues with resolution and accuracy exist when the subjective assessments used such as completeness, risk and confidence are considered. These measures are limited both by their nature – the assessment process will always include a degree of variance – as well as by the resolution that can be used, limited often by the cost of making the measure.

This cost factor is also a limit when considering the test activities. Cost effective testing must include a strategy to detect the maximum number of major defects as early as possible, with the less critical defects having a lower probability of being detected at all.

One aim of quality improvement is to find methods that will enable these limitations to be overcome. Statistical methods provide benefits both in cost and time terms, and as has been shown (45), in detection capability also.

▓ 11.7 The Role of Innovation

The start of any development process must include an element of innovation, and truly leading-edge developments will always include a large degree of innovative thought. However as the process matures, so the innovative elements reduce, and the target of a stable and repeatable process becomes self-evident. Management of the innovation process is therefore critical to developing maturity of the innovation process. It is also essential to ensuring the success of leading-edge developments.

Far from being an art form or a method of developing that is left to highly individualistic people, the innovative stage requires careful management. The process goes through three main stages:

(1) brainstorming and idea hunting,
(2) confirming and consolidating,
(3) further refining.

An innovative team will remain in the first stage for long periods of time and never arrive at the end of the confirmation stage. The task of management is to control these stages in a way that is going to maximise the output from the process. There comes a point in time when the developments are outside the scope of the project, and consequently the time to consolidate and confirm arrives. The time for this can be defined and controlled providing that the innovation is managed using techniques such as brainstorming, idea searching and lateral thinking. The time and cost parameters can be targeted by providing the environment and the techniques. The innovativeness of a product can be measured as the time taken to reach the stage of moving to confirmation. This process then becomes a measurable part of the process, and the time function becomes one of the measures of the innovative risk involved in the project. Other measures can include the number of alternatives considered, the number of dead ends researched, and the number of ideas from the brainstorming session.

■ 11.8 Summary

- Processes are different from the methods used to achieve the objective. Design and coding activities can be divided into processes which are repeated. The choice of granularity of division enables the metrics to be used for process control.
- Metrics for controlling the development process include time and cost management, process metrics and product metrics.
- Different processes are used to develop products that have different end uses, or according to the confidence and status of the supplier and customer. A process may be selected that has the highest probability of success.
- Flow charting provides a method of dividing processes into manageable parts.
- A set of metrics are used to manage the design process and another set are selected for the coding process.
- The comparison of methods is based on three product and three process metrics.
- Different processes will provide different benefits. The cheapest is simultaneous engineering or RAD using prototyping, but this may leave many defects in place. The most expensive is the simple V

model with end-of-cycle testing and rectification. This is only useful in mature processes where defect prevention is a matter of course and the rectification cycle minimal.

This chapter has provided the method for designing the metrics and charts for the design and code part of the development process. One of the fundamental processes for managing the early part of the development cycle and for in-process control of the design and code activities is that of inspections. Statistical methods of inspecting are considered in the next chapter.

▓ 11.9 Examples

▓ 11.9.1 Process control through lines of code per module

This example is of 430 modules of C code produced by a software development company. The static analysis tool used is Cantata, which provides some 76 different metrics ranging from the Halstead and McCabe metrics to the counts of language constructs and types of instruction. This data had not been used for controlling the project but has been analysed for a new release of the product which includes new code. This means that there are at least three types of code available:

(1) 'new code' – code generated specifically for this release
(2) 'modified old code' – code that has previously been released but has been modified for this release
(3) 'old code' – code that has previously been released and is unchanged.

For this analysis the Cantata metrics are provided for the old code as well as the corrections that result from detecting errors reported in the next release. In general terms it is easy to show that the length of a module has some relationship to the number of errors subsequently found in the code. The data being used is expected to have some extra complexity, because of the fact that many corrections can result from detecting one error. Fig. 11.5 shows all of the data together and while this does not portray a simple mathematical relationship it does show that generally more errors can be expected in larger modules. The reason for the lack of direct correlation is two-fold:

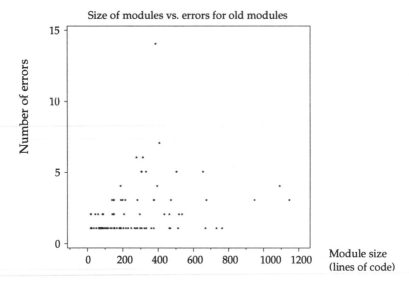

Fig. 11.5 The relationship between errors and the size of the modules.

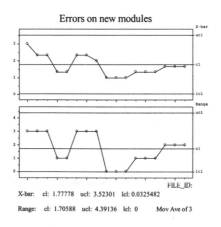

Fig. 11.6 X, Moving R chart for the new modules.

(1) The classifications of new, old and modified old code can be expected to provide at least three simple relationships.

(2) The differences in the types of code can be expected to influence the error rates.

Mathematically speaking, we should now embark on a multi-variate analysis in order to establish equations between the relationships in order to prove or disprove this hypothesis. However, our aim is to improve the

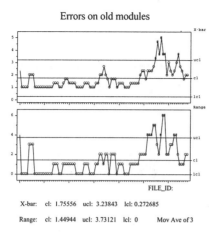

Errors on old modules

X-bar: cl: 1.75556   ucl: 3.23843   lcl: 0.272685

Range: cl: 1.44944   ucl: 3.73121   lcl: 0   Mov Ave of 3

Fig. 11.7 X, Moving R chart for the old and modified old modules.

control of the project and minimise the probability of errors being introduced. Multi-variate analysis will not provide any indication of when a module has some exceptional cause and consequent probability for higher error rates, and so is not useful for improving the control of the project. Rather we can divide the code into the three main areas and look at the control charts, identify exceptions, and then establish whether there are real causes for these exceptions. These can then be tackled enabling the company to produce better code next time round.

From the Cantata data it is easy to identify the new code, and so the defectiveness levels for this code can be charted on an X, Moving R chart, as shown in Fig. 11.6. This shows that the mean error rate for these modules is 1.78 with a mean range of 1.70. This is the error rate capability of the company for generating new code. We know that the second generation software should be better than this. The X, Moving R chart for all the other code, the modified old and old code, Fig. 11.7, provides a mean error rate of 0.4 and a mean range of 0.78. This is in line with a continued reduction in error rates expected. By analysing more historic data the capability of for error reduction could be found for the organisation.

This data disregards the type of modules included and as shown in Fig. 11.8, there are three main types of module. These are:
- the general modules, which is the bulk of the software
- the modules where high counts of the use of arithmetic functions exist
- the modules that are dominated by the use of the switch function.

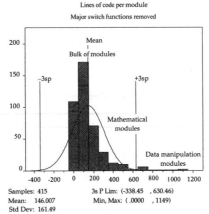

Fig. 11.8 The distribution of modules using different functions by lines of code.

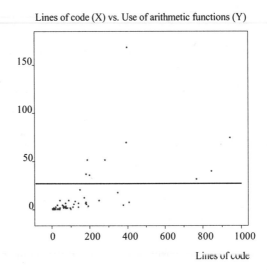

Fig. 11.9 Relationships between length of module and use of arithmetic operators.

From analysis of the relationship between lines of code and the use of arithmetic functions for general modules (no special mathematical functions), we would expect an approximation to a straight line, since the arithmetic functions are generally used for decisions operators. This is reasonably true for the lower regions of the graph (Fig. 11.9), but in the higher regions no such relationship exists. This suggests that these modules are different in some way and probably are the main mathematical operations of the system. It is reasonable to expect these functions then to

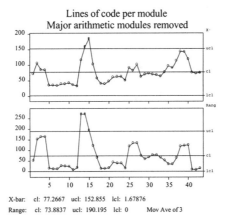

Fig. 11.10 (X, Moving R) chart for lines of code per module with different language, arithmetic and switch function modules removed.

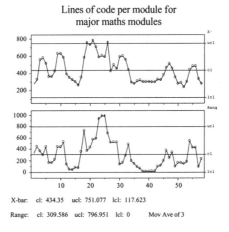

Fig. 11.11 (X, Moving R) chart for lines of code arithmetic function modules only.

exhibit a different error rate behaviour since they are of a different design nature, generally longer and more complex.

By viewing the general modules on an X, Moving R chart, Fig. 11.10, the modules that are exceptional (either very low or high, such as modules 14 and 15) are discovered. Further analysis can be used to determine whether there is a systematic cause for this or whether the cause is special and removable. The mean numbers of lines per module for this is 77 with a range of 73 and so modules can be expected to be within the three standard deviation control lines of 1.6 lines and 152 lines.

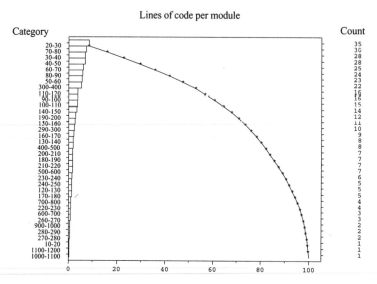

Fig. 11.12 Pareto diagram for lines of code per module.

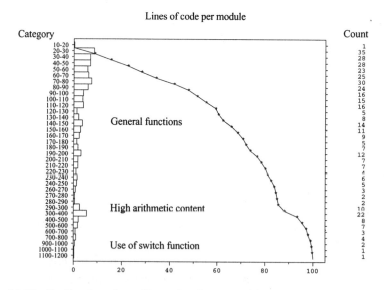

Fig. 11.13 Profile of number of lines of code per module.

By plotting only the modules with a high arithmetic function count on the (X, Moving R) chart the mean and range for these modules can be found as 434 and 309 respectively (Fig. 11.11). Again a few modules have a size outside of the control lines which are at 751 lines and 117 lines. These few can be analysed to see if they result in larger error levels than the standard.

The same analysis for the rest of the project will reveal the outliers for each of the distributions. In this example the filter used to establish the groupings was based on the use of mathematical operators in the code. While this might reflect the length of the code, it is interesting to note that the modules that make heavy use of the switch function are not included in the selection (they have few mathematical functions). It is clear that from an error viewpoint these modules are all likely to be error prone in that they are both complex and long.

The bulk of the modules have a mean of about 140 lines of code, but this can be broken down even further. The actual breakdown is shown in the Pareto diagram for the lines of code per module (Fig. 11.12), and this is presented in order of the size in Fig. 11.13. These diagrams show that the company produced large numbers of very small modules as well as very large modules (larger than 100 lines of code excluding comments). The second graph shows that there are sizes that appear to be 'preferred' and by correlating between the process metrics and the Pareto diagram the reasons for the preferences can be discovered. This is ongoing work at the time of writing and will be reported in due course.

12 Statistical Inspections

▓ 12.1 Introduction

▓ 12.1.1 Background

The inspection process for software development was first used by Michael E. Fagan, who worked at IBM Kingston NY Laboratories. As a result of work on an internal project, Fagan first announced the results of using statistical principles on text based products in 1976 (53). Work continued and the methods gained wide acceptance around IBM. Then, in 1977, AT&T Bell laboratories started using the principles.

Carole L. Jones and Robert Mays (68) have since created a number of enhancements to the techniques. In 1990 Mays (69) reported the use of the technique as a prevention process rather than the predominantly correction process that it had previously been. The techniques have been widely disseminated through the works of many authors and trainers, particularly Tom Gilb who has produced a book on the techniques in joint authorship with Dot Graham (70). This book provides most of the details of how to use the latest methods and these are followed here. However this text adds the principles of statistical charting and the principle of error mapping to find areas of high defect probability.

■ 12.1.2 The use of inspections

Inspections are now an essential part of the software development cycle and involve the use of a controlled technique for establishing the probability of error rates within a document. The principle is based on the technique of sampling and measuring the mean error rates for the pages inspected (or for the type of inspection completed).

Inspections are used in the development cycle on any of the following deliverable items from the project.

Documents: requirements, specifications, test specifications, design documents, reports, manuals and system operation descriptions, maintenance handbooks, etc.

Other items: code, pseudo-code, module lists, build lists and configuration management lists.

This means that the inspection process is an important part of the lifecycle of a product since it is a process for reducing the defectiveness of products early in the lifecycle. Inspections can be carried out on completed or half-finished documents, in the latter case to establish how well the document production process is progressing.

To understand statistical inspections it is first necessary to understand the principles of inspections and the next section provides a process outline and shows how statistics are applied to each of the stages. The following sections outline the detail of applying statistical techniques in three areas:

(1) selecting what to inspect,

(2) the methods of analysis of the metrics collected,

(3) the use of these results for process improvement.

■ 12.2 The Inspection Process

■ 12.2.1 Outline of an inspection process

The process of inspection involves a number of roles and tasks which include: inspection preparation, individual checking, logging, editing and correction, acceptance, process improvement. An outline of the overall process is shown in Fig. 12.1.

The entry to the process must meet specified entry criteria, such as all documents, procedures and checklists being available, the product document being ready for inspection, and the inspection team and resources having been prepared.

A kickoff meeting may be held to prepare the team for the individual checking tasks to be completed and to allocate responsibilities. The team members can then complete the allocated tasks separately and in private. The logging meeting is used to identify the issues raised and to categorise them. The document is then returned to the author for checking or is prepared for release. Any issues that could improve the process of both the document preparation and the inspection process are prepared for use in management and process improvement meetings.

▓ 12.2.2 Statistical control during preparation

The main activities are the individual checking and the correction processes. The preparation process is gathering the source and control documents and the inspection team together. The main statistic that can be gathered from this activity is to ensure that the document to be inspected is ready

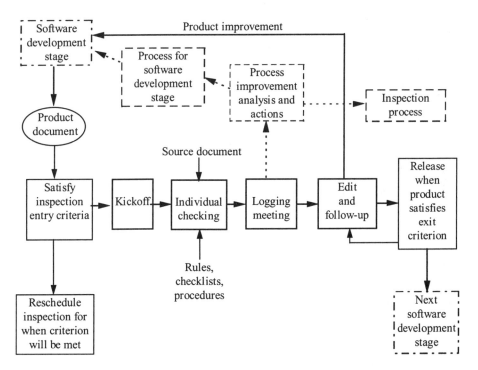

Fig. 12.1 The inspection process (source – modified from Gilb and Graham (70)).

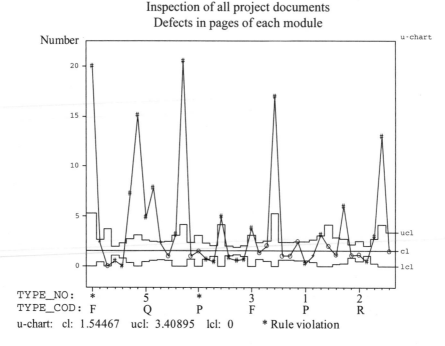

Inspection of all project documents
Defects in pages of each module

Fig. 12.2 u chart for error levels in documents being accepted or rejected to inspection.

for inspection. This can be completed a using a statistical approach so that the document is not rejected for reasons of one poor area, or accepted for one good section.

The time taken for preparation can be charted on (X, Moving R) charts. The results of the decision to either accept the product to inspection, or reject and return it to the author, can be logged as the percentage of defects found per page, line or paragraph, and charted on a u chart as shown in Fig. 12.2. In this way an acceptance level (entry criterion) can be established that is based on the error rates that authors are capable of producing prior to inspection. This also gives a chart that will monitor any improvement in the production process. The charts can be used for specific types of documents so that like is always compared with like and action is taken to improve the process of products that fail at this stage.

The method of selecting a sample for inspection that will provide the data to support the decision to accept a product for full inspection or not, depends largely on the type of product being inspected. If there is a need for frequent and regular inspections of highly structured documents, then this document type can be modelled. Statistical selection rules can be established to ensure reasonable coverage of the areas that are most likely to have serious errors, or are critical to the success of the project. This selection is of a smaller set than that used for the main inspection task. Inspection of 10% of the total document will often provide adequate data for this decision. Sometimes, however, the first page that is checked provides adequate information for failure of a document to meet the entry criteria. Acceptance of a document to inspection takes a larger sample and more careful inspection.

▓ 12.2.3 Metrics from the checking and logging activities

The individual checking activity is expected to be completed at a lower rate than the rate inspectors would naturally choose. The suggestion is that the curve for detection rate is as shown in Fig. 12.3. The optimum for most people appears to be between 0.5 and 1.5 pages per hour. This information is logged during the inspection meeting together with the number of defects found, and their severity.

These metrics can be charted on (X, Moving R) charts for the rate and multiple variable charts for the defects, where the types of defects found provide the multiple variables. Figs. 12.4 and 12.5 show examples of both these charts.

The logging meeting can use the manual charts in order to quickly identify whether the document is in any way exceptional compared with results from previous logging meetings. The charts are set up for each type

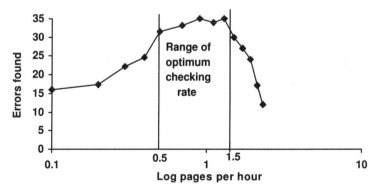

Fig. 12.3 A checking rate curve showing optimum rate.

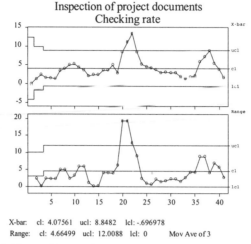

Inspection of project documents
Checking rate

X-bar: cl: 4.07561 ucl: 8.8482 lcl: -.696978
Range: cl: 4.66499 ucl: 12.0088 lcl: 0   Mov Ave of 3

Fig. 12.4 The (X, Moving R) chart for checking rate.

of document regularly being inspected and the limits are calculated once adequate numbers of points have been collected. These limits are then used for all future charts until a history of results with a standard deviation of 2/3 of the current value is observed. This is the point where it is useful to recalculate the limits for the next process improvement cycle.

■ 12.2.4 Overall inspection metrics

The inspection process involves collecting several metrics regarding the efficiency of the inspection process and the effectiveness of the product improvement. Typical metrics are included in the standard log chart shown in Fig. 12.6. This layout proposed by Gilb and Graham (70) shows data for the checking rate, the major and minor issues, the improvement and the questions noted, as well as providing an average checking rate and the logging meeting rate. The summary data is recorded on a second multiple variable chart and this is used to establish whether the inspection process is in statistical control. Fig. 12.7 shows the summary chart for the error reports received from many logging meetings, and Fig. 12.8 provides the individual charts for the different rate readings as multiple (X, Moving R) charts.

In addition to these metrics the follow-up actions are recorded for editing to achieve the exit criteria. They include the major defects, the minor defects and the number of change requests raised. The edit time, follow-up time

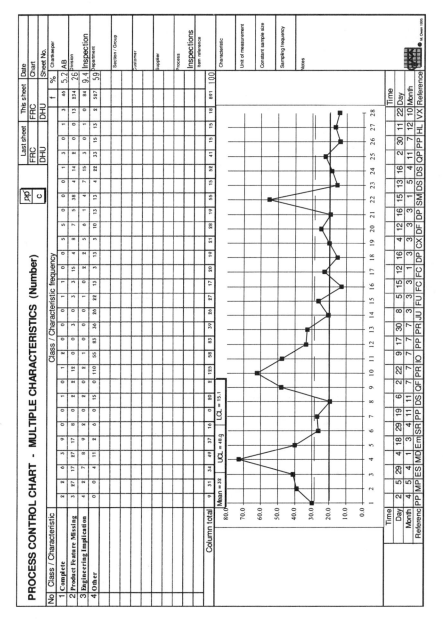

Fig. 12.5 Multi-variate chart for quality characteristics of product.

Inspection Data

Date 5/7/92   Inspection Number INSREP3/6   Leader DS

Document AI1_QFD_R7_92   Total Pages 10.5

Inspection Date: 8/6/92   Entry Criteria Passed: 2/7/92

Requested By: ASD

Planning Time 6.5   Entry Time: 0.5   Kickoff Time. 0.5

Individual Checking Results

Inspector	Checking Hours	Pages Checked	Major issues	Minor issues	Improvements	Questions	Checking rate
1	4	1.5	2	6	1	5	2.7
2	6	2	3	13	1	3	3
3	3	1	2	8	0	0	3
4	4	1	2	11	0	3	4
5	5	1	1	2	1	2	5
6	3	2	1	17	0	0	1.5
7	5	2	2	6	0	0	1.5

Checking Time: 10.5   Average Checking rate: 2.96

Logging Summary

No of people 7 Logging duration Logging time ⌐

Major Issues Logged	Minor Issues Logged	Improvement Suggestions	Questions of Intent	New Items found in meeting
7	45	3	8	2

Logging rate _____ Detection Time _____ Logging Meeting rate _____

Editing, Follow-up and Exit

No Major Defects ___	No Minor Defects ___		No Change Requests ___
Edit Time ___	Follow-up Time ___	Exit Time ___	Exit Date ___
Control Time ___	Defect Removal Time ___		Estimated remaining major defects/page ___
Estimated found/total) ___	Effectiveness(major defects ___		Efficiency (major/wk-hr) ___
Development time saved by Inspection ___			

Fig. 12.6 The summary chart from the logging meeting.

and the exit time (the final check that all exit criteria have been met) are recorded. The control time, defect removal time, and the estimated remaining major defects/page, plus the estimated effectiveness, efficiency (major defects/work-hr) and the estimated development time saved by the inspection are all on this exit data sheet.

To establish whether inspections are continuing to be effective and whether the development (document production) process is improving, these metrics can be charted on standard (X, Moving R) charts and exceptions detected can be investigated for causes.

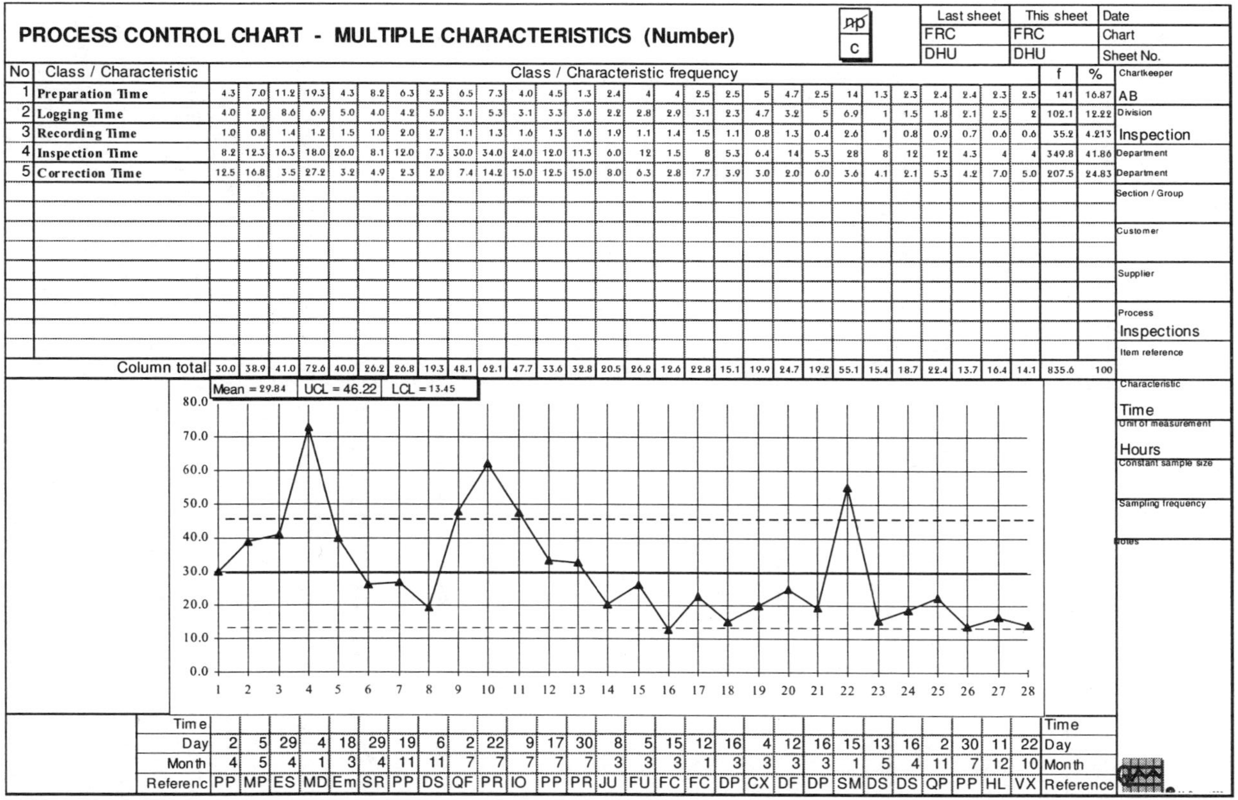

Fig 12.7 Multi-variate chart for inspection related time.

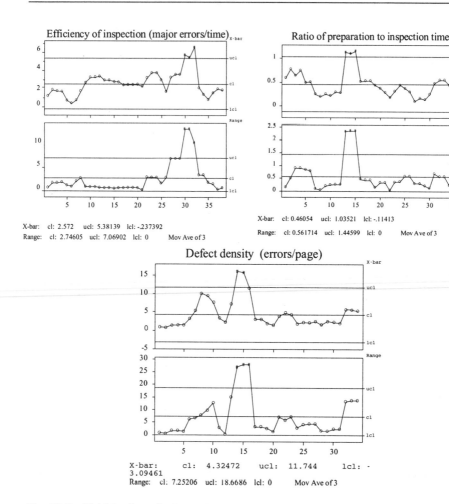

Fig. 12.8 Multiple charts for inspection summaries.

■ 12.3 Statistical Selection

To inspect all but the smallest documents, a method of deciding what to inspect is required. This is because it is not effective or efficient for any individual to be involved in more than two inspection meetings per day. Consequently this limits inspection time, and therefore page numbers, to only a few per week for any one inspection team.

If the document to be inspected has over 100 pages, then the inspection process can be expected to last 100–200 work hours, which with a small team of people, can be upwards of three person weeks of effort. Given that it is essential to limit the number of pages per elapsed week to 30, then the whole process will take 4 elapsed weeks and possibly 12 weeks of effort.

However if the first inspection is targeted to areas of high risk, then the usefulness of the initial stages of inspections increases.

We can take this analysis one step further – the inspection process is very like the test process. When there is only one defect left to be found we are likely to be spending large amounts of time looking for it, i.e. the efficiency of inspections reduces as the product quality improves. Consequently a mechanism is required for managing the efficiency of the inspection process.

The efficiency calculation, provided in Gilb and Graham (70), of the number of major faults found divided by the effort hours, provides one way of controlling efficiency, although the combination of both major and minor errors might provide a more effective result.

Many companies divide the errors found into more than just minor and major errors. The use of categories such as:

Major categories
- Interface errors (visible to the user)
- Mathematical or algorithmic errors (giving incorrect results)
- Errors of functional omission
- Errors of functional addition
- Errors of function (the function could not be implemented without great project risk)
- Errors of control (probable system control failure due to specification error).

Minor categories
- Spelling
- Language usage
- Document conformance to standard
- Layout
- Omission of section
- Cross-reference error.

The efficiency measure can be provided for each of these categories so generating an efficiency profile. This can be charted over time to ensure that no team is generating a profile that will have a probability of not detecting particular types of categories of errors. This enables balanced teams to be assembled that have an ability to detect different types of faults and errors.

The second advantage to be gained from using this type of profile is that, for the inspection of a sample of pages, the probability of missing categories can be calculated from the difference between the normal profile and the current inspection. This will indicate when the inspection should be halted. This of course also depends on the type of sample taken.

■ 12.3.1 Profiling

The normal method of initially sampling a large document is to take a set of pages at random. For a 100-page document this could be 20 randomly selected pages. However this will result in pages being inspected that are of little importance to the actual functionality of the system under development. Worse still, it can result in critical parts of the system being left out of the initial sample.

The aim of sampling at the inspection stage is to start to produce a profile that will also be useful for the testing stage. This means weighting the sections within the document according to the risk that they contribute to the failure of the project.

The second purpose of sampling is to maximise the errors found in the first pass and every subsequent pass of the inspection. This requires confidence in the knowledge of where the maximum number of errors are likely to be found within a document. This, as with code, means developing a sampling plan for the document under inspection based on the knowledge of its originator.

The first pass of an inspection will consequently look at not the first few sections, but at a selection of those sections that are:

(1) most complex
(2) most likely to be error prone (for reasons such as originator, simplicity, time of production, rate of production, management pressure, external pressures, weather, etc.)

Table 12.1 Section types and error-proneness metrics.

Section type	Mean error history	Range of error history
Non-technical	5.5/page	3.2/page
Technical – descriptive	7.9/page	4.1/page
Technical - mathematical	6.3/page	4.2/page

(3) highest risk to the project (may be simple functions but critical to system operation)

(4) visible to the user

and the result of the inspection is used to determine whether these objectives were achieved.

The sample size to be used will depend on the density of the document. If it is full of mathematical descriptions then it is probably sensible to take a larger first sample. For a document that has a high word count but less content, the sample size can be smaller, since the probability is that a larger number of minor errors and a more even distribution of major errors will exist.

▓ 12.3.2 Sampling to find maximum numbers of errors

The profiles to be used are basically the categories of the normal cause and effect diagram. The profile aims to optimise the inspection to maximise the probability of detecting errors and the profile takes a model of the document (say the section headings) and allocates a risk factor to them. This means that for a specification the guidelines of what should be contained in the document can also provide initial guidelines for the risk factors. These are then used to weight the section in a selection table. For error-proneness a factor between 1 and 5 is allocated according to experience of the types of modules and the errors found in the past. A table, as shown in Table 12.1, can be produced over time, which may categorise sections according to content type. The table may also refer to development teams, experience of the producers, the method of development being used, etc.

This error-proneness may then be used in conjunction with a risk profile to establish the probability of inclusion of a particular type of document within a particular project in the sampled inspection plan (Table12.2). This does not mean that other parts of the document are not reviewed, only that the detail emphasis is placed where the most probable cause of both future errors and project risk occur.

The sample of the sections to be inspected is taken using a random number generator that has an equal probability profile for all numbers. If a sample of 20% is taken from the above document, then section 3.2 is the most probable to be selected – it has 15 chances in 25 of being selected. The next most probable section is section 2.2 and so on. In a large document this would give a realistic profile for selecting the parts of the document to be inspected at the optimum rates.

Table 12.2 The calculation to determine the selection for inclusion in the inspection.

Section	Error-proneness	Risk weighting	Entry count
Section 1	1	1	1
Section 2.1	2	1	2
Section 2.2	2	2	4
Section 2.3	1	2	2
Section 3.1	3	1	3
Section 3.2	5	3	15

The rest of the document may be subjected to a different type of inspection. This is aimed at finding the areas where unacceptable levels of errors appear to occur.

▪ 12.3.3 Sampling to find probability of high error density

The areas of a document that are not as critical to the success of project may be subjected to a second type of sample. This sample is based on the principle that the resulting quicker inspection process may provide far less information about the absolute numbers of errors. It will, however, profile the whole document for the error density and the types of errors in the different sections. The results of an inspection by the team as a quick scan will provide results typically as shown in Table 12.3. For each person involved, a profile for both the errors found and the type of errors for each section is calculated. Error mapping is used to identify those areas where highest error densities are found. This means that instead of individual results being recorded only the standard deviation band in which the value lies is recorded, i.e. 0 to $+1\sigma$ recorded as 0, $+1\sigma$ to $+2\sigma$ recorded as 1, $+2\sigma$ to $+3\sigma$ recorded as 2, -1σ to -2σ recorded as -1 etc. This immediately shows up the areas of criticality of the document.

The calculation for the standard deviation values uses the mean of the values calculated from each individual inspector. For the example five inspectors are involved and so the values are the means of the results from these inspectors. This is because the process of inspection is being taken into account. The error classifications will be subject to a distribution of interpretation with some errors being less serious than classified and others being more serious. Using the mean of all inspectors we can to some extent

Table 12.3 Results of rapid inspection scan.

(a) The logging table.

Section	Type of error			Individual inspector results				
	Critical	Major	Minor	1	2	3	4	5
1	///	卌	卌 ///	///	卌 //// ///	//// ///	卌 /卌	卌 卌
2.1	卌 //	///	卌 卌 卌 //	卌 /卌 卌 /卌	卌 /卌 //	卌 /卌 卌 ///	卌 //	卌 卌 ///
2.2	/	卌 卌 /	/	卌	卌 ////	////	卌 ///	卌 //
2.3	/	//	///	//	///	卌	////	///
3.1	卌	卌	卌 卌 卌 /卌 ///	卌 卌 ///	卌 卌 //	卌 /卌	卌 卌 卌 /卌	卌 ///
3.2	卌 /卌 ///	//	卌 ///	卌 卌 /	卌 卌 ////	卌 卌 卌 /	卌 卌 卌 /卌	卌 卌
3.3	//	卌 /	///	////	卌 ///	卌 //	卌 /	////

(b) The calculated results.

Section	Type of error			Individual inspector results				
	Critical	Major	Minor	1	2	3	4	5
1	+1				+1		+1	
2.1	+2		+1	+2	+1	+2		+1
2.2		+2			+2		+1	+1
2.3						+1		
3.1			+1				+1	
3.2	+3				+2	+2	+3	+1
3.3								

reduce the effect of this.

This example shows that section 3.2 has a higher than normal error density and section 2.1 is another area where it may pay to concentrate more inspection effort. The individual inspectors contribute to the results by providing confidence that the range of results is typical of all inspectors. If the range of results is too large then the highest and lowest readings may be suspected and analysed. If however there is broad agreement then the results can be taken to indicate that there is an error density problem.

This technique is not designed to find the single individual error – it provides a measure of the probability of defectiveness of the document.

These tables can be drawn up using standard spreadsheets. The standard deviation, σ, must be calculated using the range, ($\overline{R}/d_2$), and not the formula provided for standard deviation within most spreadsheet packages. The calculation for each value is based on the formula:

$$UCL = X + A_2 R$$
$$\text{and } +2\sigma = 2/3UCL,$$
$$+1\sigma = 1/3UCL$$

This ensures that the fact that we are taking the results from subgroups is taken into account. The subgroups in this case are provided by the number of inspectors and the values are calculated from the mean for all the inspectors. This is because we are dealing with an inspection process which in itself is subject to variability. Some inspectors may grade an error as critical whereas others may not even consider it to be an error. By taking the mean we remove much of this subjectiveness. As stated previously, the range of values received from each of the inspectors also provides an opportunity to find the cause of the variance. This in turn will provide information that can be used to take action to reduce the variability in future inspections. This can be achieved through training, staff reallocation and improved guidelines.

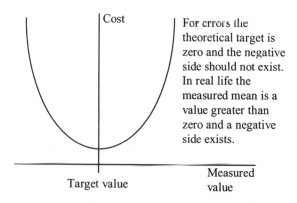

Fig. 12.9 The Taguchi loss function for errors in inspected objects.

▓ 12.4 Presentation of Results

Inspection metrics are wide ranging and, if presented as a series of numbers from many inspections, pose a daunting analysis task. The techniques for presenting the results in a way that will reveal information about the products and the inspection process provide management with a control mechanism for continually improving the process.

The types of chart that are useful are:

- the multivariate charts shown earlier in the chapter (Figs. 12.5 and 12.7)
- the error map that shows the most probable area of defectiveness
- the management charts (both the line and the star chart) which provide week-on-week comparison of the effectiveness of the process.

The examples at the end of this chapter show some of these charts from real examples in the software industry.

▓ 12.5 Product and Process Improvement

▓ 12.5.1 Product improvement

The inspection process is about improving the product – in this case the object under inspection such as a report or document – in order to remove errors and inconsistencies that may cause problems later in the development cycle. In some cases it can be argued that it is unimportant to remove the trivial errors. However the Taguchi loss function, Fig. 12.9, suggests that any errors left in the document are likely to have a price attached to them. If the errors can be prevented rather than removed, then the cost will be minimised.

Note that the function was developed for physical measurements of objects and consequently suggests that there is a target value. This may also be true for errors where the cost of prevention and removal is considerably higher than the cost of leaving them in the product. For most cases the target value is zero and this suggests that any value higher than this will result in an added cost.

Arguing this case for removal is not a simple problem. Many of the errors may be simple spelling mistakes of words that have only one alternative in

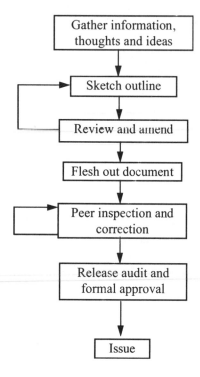

Fig. 12.10 A formal document production process.

the context in which they are being used. The only added cost due to the error is the cost of a reader establishing what the word should be, and assessing this will probably cost more than interpreting the error itself. The actual cost of changing the mistake may be many times more than the cost of error correction by the reader. The Taguchi loss function then, even in trivial cases, can be seen to be true. If these errors can be prevented then the costs will be minimised.

However for less trivial cases the function provides the justification for both preventative and corrective actions. Any deviation from the zero defect position adds cost to the development cycle and should be corrected as early as possible, or prevented where possible.

■ 12.5.2 Process improvement

Prevention is only achievable through process improvement. In terms of the documents that are being produced the prevention activities are usually training, and the use of spell and grammar checkers, but can also include the use of formal writing techniques. It is surprising for an industry that relies so heavily on the written word to describe and specify systems how little training is given to engineers in writing technical documents. The assumption is made that this is a skill obtained at secondary or high school. However few of these organisations actually teach the skills of gathering information together, sorting thoughts, drafting and reviewing an outline, and then producing the final document. Fig. 12.10 shows a typical flow diagram for document production including the inspection process. This provides several opportunities for ensuring completeness and correctness of the document before formal release.

The second area of process improvement is in the inspection process itself. The measure of the effectiveness of an inspection is given as:

$$\text{Effectiveness} = \frac{\text{major defects found}}{\text{total defects found}}$$

and the efficiency is given as:

$$\text{Efficiency} = \frac{\text{major defects found}}{\text{work hours}}$$

A further measure used is the estimated time saved by the inspection process based on algorithms that are historically proven for particular organisations. The final measure is based on the percentage of major errors found at inspection as a proportion of the major errors found at all stages of development including the post-delivery stages.

Each of these metrics provides a measure that can be targeted at improving the inspection process. However reaction to an individual figure that is higher or lower than the previous history can lead to actions that provide no benefit to the organisation. In other words an inspection can only be judged on its achievements compared with the normal capability of the inspection team. Process improvement is then based on reducing the variance of the process and increasing the capability of the effectiveness of the team.

The three measures outlined can be plotted on separate (X, Moving R) charts with control lines set according to the historical data. However it may also be beneficial to provide sloping control lines for the expected improvement of the effectiveness of the process.

This process improvement will only be achieved by providing training, experience and through the use of historical knowledge of the process.

However process improvement can also be achieved by using the techniques to advantage. The inspection process suffers from the fact that the last defect will always take the longest time to find. Consequently any method of reducing this time will increase the efficiency of the process.

We have already seen how a model of the process can reduce the timescale by detecting errors in the places where the highest probability of detection exists. To improve on this further requires models not only of highest probability but also models of what methods of inspection are likely to find particular types of errors. Inspections, like tests, can be defined by the search method used, such as whether the inspector is looking for errors in cross-references, logic, language, translation or definition. The methods of identifying these things require a different inspection strategy and consequently combining highest probability with the correct strategy of inspection can result in reduced effort to find the errors. By defining these methods the skills required for the most successful inspections can also be taught to a wider audience. How often do inspections suffer from the lack of knowledge of how to detect errors? This is currently a rhetorical question because the methods have not been defined. The variance of the process has been observed in the many inspections completed around the world. This can be reduced by applying techniques of detection to the different types of errors that the inspection is trying to find.

Some of the methods that can be used are:

Cross-references (X) – search the document for all occurrences of individual items as they are come across and check that the context is correct in all cases.

Logic (01) – the document is redefined in logical terms as it is being read in order to ensure that adequate cases are covered for all statements that include logic.

Language (L) – this is the use of language and usually requires two or more people to agree to ensure that the readability and understandability are not going to hamper the future readers. A strategy for agreement on the general use of language is required as a result of the events raised in the logging meeting.

Translation (T) – most documents, in a software development context, are the result of translation of, and addition to, one or more source documents. The additions should all provide increased detail whereas the main body is a translation into another form such as design, pseudo-code, program language, etc. The checking here is a one-to-one comparison with the source documents, identifying the translations and ensuring that they are correct, and identifying the additions for future checking.

Definitions (D) – are the additions made to the document. They are the source of knowledge for the project and consequently can only be checked for consistency in their relationships with the sources and the associated translated text.

There may be other categories of checking that can be used although most books on the subject suggest a freedom to select methods natural to the checker. Checking is however a skill that can be taught as well as gained by experience and so definitions of a few core methods may reveal techniques that improve efficiency.

The use of these methods in an iterative approach first applied to the critical and most probably defective areas of the document will result in higher error detection rates at the start of the process. This will be maintained for several inspection passes because the method and the inspected parts are always those areas of greatest criticality and probability of defectiveness. Note that the second pass inspection will use a different weighting for the parts inspected in the first pass because the inspection results of the first pass give a lower probability of defects. This means that new areas are now more likely to have defects and so the new areas are being inspected and for new reasons.

An inspection form might be designed as shown in Fig. 12.11.

12.6 Summary

- The inspection process finds faults during product development early on in the development cycle. It is a useful tool in its own right, and with unstable and uncontrolled processes is efficient and effective without statistical control.
- As the processes are brought under control the inspection process can utilise the statistical charting and analysis tools for improving the processes and improving the efficiency of the inspection process itself.
- The use of (X, Moving R) charts provides a picture of the current inspection in comparison with previous results. Anomalous figures result in immediate corrective action even after a first trial inspection.
- The multiple variable chart enables the inspection results to be analysed both as a whole and separately in order to find exceptions in the whole document and amoung the individual types of errors.

| Name | | Date | | | Document Inspected | | | | | | Version | |

Pages inspected

Inspection Type	1	3	7	9	15	18	26	31	40	43	48	50	63
X	1	3	1		7	1		1			1		
01		1	5	1	?	1	4		4		3	3	
L	1		1	3			2	2		3	3	2	2
T	2									2			
D		2	1		2	3	2		2	5		2	2
Other	1			1		2		2		1	1		1
Total X	5	6	8	5	11	7	8	5	6	11	8	7	5
Range	2	3	5	3	5	2	2	1	2	4	2	1	1

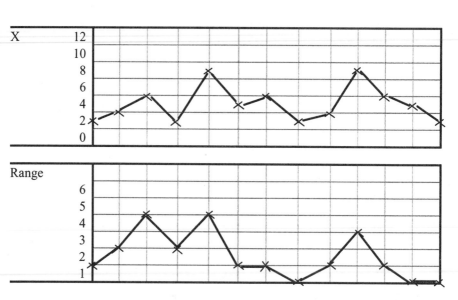

Fig. 12.11 An individual preparation inspection form.

- Mapping of the errors on the document will reveal places of high probability of errors. It will even find the odd lonely error that is lurking in one part of the code.
- Repeated statistical samples of the same product using different error finding strategies will help to find both the concentrations and the lone errors. This can greatly influence the efficiency of document inspection with few errors left in them.

This chapter has shown how to reduce the probability of errors occurring by inspecting early documents and products as they are being developed. However the probability is that errors will remain in the product at the end of the development stage. Consequently the modules and the system will require testing before being finally accepted by the client or customers. The next chapter looks at how statistical techniques can help to improve the efficiency and effectiveness of the testing process.

▥ 12.7 Examples

▥ 12.7.1 Inspection results from a multi-user integrated office product

This section provides results from inspecting the product that has been the leading integrated office system in the office automation market since the 1980s. Engineered in the United Kingdom, an important characteristic of the product is its ability to support very large user populations, for example in excess of 10,000 users on a single system or more than 60,000 users in a network. This product provides users with an extensive range of office tools such as electronic messaging, word processing and calendaring, through a large number of integrated modules. All of these tools have a very rich set of features and all of them are integrated with each other through a common file cabinet.

In addition to the user tools, a significant feature of the office integration product is its capability in allowing customised applications to be built from the same constructs as used for the supplied tools. It can even allow the supplied tools to be heavily modified to meet customer requirements. This capability, coupled with the ease with which existing external applications can also be integrated seamlessly into the overall user environment, means the product provides a high degree of flexibility in creating applications, together with rapid application development. This capability is reflected in the results shown in this section.

The results to be analysed are the result of commercial decisions taken by the developer to counter the slow decline from a peak of about 5 million users in the early 1990s. This decline is largely due to the market trend towards PC based productivity tools and client server environments. Over the period of the mid 1990s the company responded to the shift in the market by re-engineering many of the core components of the product in order to bring the benefits of wide-area document distribution, robustness and scaleability to the Local Area Network (LAN) based community. As a result, the declining terminal base population is being replaced by PC and Macintosh based users using the TeamLinks client server software accessing the products servers.

The engineering quality data, which are the basis of this and the Chapter 13 examples, are derived directly from the engineering work that has been undertaken in moving the product from being time-shared to a true client server product.

■ Use of inspections

A feature of the development process for this work has been the use of formal inspections of the documentation for the project. This has been established within the development team for many years and so the methods are mature in operation.

The examples here demonstrate from the real data what can be achieved using statistical control charts for controlling the inspection process for improving the product. The measures defined by the formal inspection process provide the ideal opportunity to measure how the process is operating and ensuring that statistical control is achieved. It also provides the opportunity for correlation between the process control variables and the product quality defectiveness and this example provides the charts for control of the process, the product and the correlation.

■ The inspection process

Guidelines for the inspection process are provided by the company in terms of the main controls of the inspection process. These include factors such as the checking time, inspection time and logging rate. The guidelines are not in any way mandatory and so the data from inspecting product documentation shows that the time taken varies and this variation is not in proportion to the size or complexity of the document being inspected. The data shows that for some small documents that have few errors too much time is being spent, while for other larger documents too little time is being spent. This is observed from the correlation graph which shows the number of defects found per hour of effort in the total inspection process against the number of pages inspected (Fig. 12.12).

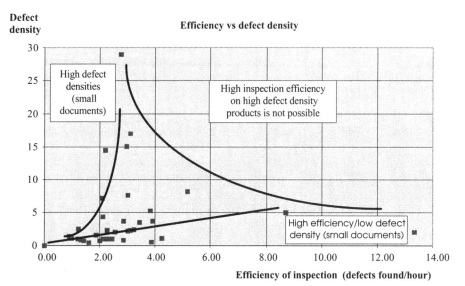

Defect
density

Efficiency vs defect density

Fig. 12.12 Correlation of defects found per hour versus pages inspected.

The data indicates that the main of the documents were inspected using an in-control process, i.e. the ideal rates were being used and the inspection effectiveness was maximised. However for the product where few faults were found, despite a long inspection process (relatively speaking), the process was clearly out of control. Either these products were of such quality that few defects could be found, in which case the inspection should have been relatively short in duration, or the process was not effective in finding the defects despite the time spent. Which of these is the case is not clear from the data presented and requires further study. It appears from the data that the inspections are continued until an exit criteria of a particular number of defects per page has been achieved and this is shown on the defects per page data which in all circumstances is within the control lines for the guideline mean.

This is clearly seen from the control chart on the defects per page data – it follows a characteristic pattern and most points are within 3 limits as shown in Fig. 12.13. The two points that are outside the control limits are attributed to documents that were undergoing major change for this particular project. At this pass they should not have been accepted as working documents for release. As we will see later in the testing phase (section 13.13.1), the result was a product that also has higher error rates.

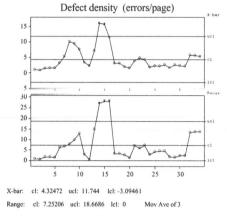

Fig. 12.13 The control chart for the defect rate data.

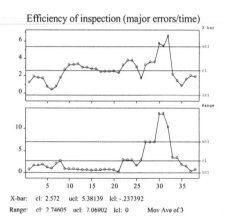

Fig. 12.14 (X, Moving R) chart for efficiency for all inspections.

■ Process efficiency

The definition of process efficiency is the number of major defects found per hour, and the control chart for process efficiency for all inspections is shown in Fig. 12.14. As we have already seen from correlating efficiency with defects/page data there are clearly several levels of efficiency being achieved. The analysis aim is to correlate these efficiency levels with the type of product being inspected. The task of inspecting a requirements document is obviously different from the task of inspecting a standard or a quality plan, and so the efficiency can be expected to be different for the different levels of complexity of the documents.

Type of document (X) vs. inspection efficiency (Y)

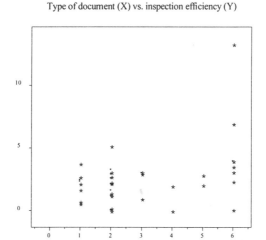

Fig. 12.15 Relationship between document types and the inspection efficiency.

Effeciency of inspection (majors/time)
without list type documents

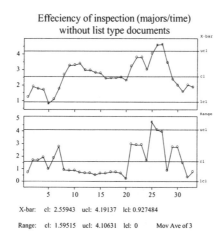

X-bar: cl: 2.55943 ucl: 4.19137 lcl: 0.927484

Range: cl: 1.59515 ucl: 4.10631 lcl: 0   Mov Ave of 3

Fig. 12.16 (X, Moving R) chart for the inspection efficiency based on all but list types of documents.

The aim of this analysis is to find target efficiency levels for the different types of document, for future control of the inspection process. Fig. 12.15 shows the relationship between efficiency and the type of document and this indicates that all documents are inspected with about the same efficiency except for two standards type documents. These documents were

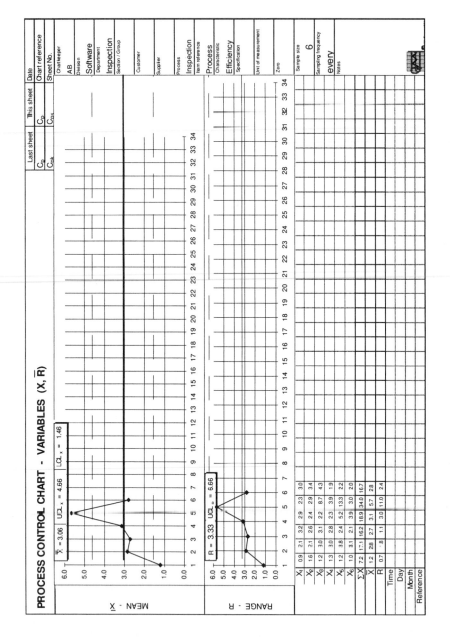

Fig. 12.17 Inspection efficiency control chart.

both lists of codes or activities and consequently should be categorised differently again.

From a company viewpoint, Fig. 12.16 shows the control chart for inspection set up with the historic control limits excluding the list type documents. This shows that the mean efficiency that can currently be expected is 2.6 errors per hour and the range is between 1 and 4 errors per hour.

The aim for the organisation is to continually increase the efficiency and to reduce the range. This can only be achieved by changing the inspection strategy to improve chance of detecting the major defects earlier as described earlier in this chapter.

Fig. 12.17 shows the control charts used for controlling the process set up with their control limits. These are ($\overline{X}$, R) charts and, since the company completes many inspections per month, are completed using data for every inspection, but grouped in sub-groups of six.

13 | Software Product Testing Techniques

■ 13.1 Introduction

Testing, usually considered as a means of finding errors and defects in a software product, can never be 100% completed. There are always more test cases available. Indeed it has been stated that for even the simplest system all the test cases would take some tens of years to complete.

Secondly, the efficiency of testing in a straightforward approach appears to be directly related to how far removed the tester is from the development. As we will see later, this is more to do with test process design, than the relationship of the people to the code. However it is because of this that many companies now employ independent test teams to find the error content of the product. These teams are provided with a product that has not been previously tested for the sole purpose of finding the errors and this is directly the reason that the time and effort of the test team cannot be determined (since the workload is variable and indeterminate). It is also often the cause of project over-run in terms of both time and cost.

Analysing this for the cost of testing we see in Fig. 13.1 that the total development cycle costs are made up of three main elements:
- producing the product
- finding fault with the product
- correcting the product.

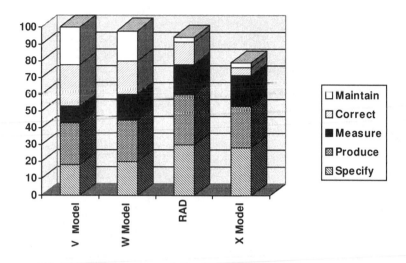

Fig. 13.1 Software development costs in different development cycles.

While much is said about the RAD method, prototyping and simultaneous engineering, the danger, as shown in Fig. 13.1, is that the cost ratios may not reduce as much as predicted. Changes in these ratios are usually caused by committing to quality at the earliest stages of development, and not by changing the development strategy. The X model provides the measurement techniques (test methods) that provide the assurance that the commitment to quality is being translated into action throughout the project lifecycle.

A parallel to this is drawn from manufacturing industry where the original processes provided defective product to customers. Inspection was brought in-house and only good product was delivered to customers. This left a pile of defective product for rework or scrap with all the consequential costs involved. The next step was to inspect earlier in the process and thus avoid any defective reaching the end of the process. The result is rework throughout the production process and a small reduction in costs. The move is now into the control of the process to prevent defective production and this has meant understanding the processes better to understand why defects or errors ever occur.

For the software industry the parallel is clear. The V model used post-development inspection and testing combined with a rework cycle aimed at removing the defects. The W model moves inspection and testing back through the cycle to the earliest point in the process, still with the difficulty

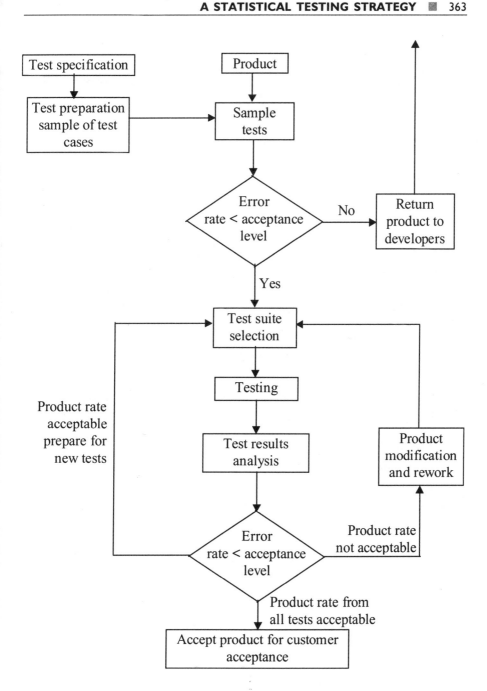

Fig. 13.3 The test cycle.

weighting is carried out for a number of reasons such as criticality of the code, use of the code, use of data, or the criticality of the set up criteria. This weighting will be detailed later in this section. Once the selection has been made, then the test outputs are defined. The test activity is now prepared with:

(1) inputs including set up data

(2) test selection methods

(3) a definition of the acceptance criteria for the test in terms of both the system outputs and the error rates.

Table 13.1   The metrics used for each stage of the testing cycle.

Test activity	Inputs	Method	Output	Metrics
Design	Software specification	Break down system by functions, inputs & data points	Test specification	Number of test cases Coverage per case Acceptance criteria
Accept product to test	Product Test design suite	Sample product and compare with acceptance criteria from test cases spec	Test errors Error histogram	Mean and range for small sample of tests completed Error Records
Test suite selection	Test design Statistical selection criteria Weighting	Even chance random selection on list of all possible test cases by function, data and test method & weighted by usage, criticality	Selection of test cases to be completed	Number of tests as a proportion of total number possible Coverage expected of the tests
Test preparation	Product specification Test cases selected	Generate the expected outputs for selected cases from the specification	Outputs expected from test cases Acceptance criteria	Possible confidence index for number of unidentified outputs in the specification
Test	Test Methods Tools	Complete tests (manual or automated), record & grade errors found	Error log Statistical Measure of Errors	Number of errors as a proportion of coverage Errors mean and range
Results analysis	Statistical tools Test results	Use cause analysis with error dependency mapping to find causes	Error map Error rates Error reports	Errors by dependency
Product acceptance	Test indices	Compare acceptance criteria with test results on a statistical basis	Accept or send back to development with error details	Number of referred parts compared with total test and coverage

▨ 13.3.4 Testing

The product is tested by running the selected activities completed during preparation. Errors are noted and classified according to type. These values are then charted on a multivariate chart to establish the mean and range index for the system. Any deviations are noted for further analysis.

▨ 13.3.5 Results analysis

The results from the tests are charted to establish their significance, and any outlying points are highlighted for cause analysis. The product is accepted or rejected by comparison with the acceptance criteria for each individual test completed. This usually leads to some parts of a system being accepted while others are rejected. The rejected parts of the system are studied for similarity in terms of complexity, number of paths size or function, so that they can be grouped for further work according to their statistical compatibility. The developers can then use this information to determine where the most error prone parts of the system are. Analysis also takes into account the original weighting used so that critical parts of the system can be identified and grouped for further analysis if necessary. Table 13.1 shows the inputs, methods, outputs and metrics used for each stage of the testing cycle.

▨ 13.4 Test Preparation

The design of a test is based on the specification that has been generated for developing the system. For statistical testing the design requires one extra input. This is the numbered list of the functions, entry points and data points for the system, so that each can be selected as an individual test set. There are several standard methods for decomposing a system into a list that have been developed by various researchers over the last 20 years.

Once the program has been decomposed the test data sets can be generated for every testable item on the decomposed program list. Also a set of appropriate test methods can be generated for each of the test items and data cases. This list is used as input into the weighting and statistical selection stages that are completed before testing. The example program has an input domain as shown in the flow diagram (Fig. 13.4).

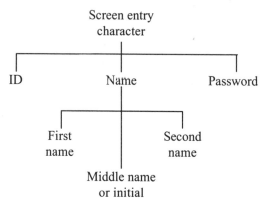

Fig. 13.4 The inputs for the decomposition example.

▩ 13.4.1 Decomposing functions

This method is the simplest of the decomposition methods and relies only on identifying the functions that are to be tested. This method does not provide enough detail to assure that full coverage can be achieved for every path, loop or decision for every part of the input domain.

The method involves taking each specification statement in turn and identifying the functions that lie behind that statement. Each of these is then listed out in turn and, for statistical testing, each point is numbered sequentially as shown in Table 13.2. The list is then input to the statistical selection procedure.

▩ 13.4.2 Linear decomposition

Linear decomposition is similar to function point analysis except the program is considered in a linear fashion. It takes into account the data domain, its limits and non-valid regions, and the constants, as well as the individual functions to be performed both from a users viewpoint as well as an internal function viewpoint. For the same example a much lower level of detail is obtained and the data table might be 30 to 35 points long rather than the 18 of the previous example. The data table will also take into account such things as dynamic allocation of memory, file fetch, unscramble of passwords (or encode), and the actual paths taken for errors. If the system is designed for multiple users, then the decomposition will take into account:

- the number of other users at this point of the program at the same time
- the number entering data
- the number already using the system
- close derivatives of the names, IDs and passwords
- other less direct test attributes.

▓ 13.4.3 Dependency decomposition

This method is designed to cope with the problem of decomposing a system that can be multi-user and multi-tasking. The decomposition takes into account directly the tasking and user segments of a system and expects as input the limitations of the system. An example may be:

- many users at different points
- many users at the same point
- few heavy users
- a mix of heavy and light users.

Table 13.2 Decomposed program with number associated with each function.

Statement	Function points	
The system is to contain a log on screen consisting of 3 entry fields: the user ID, user name and a password.	Screen generation	1
	ID display, ID entry, ID validate	2,3,4
The ID field will allow up to 20 ASCII characters to be entered in the range A–Z, a–z	ID move to user name or move to error	5
		6
The user name will allow up to 25 ASCII characters to be entered and stored in the range A–Z, a–z, and SPACE (ASCII Code 20).	User name validate	7
	Compare with data	8
	Move to new user entry	9
The password field is 8 characters and expects input	Accept user and set up access	10
		12
	Move to password	
The system will validate each field on entry	Check password	13
	Fail password, increase count,	14
	fail after 3rd try	15
	Logout	16
	Move to next screen	17
	Password fail log	18

Table 13.3 Data tables from dependency decomposition

Index	Users and tasks	Rules
1	Single user with full access authority	1
2	Two users, different access authorities	1,2
3	Two users, same access authorities	1,2,3
4	Two users, multiple tasks	
5	10 Users, multiple tasks	
6	Maximum users, maximum tasks	

RULES

Rule index	Description
1	Using only one program at a time
2	Using programs 1,2,3,4
3	Using programs according to usage weighting

This information is used as basic data selection criteria for the tests. A typical dependency decomposition table would be as shown in Table 13.3. The length of this table is dependent on the actual usage profiles expected for the system. These can be calculated either from experience on exiting systems or estimated from the volumes of information to be input and the time taken for an analysis action.

An example of a usage profile for a multi-user system is shown in Fig. 13.5. This is based on the number of people expected to be employed on data entry and data analysis as well as the estimates of the times for these tasks.

■ 13.4.4 Test generation tools

Many of the standard test generator tools provide some method of decomposing programs into numbered paths, numbered data sets, numbered decision trees, entry states, control flow graphs and cause and effect graphs. New decomposition techniques will be developed as the tools become more mature and as more is discovered about the effectiveness of many of the decomposition methods. For the purposes of statistical testing

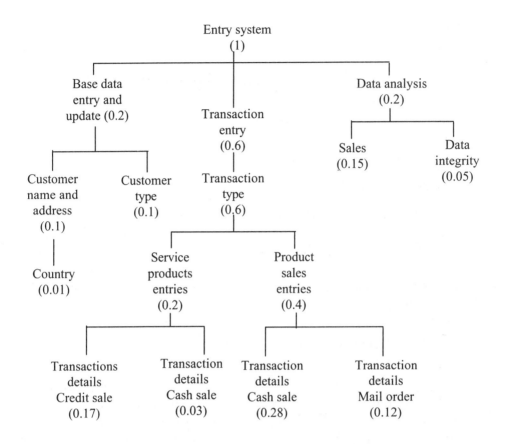

(0.XX) – Usage weighting

USER PROFILE

Function	Number of users
Base data	3
Data analysis	15
Transaction analysis	10
Service transaction entry	2
Product transaction entry	8

Fig. 13.5 Usage and users profile.

any one of the listing mechanisms as described in the test tools or the paragraphs above may be used. The choice of the method will depend partially on the type of software being tested and the target coverage level.

To get the most effective testing as many of the non-overlapping decomposition methods as possible should be used. However for all but the most critical software this is impractical due to time and effort constraints.

■ 13.4.5 The data set

There are several ways of developing a data set for each of the functions, but the most important factors are to include examples from the valid domain, boundary conditions, and invalid data from all possible sources. Details of boundary analysis and input domain analysis can be found in any of the main texts on testing. The principles are embedded within the SIAD decomposition method.

■ SIAD decomposition

This method, called Symbolic Input Attribute Decomposition (SIAD), was developed by Cho (6) in the 1980s for use in statistical development of software and based on the work of several researchers into decomposition methods. The total methodology described by Cho is not the same as the work described here. It is more closely related to reliability testing, but symbolic decomposition is a useful way of developing input lists for future statistical selection based on the input domain of a program.

The method uses a tree breakdown of the proposed system and includes all data entry points for the program. It takes account of both the program flow and the data entry requirements by preserving the tree structure of the data entry flow. However as described in Cho's book, it does not take account of data storage size and quantity, or interaction between multitasking and multi-user systems. The tables resulting from SIAD analysis provide the decomposed input list, together with the rules and sub-rules for these inputs.

A typical SIAD tree for the user entry screen will be as shown in Table 13.4.

By combining the entries in each of the tables the total test set provided by this analysis is the number of lowest level rules and sub-rules for each of the data entry points. This means that for this simple case the total test data set is 20.

Table 13.4 Typical SIAD decomposition.

Index	Tree symbol	Tree element	Rule index
1	X1	ENTRY SCREEN	1,6
		N1 Screen selection character	
2	X1,1	ID, N2 alphanumeric characters	2,3,4,5,6
3	X1,2	NAME, N3 alphabetic characters	3,4,6
4	X1,2,1	FIRST NAME, N3 alphabetic characters	3,6
5	X1,2,2	MIDDLE NAME or INITIAL, N3, N4 alphabetic characters	3,4,6
6	X1,2,3	LAST NAME, N3 alphabetic characters	3,6
7	X1,3	PASSWORD, N5 alphanumeric characters	3,5,6

INPUT DOMAIN RULES

Rule index	Rule description	Sub-rule index
1	N1 single character input	1
2	N2 = 3 + 4 + 5	2
3	N3 = Alphabetic characters	3,4
4	N4 = Including single space	4
5	N5 = Numeric characters	
6	N6 = Invalid data characters	

SUB-RULES

Sub-rule index	Sub-rule description	Remark
1	1	Length of menu entry
2	$1 < N2 < 3$	Length of ID string
3	$1 < N3 < 10$	Length of name string
4	$1 < N4 < 1$	Minimum middle name string
5	$1 < N5 < 8$	Length of password, displayed as Xs

■ 13.4.6 Test methods sets

For each item in the numbered set we now require a method of testing. The methods are usually quite few for each data set since we have simplified the test cases in the functional and data partitions. However in our password code there are a number of validation paths and count loops to be considered. Consequently further test methods can be considered for each listed item. An example of the test list is provided in Table 13.5. Our test sets are now 50 in number and to complete them all even for this simple case would take an automated system tens of minutes and a manual system, several hours. These cases are the simplest statements of entry and do not take into account the sets of data required. The full combination of tests for the data entry in the name field may be required to validate repeated letters. An example might be allowing particular letters to be repeated but preventing 'ww' and other combinations that are not expected within the name field. The full alphabetic range will be required to be tested in each of the fields as well as the non-valid characters at each of the entry points. The use of keys such as 'delete' and 'backspace' will also be included in these tests. Once all these are added to the data set the total set gives over 1500 test cases.

From this point there are two actions. The first is to find the mean defectiveness of the whole product and discover the areas of exceptional variance. The second is to prepare the test set for assurance and reliability testing.

▓ 13.4.7 The complete test set

The complete test set is a combination of all the previous analysis of the program, the data and the test methods to be used. For a simple example the set builds up as follows:

- Decompose the program by data entry, function or path.
- Decompose the data test sets by domain boundaries considering all dimensions of the set.
- Number the resulting lists.
- Weight the functions by determining the criticality and usage index for the decomposed program and weight the entries in the lists according to a linear, logarithmic or exponential function. The choice is dependent on the difference in the weighting functions. Life threatening functions should have more than one chance of being tested. The sample rate should ensure that the number of entries in the table has a probability of being selected greater than one and usually greater than three. This weighting is used for the final tests.

For acceptance of a product to test the weighting is usually based on a combination of the number of developers, the number of languages and the number of different types of code. The aim here is to get a list that will test the processes, not the system, so that the main corrective action effort can be placed where the highest probability of error exists. Some effort will also be placed in areas of lower probability as a method of assuring the effectiveness of the test method.

The weighted table provides a list at least three times as long as the start list depending on the weighting factors used. For instance in our test of the entry screen the usage is only dependent on number of users, not on frequency of use and consequently only the test cases for multiple simultaneous users are tested. This provides a table of $1500 \times 4 = 6000$ entries and this is for only four data entry points on a multi-user system and a solution that is unlikely to be no more than 100 lines of C code. Multiply this up for complex software with tens of thousands of lines of code and

Table 13.5 The combined test set.

Number	Function	Data set	Test method	Number	Function	Data set	Test method
1	X1	1	1	26	X1,2,1	6	3
2	X1	6	1	27	X1,2,2	3	1
3	X1,1	2	2	28	X1,2,2	3	2
4	X1,1	3	2	29	X1,2,2	3	3
5	X1,1	3	3	30	X1,2,2	4	1
6	X1,1	4	2	31	X1,2,2	4	3
7	X1,1	4	3	32	X1,2,2	6	1
8	X1,1	5	2	33	X1,2,2	6	2
9	X1,1	6	1	34	X1,2,2	6	3
10	X1,1	6	2	35	X1,2,3	3	1
11	X1,1	6	3	36	X1,2,3	3	2
12	X1,2	3	1	37	X1,2,3	3	3
13	X1,2	3	2	38	X1,2,3	6	1
14	X1,2	3	3	39	X1,2,3	6	2
15	X1,2	4	1	40	X1,2,3	6	3
16	X1,2	4	2	41	X1,3	3	1
17	X1,2	4	3	42	X1,3	3	2
18	X1,2	6	1	43	X1,3	3	3
19	X1,2	6	2	44	X1,3	5	1
20	X1,2	6	3	45	X1,3	5	2
21	X1,2,1	3	1	46	X1,3	5	3
22	X1,2,1	3	2	47	X1,3	5	4
23	X1,2,1	3	3	48	X1,3	6	1
24	X1,2,1	6	1	49	X1,3	6	2
25	X1,2,1	6	2	50	X1,3	6	3

the test time requirement becomes impossible for 100% testing.

Test selection is by taking a sample based on an even distribution from the list of test cases. The sample size for acceptance to test must be more than the number of developers to avoid aliasing with an individual developer. This will also provide adequate samples to measure the quality of the whole development process and not the performance of just one individual developer.

■ 13.5 Acceptance of Product to Test

This phase of testing often happens informally but provides the developer with little information about the product or the process (the developers own process).

Acceptance of a product into a test area is based on comparison of the normal error rates and the rates for the product being supplied to the test team. Two measures are taken from a small sample of all the possible test cases:

- the mean number of errors for each module
- the error rate range for each module.

These figures are based on either the number of errors for individual functions within a module (mean number of errors) or the mean for a small sample of modules (the error rate). The method of measurement is dependent on the error rate of the whole. If most of the functions have either one or no errors then the calculation is based only on modules where the total is greater than two. If the mean error rate really is less than one, then a more strict definition of an error is used. An example may be to define serious errors, major errors, minor errors, and major flaws and minor flaws.

The results of detection are plotted on a multivariate chart and if the results are within the capability of the company (all points with the control limits), then the modules are passed to test. If an individual or group of modules are outside of the control limits then these are passed back to development. The long term is to continually reduce the error rate. An example of this is shown in Fig. 13.6.

On the first pass through this process there is no historical comparison information and so charts are not useful. Instead the measurements are taken and then used to provide an error map that will indicate where the most defective areas are likely to be.

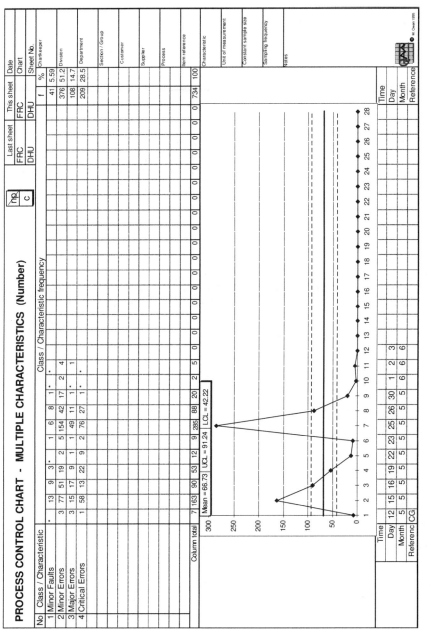

Fig. 13.6 Multivariate Chart for release to test based on samples of tests.

Table 13.6 Test cases for different types of software.

Type of software	Test cases based on
Single user time domain software	System timing
	Repeated functions
	Mathematical error accumulation
	Decision paths
Multi-user time domain software	User timings
	Task switching
	Multiple function operation
Single user non-timed application	Paths and data
	Functions

Table 13.7 The tests method.

Test number	Selected test	Test number	Selected test	Test number	Selected test
1	1291	26	867	51	1234
2	1371	27	381	52	595
3	1364	28	523	53	715
4	1344	29	570	54	1149
5	1054	30	413	55	747
6	1378	31	1219	56	1412
7	831	32	1459	57	569
8	354	33	1298	58	1053
9	163	34	4	59	13
10	1006	35	495	60	1055
11	948	36	846	61	690
12	375	37	1357	62	912
13	862	38	1047	63	146
14	1499	39	91	64	401
15	1076	40	265	65	796
16	38	41	1346	66	542
17	599	42	709	67	293
18	476	43	1091	68	226
19	955	44	686	69	898
20	1348	45	706	70	374
21	213	46	1137	71	751
22	390	47	148	72	859
23	817	48	1359	73	858
24	321	49	1026	74	1296
25	486	50	1040	75	458

The process consists of three stages:
- generation of a test set suited to finding the error rates
- test completion and collection of the metrics
- analysis of the results for error rate variance and error mapping.

▦ 13.5.1 Test case generation

For acceptance into test the program is decomposed and a small sample of tests is completed covering the whole of the system to be tested. Once testable items are listed then a statistical test set can be generated that is suitable for checking on the acceptance of the systems to test. In normal terms this means breaking the system as quickly as possible. However if the breaking occurs very early in the test cycle on totally non-critical functions, then the failure detection is not very useful. The aim is to find out whether the defect rate across the whole product is evenly distributed, or at least find those areas where the most defects occur.

To achieve early critical defect detection, test cases are required that will find difficult defects early, and along the way detect some of the less difficult defects. The testing at this stage is aimed specifically, not at functionality testing, but at the errors that occur due to overload and repetition such as data area boundary problems and multi-user boundary problems. These functions are weighted in the test selection suite rather than the simple user interface problems (although these may be equally critical from a financial risk viewpoint).

The test cases are therefore generated by weighting those that will have the highest probability of causing a failure. This is of course dependent upon the type of software being developed. A few examples are shown in Table 13.6.

The selection process is based on a non-repeated even distribution from the resulting list of test cases. An example for a real time and a single user system illustrates how this process works and these are provided in the examples at the end of this chapter.

The size of the sample is dependent on the resolution required of the variance of the product. A 5% sample based on an even distribution will provide a test set of three cases for our example that is both manageable and can be completed in a reasonable time. The test cases are charted according to the type of test completed and the part of the system tested. Table 13.7 and Fig. 13.7 show the selection and the even distribution for the example.

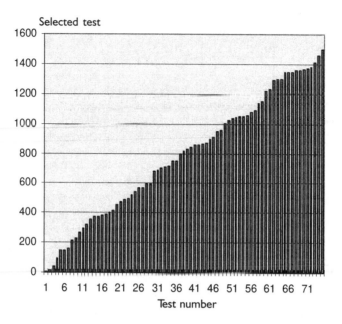

Fig. 13.7 The distribution of the selected tests.

The consequence of this is that some of the tests will uniquely test one part of the system only, whereas others will carry out a number of different tests on one part of the system. The result of completing the tests shows where the most defective areas of the product are (Table 13.8).

This map shows where the highest values are, but it does not provide us with the answers of the significance of the numbers of defects being found, or the coverage obtained for each of the tests.

▓ 13.5.2 Metrics generation for test completion

The test coverage for each of the tests is provided by analysing the coverage possible and comparing this with the coverage obtained as a percentage figure. This figure measures how completely the 5% sample has covered the code and therefore provides an estimate of how well the results can be compared across the whole of the product.

Table 13.8 Map of defects against test method and function.

Test number	Test method used					
	Function	1	2	3	4	
1	1			3		
2	3					
3	1	2				
4	2		2			
5	2			3		
6	4	1				
7	2		2			
..	..	..	..	..	..	
74	7				5	
75	6		2			

▓ 13.5.3 Test metrics analysis

Two methods are used to analyse the number and severity of defects information gathered. Each test completed is plotted on a multivariate chart as shown in Fig. 13.6. The resulting c chart shows the consistency of production of the product, and the severity factors are shown in the table used to make up the chart.

If the consistency of the process shows that all errors are within the control lines – within the bounds of the 3SE limits for the chart – then the product can be accepted for system, acceptance and reliability testing. The areas where the error levels are above the expected levels (above the 3SE levels) can be sent back to development for further investigation. A secondary question is also asked. Why are the error levels higher in these particular places?

To answer this question the second analysis method used. This aims to determine the causes for the types of errors that are occurring most frequently and to find some way of eliminating these causes. The technique used to achieve this is through the 'house of quality' mapping process, shown in Fig. 13.8, which enables severity factors to be related for each of the different causes identified.

This house of quality is developed through the use of Pareto analysis, brainstorming, and cause and effect analysis. The engineers involved in the development are key people and without their cooperation in finding these causes the effects can remain hidden while managers chase after minor causes.

DIRECTION OF IMPROVEMENT	IMPORTANCE	PROCEDURE			TRAINING			LANGAUGE USE			CUSTOMER RATING
HOWs / WHATs		Define Process	Control LOC	Control Complexity	Language	Tools	Product	Define Limits	Classify Modules	Control LOC by Class	0 1 2 3 4 5
Tools Language	10	○	○	◉	○		◉	○	○	
Machines	2				◉					
Networks	7				◉					
Environment Pressure	30		◉	○						
Responsibility	28					○				
Environment Pressure	30		◉	○						
Responsibility	28					○				
Motivation	55					○				
Methods Definitions	50	◉						◉	◉	◉
Measurement	40	◉						◉	◉	
Audit & Revie	35	○	○					○		
ORGANIZATIONAL DIFFICULTY		50	20	50	35	10	50	75	35	66

TARGETS

ENGINEERING COMPETITIVE ASSESSMENT	5 4 3 2 1 0

ABSOLUTE IMPORTANCE		915	135	300	180	111	249	1005	840	480
RELATIVE IMPORTANCE		21%	3%	7%	4%	2%	5%	23%	19%	11%

ROOF	MATRIX	WEIGHTS	ARROWS
Strong Pos ◉	Strong ◉	9	Maximize ↑
Positive ○	Medium ○	3	Minimize ↓
Negative ✕	Weak △	1	Nominal ○
Strong Neg ✖			

Fig. 13.8 House of quality.

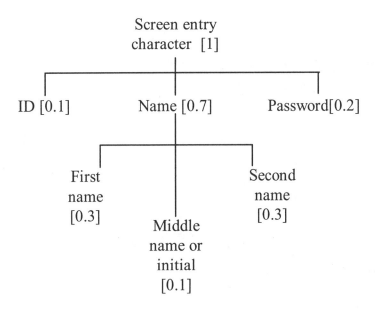

Fig. 13.9   A usage map for the password entry system.

▨ 13.6 Test Selection

Once the product is accepted into testing then a new test set is required. This will generate metrics not only to refine the rates and consistency information, but also to find the critical cases and the more difficult results. This is completed by weighting the test cases, carrying out statistical selections, repeatedly testing, and providing metrics for the defect detection rate, the consistency and the detail failures of the system. The purpose of the weighting here is to try to generate a test suite that will thoroughly test the critical components, and will ensure a rate of defect detection that maximises the testing effectiveness. In work completed by Thevenod-Fosse (45) we have seen that the detection rate for errors falls rapidly after the first tests are completed. However that does not mean that there are fewer errors left, just that the test strategy is not aimed at finding these new errors.

The first stage of this process is to base test case selection on a weighting of the decomposed program. There are several common methods of weighting a program – no doubt new methods will arise over the next few years.

▨ 13.6.1 Test weighting – usage

If all the commonly used parts of a program are error free then the satisfaction of the customer can be expected to be greater than if the system fails at the first few attempts at live usage.

This weighting is based on a map of the functionality of the system with each part being weighted according to the expected frequency of use. An example of this is for the password control system that we looked at earlier. The entry code has a probability of being run of 1. The different access level paths each have a different usage level based on the profile of the expected users. The usage map is proportioned out according to these usage levels as shown in Fig. 13.9.

Once the chart has been produced the weighting levels can be applied to the decomposed test suite list by adding an entry for each item on the list according to its weight. The weights are multiplied up so that if the least probable item still has a factor of 0.2, it is given one entry in the table and consequently the entry code (factor 1) will have five entries in the table. The weighting is usually only carried out for sub-systems since the entry system is often tested on entry to every sub-system and consequently is tested according to the number of lower level functions. However where testing is to be carried out independently on sub-systems without first running the dependent path, then this path requires its full number of entries in the test list.

▨ 13.6.2 Test weighting – criticality

With the previous weighting system we looked at frequency of usage. For many software systems the part of the software that should only run once, and only in critical fail mode, is the part of the software that absolutely must be error free.

Two models of the software are used for analysis of the system to find these systems. The first of these is the model of how critical the software is to the success of completing the task. During the development and design of the test requirements each part of a system is provided with a comparative estimate of its criticality. These parts then obtain the highest priority in the map of probability of being tested.

The test activities that will test these parts are given a high probability of being tested by having more entries in the table. The weighting is linear between the items of least criticality (one entry in the table) and the most critical items. These are given a weighting equal or greater than the most frequent item in the table at this stage of developing the test suite.

The second test criticality weighting relates to the internal criticality of a function based on the likely failure consequences to the ability of the system to continue to complete its mission. This is sometimes called 'call' weighting, but is not just a relative weighting on the number of calls to and from a particular module, but also a weighting of the consequential damage to the total system because of this failure mode. This weighting is less than that of the external criticality weighting. Consequently the number of entries in the test list for the most critical function is likely to be less than for the externally critical function.

▓ 13.6.3 Test weighting – data usage

This weighting is related to the consequences of failure of a data item. There are many systems that have no method of continuing to function if the password validation bit for the system becomes invalid during operation of the system. This means that failure of this one data bit will always cause system failure.

This is a consequence of coding the system with the 'WHILE... TRUE... ENDWHILE' function surrounding the body of the code. The failure of the TRUE or valid bit during the rest of the operation causes the function to be in an invalid state. If the checks have been built in (to provide security against entry into parts of the system), then failure of this part will always call total system close down. This is not the only data type to cause this failure and a model of data criticality in this sense can reveal areas where externally provided data can cause the whole system to fail.

The model of the data criticality in this system is used to provide tests as data states that will ensure coverage of the most critical data items. This model is used to cover as many parts of the system as possible. This criticality is coupled with the previous set (the criticality of functions) providing a data set criticality list that is additive with the function list.

▓ 13.6.4 Test weighting – entry condition weighting

How many systems continue to operate successfully and then fail when they are entered with a particular state either due to hardware or software limitations? This weighting system aims to find all the possible entry conditions for a function and then weight the test cases with each and every entry condition. In reality for non-critical systems the entry conditions that are within the design specification are used, but for critical systems, the weighting must include boundary and non-valid states of entry as well.

13.6.5 Test weighting – multi-tasking weighting

A special instance of this last weighting is the operation of multi-tasking systems. These environments have infinite numbers of entry conditions and consequently sets are established that will provide tests for valid entry to the system. They also provide sets to validate the ability of the system to run in parallel with the other software. In GUI interface software of Windows-type developments this testing can provide the largest test set of all the test methods.

13.7 Test Preparation

Once the complete test suite has been produced using the same statistical models as used for acceptance to test, a test suite is selected. However the weighting now ensures that the most critical, most often used code, and most critical data all has a probability of being tested at least once. It should be designed to ensure that these tests are selected several times with many different dependency and startup conditions. This provides a method of detecting errors that would otherwise remain undetected.

The first time the testing is completed the detection rate is unknown. However the acceptance to test data will provide some indication of the likelihood of finding errors with a particular technique. A control chart for the error detection rate is set up for each different test technique with the control limits determined by the acceptance to test data.

13.8 Test Execution

A feature of this type of testing is that instead of the normal error detection rate, shown in Fig. 13.10, the aim is to provide tests that are more likely to detect new errors as testing progresses. To achieve this a detection history for the test techniques is required but initially the control chart is set up from the acceptance to test data.

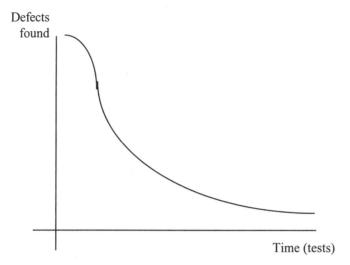

Fig. 13.10 The normal test effectivenss curve (detection rate).

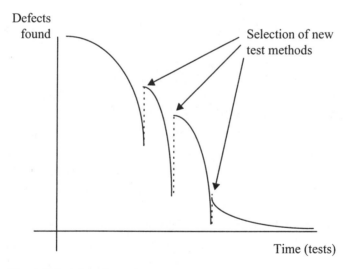

Fig. 13.11 The statistical detection rate curve.

Function	Error type				
	Fatal	Serious	Major	Minor	Flaw
A101	1	1		2	
A102			1		
A103	1		3	3	3
B101			2		2
B102		1		1	
B103			1		1
B104			1	2	
C101		1			
C102		2	3	3	
C103	1	2	1	2	
C104				2	
C105			1	1	1
D100	2	2			
E101					
E102			1	2	2
E103		1		2	
E104		1	2		2
F101				2	
G101	1		1		1
H101		1			

Fig. 13.12 Error map of error types vs. functions for the completed tests (σ values for the whole product).

An even distribution sample is taken from the test list and the tests completed. The results are plotted on the control chart and when the detection rate falls below the 3 standard deviations limit the method is abandoned in favour of more productive techniques. The resulting test detection curve now becomes as shown in Fig. 13.11. This is an improvement both in error detection rates and in the effectiveness of the testing, since the test method is only abandoned when the areas fall below a known threshold.

Once a complete single pass of all tests in the selection is complete, a second set is selected. This will include a repeat of some previously executed tests, but by doing these tests a second time we can gain confidence that the results are identical and no errors have been left undetected. The new tests will indicate where the error rates are still highest and these two sets of data provide input for system mapping.

A typical system map for errors is provided in Fig. 13.12. The errors are reduced to a standard deviation (σ) value based on the mean for the whole system. The areas where most errors are to be found are identified and

Function	Test method				
	1	2	3	4	5
A101	1	3			
A102	1				
A103	2	2		1	
B101	1		1	1	1
B102	1			1	
B103		1		1	
B104	1		1	1	
C101	1				
C102	1	3	1	1	1
C103	3				1
C104		2	1		
C105	1	1		1	
D100	3		1		
E101					
E102	1		1	3	
E103	1	2			
E104		3	1	1	
F101	1	1			
G101	1		1	1	
H101				1	
Mean	1	0.9	0.4	0.65	0.15

Fig. 13.13 Errors detected by test methods for each module.

cause analysis in these functions and data types is used to find and eliminate the causes for future projects. This process is also used to remove individual

The effectiveness of the testing can be found by charting the error types against the test method in a similar fashion. Fig. 13.13 shows the errors detected by the different test methods in each of the modules as compared with the whole. This is corrected for the number of defects found in the module.

▨ 13.9 Test Results Analysis

The results obtained from testing are three-fold:

 (1) actual error information and a first level of classification
 (2) density information
 (3) test effectiveness information.

The purpose of analysing these results is also three fold and is represented by the statistical model we saw in section 13.1.

The first stage is to find the errors in the product and discover the underlying defects in the code and the causes. Several types of analysis can be used including cause and effect charts. Other techniques include debugging and code tracing, code and compiler output walkthrough, code break point insertion, and data tracking. Once the cause is found the error type can be re-classified since it is at this time that errors can clearly be attributed to a development stage or an activity or process.

The second stage of the process is to establish how effective the testing has been in finding all the errors. The argument against statistical testing is usually that 100% testing is necessary to find the last error. This is usually put forward by people who cannot define 100% testing!

Defining the test effectiveness means taking information such as error detection rate and coverage and establishing their relationship. The areas where most errors occur are likely to contain more although individual errors will be scattered throughout the product.

Coverage is defined in two ways: The amount of code covered by a particular test and the number of tests that have covered a particular module of code. These two figures show how well the code has been tested and where there are possibly more tests to be completed. This analysis can be carried out using the error mapping methods described earlier. The functions are listed vertically and the test methods horizontally. The inverted coverage figures are calculated as being between 0 and 1σ (0), 1 and 2σ (1), 2 and 3σ (3) and above 3σ (4). This means that areas of 4 are not well covered by the tests and consequently can be concentrated on for further investigation. However the second number added in the box is the number of errors found, also plotted as 1, 2, 3 and 4σ. The combinations can then find the areas where both poor coverage has been achieved and high error rates can be expected.

This provides an indication of the most effective test methods for a particular area of the code and can be used to refine the test suite model of the software.

■ 13.10 Product Acceptance

The results from testing are used to either accept or reject a product. In the traditional sense this means either accepting the product because no or few faults have been found, or rejecting the product because errors have been found and these require fixing before delivery. This strategy does not prevent errors – have you heard an engineer state that 'testing will find any errors left'? The testing phase indicates how well the product has been produced. It is impossible to 100% inspect and consequently it is impossible to remove all the errors through a testing process. The measure of how well the product has been produced gives confidence in the development process providing that:

- the test process itself can inspire confidence by measuring its ability to detect errors
- the test process has been performed to known standards and measures.

In software we are already aware of the relationship between error detection in a document and the rate of inspection. This is well documented in (70). However significant amounts of testing are based on the same theory of manual inspection – usually of pictures and images and not text. Our ability to spot minor defects in images as complex as an interface screen is not any more effective than our ability to detect errors in text, and consequently the same rules are applied. By selecting a sample from a screen that can then be subjected to longer than normal scrutiny, and calculating the error rate per inspected object, an estimate of the total errors in the product can be extrapolated.

■ 13.11 Developer Testing

The strategy outlined above requires the developer to understand the defect levels left in the code at the time it is submitted to test. This means that the developers themselves must take responsibility for measuring the error levels or be subjected to the test teams independent initial assessment. The subsequent risk is that the product will be returned with only an error level assessment based on a small percentage coverage (the first actual tests completed by the test team).

Random test strategies assist developers in objectively finding more faults in their own code. A good example of this is the inability of an author to find the errors in written text. Random selection and reading highlights the areas where probable errors have occurred. The improvement in efficiency of this type of inspection is many-fold, however the expected results are still likely to be less than 80% effective.

▥ 13.12 Summary

Testing described in this chapter provides methods of ensuring that software will function under as many user states as possible once development and testing are completed. However the statistical sampling provides reliability estimates for a number of different test areas.

- Coverage for even the simplest function is not feasible. A method of selecting tests is required that removes the temptation to complete the easiest tests.
- Random testing provides no mechanism for ensuring critical tests are completed.
- Statistical modelling of systems usage, criticality, data usage, entry conditions and multi-tasking provide a test suite where the probability of selection can be calculated.
- A 10% completion of all tests will provide confidence that testing to a set level of criticality has been achieved. Experience shows that this testing reveals errors not identified by non-statistical testing.
- This testing will never find the last bug. Combined with acceptance to testing it will provide confidence that the most critical parts of the system have been tested.
- The argument for random or selective testing cannot be justified in terms of reliability measures, reduced testing terms, or for financial benefit.

▥ 13.13 Examples

▥ 13.13.1 Test resources management and defect detection

▥ Background

The major office integration software package that is the subject of this section provides the features required for office inter-connectivity and communication via e-mail as well as document and message management. Two versions of this software were produced over a development period

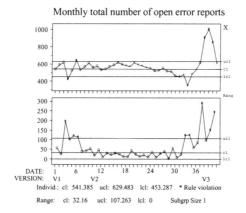

Monthly total number of open error reports

Fig. 13.14   Outstanding defect reports by release.

of 3 years and statistics have been gathered. These include the number of defect reports open at the end of each month and the types of defects found during testing during each of these development stages. This information has been used to indicate whether the new product is less defective than the previous version and to show how the profile of the types of defects being found is improving with time.

This example uses this historical data to show how the same information can be used to define the resource requirements for the project, and how, by using statistical control charts, the rates of defect detection can be controlled by responding to the out-of-control conditions that arise.

The information has been used to provide Pareto diagrams for the defect types and to produce a cause and effect diagram for major defect types so that the company can initiate a policy of tackling the introduction of defects.

▓ The project statistics and charts used during development

The development company has been innovative in their use of statistics gathered during the project to show improvement over previous releases. The data includes the number of defect reports remaining open at the end of each month, with the defects reported categorised for type. This information is used to produced the release quality level based on the remaining outstanding defect reports (shown in Fig. 13.14), and the residue defect level for each module for each release (shown in Fig. 13.15). The month-on-month average is also calculated to provide a mean rate of clear-up shown in Fig. 13.16.

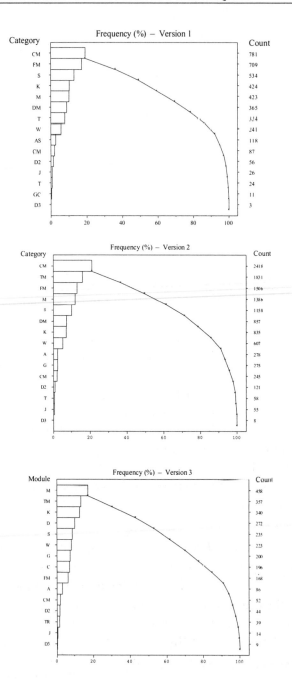

Fig. 13.15 Module open defect report levels accumulated for each month during development.

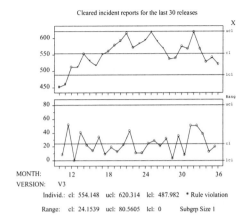

Fig. 13.16 Mean clear-up rate of defect reports.

These diagrams show how the process has improved over the development period and provide management reports that can be used to justify the expense of data collection and process improvement activities that have been completed. The aim of the data collection and analysis activity is to help the developers to complete their tasks more effectively.

Returns and re-submission charts

The charts shown in the previous section provide monthly trends and levels which provide an overall view of the information. The data for the number of submitted, rejected and reworked reports provides a mechanism for establishing the state of control of the development–test–rework cycle. This data is about both the product (number of reports opened) and the process (number of failures, number of re-submissions, etc.). The control charts show that the company has a capability of achieving a ratio between %returns and %clean corrections of 1.3. The target figure is obviously one and so a control chart is set up with a target of one and a UCL calculated from the first 20 readings. The aim is to find ways of reducing this figure to as small a value as possible (Fig. 13.17).

Using control charts for test effectiveness

The effectiveness of testing is based on the quantity of defects observed in a given time period. The ideal rate is a constant level for each of the individual testers which can be used to provide an overall figure per unit

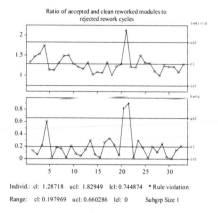

Fig. 13.17 Control chart for ratio of accepted plus clean rework cycles and rejected cycles.

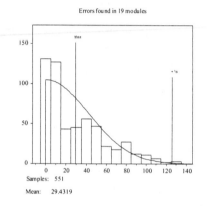

Fig. 13.18 The distribution of errors found in modules.

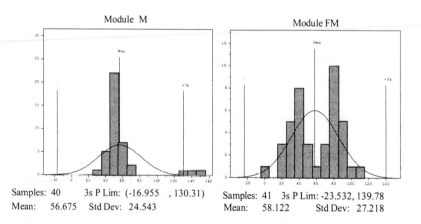

Fig. 13.19 The distributions of the errors in different modules.

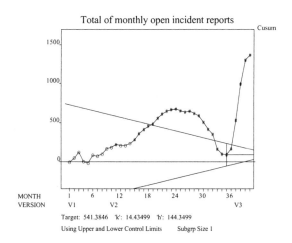

Target: 541.3846 'k': 14.43499 'h': 144.3499

Using Upper and Lower Control Limits   Subgrp Size 1

Fig. 13.20 The cusum chart for open incident reports.

of test effort. However in practice test effectiveness is an S-curve, with few defects being found in the early stage of a project (there is little to test). A maximum rate is achieved during the middle stages, limited by the resources that can be put into the task. Then an ever reducing level is experienced as the defects become harder to find (limited by the task difficulty and consequently by the shear volume of testing required to detect individual defects).

The rate of detection chart is an (X, moving R) chart with sloping control lines, since the aim of testing is to continually decrease the number of remaining defects in the product. We can see from the distributions (Fig. 13.18) that modules are produced with either a large, medium or small number of errors present. These are identified during testing as defects and then, once causes have been found, the underlying errors are removed.

The effectiveness can also be monitored using cusum charts. These charts accumulate the differences between measurements and consequently provide a rate of detection chart. If a mean rate is expected then this is used as the zero level and the chart is continued until the data moves too far from the zero. The chart is re-centred at this point by recalculating the mean levels.

For this project the mean rates are calculated from the monthly figures. The distributions (Fig. 13.19) show that there are three mean rates expected for the different types of modules. (We have no indication in this project as to whether these levels can be correlated to complexity, lines of code or any other module metric.) A cusum chart is set up for each module being developed with a mean based on the first readings (see Fig. 13.20). This

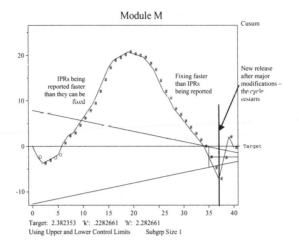

Fig. 13.21 The cusum chart for a balanced resource level.

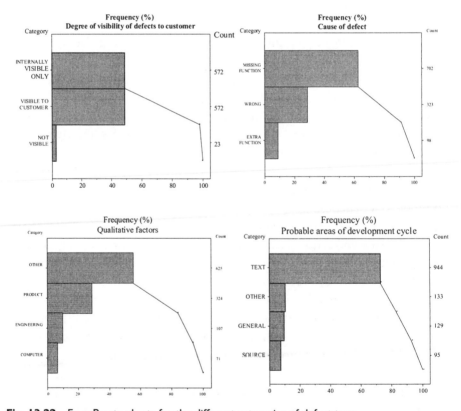

Fig. 13.22 Four Pareto charts for the different categories of defect type.

provides a target level for the continued working of the chart, but if the process changes significantly (as expected in a testing environment), then the chart is re-centred using the new mean value. One difficulty of this is that manual charting will not provide an appropriate centre until the end of the activity. The characteristic curve depends on the testing rate and the fault correction rate.

▓ Using cusum charts to manage test resources

The cusum chart also shows the effect of changing test and rework resources since the process is an effective pipe-line. The flow is determined by the test effectiveness on the input side and the rework effectiveness on the output side.

The test effectiveness is determined either from the selected types of automated tests or from the availability of human resources. The rework effectiveness is also determined by the ability of staff to find and successfully correct defects. The minimum time to complete a project is given by whichever of these two resources is smallest.

The cusum charts show this as move away from the static target level for the module (Fig. 13.21).

▓ Using Pareto for defect type analysis

The Pareto chart is useful for establishing the type of defects seen in a project and for relating these types. In this instance we have several different types of Pareto charts. The defects are identified for:
- their visibility to the customer (a severity measure and possibly a test selection measure for future characterisation)
- their cause in terms of the detected defect (missing, wrong or extra function)
- an engineering classification aimed at finding the most probable areas for error in the development cycle
- the qualitative factors aimed at improving either the product or the costs.

These four charts (for the same defects, Fig. 13.22) provide a profile of the defectiveness of the product. They consequently indicate how a future quality management system could be used to identify the causes of error and start the elimination process.

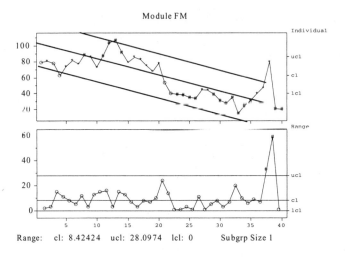

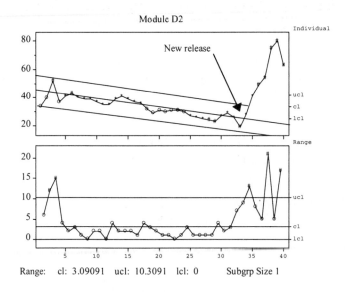

Fig. 13.23 The two control charts.

■ The control charts for defect management for different modules

The control charts for the 15 different modules cannot all be drawn here, but two examples are provided (Fig. 13.23) to show the type of variation seen with time. These clearly demonstrate when resources are being used to test and find errors and when resources are reducing the errors left in the product. The charts are drawn with sloping control lines and the new

Component	Jul	Aug	Sept	Oct	Nov	Dec		
M	47	147	136	128	70	57		
D	2.9	5	5	2.9	2.2	1.1		
DM	4	5.4	5.4	4	5.4	2.9		
TM	36	82	89	79	62	63		
F	20	21	80	47	40	31		
SM	26	38	54	33	19	11		
C	10	16	33	35	44	38		
D1	40	51	48	35	31	26		
W	75	47	46	55	60	46		
D2	4	3.2	3.6	3.2	2.9	1.4		
J	0	4.5	4.5	0	0	0		
G	13	35	41	38	7	7.7		
A	14	6.1	6.8	3.6	2.5	2.2		
K	94	80	96	70	31	24		
D3	2.2	0.4	0.4	0.4	0	0.4		
Sum X	389	542	648	534	376	312		
Xbar	26	36	43	36	25	21	17	Grand X
Range	94	147	136	128	70	63	58	Rbar

σ	15.722
X +3σ	64.2
X + 2σ	48.4
X + σ	32.722
X	17
X − σ	1.278

$(= Rbar/d_2)$

Fig. 13.24 The start of an error map with the control data calculated.

release shows how the charts are restarted once the error levels have stabilised.

▓ **Using the error map to determine the overall quality of the product**

The error map demonstrated here shows a way of quickly determining which modules are likely to cause problems to the future completed product. The initial stages of the map are shown together with the calculations of standard deviation (σ) values for future use in the project (Fig. 13.24).

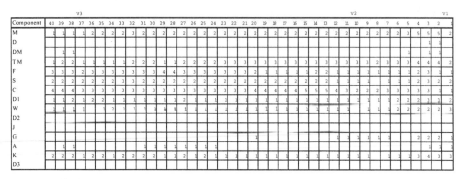

Fig. 13.25 Error map to October 1994.

Component	40	39	38	37	36	35	34	33	32	31	30	29	28	27	26	25	24	23	22	21	20	19	18	17	16	15	14	13	12	11	10	9	8	7	6	5	4	3	2	1	
M		2	2	2		1	3	4	4	5	6	4	5	3	3	4	4	4	4	3	4	3	4	4	4	3	4	4	3	3	3	4	5	4	5	5	6	13	14	16	3	
D																																										
DM																																										
TM			2	4					1	2	2	2	1	1	2	3	3	3	5	5	6	6	6	5	5	4	5	5	5	5	5	6	4	3	5	5	5	7	8	8	2	
FC	7	7	7	5	7	8	7	8	8	6	8	10	11	9	7	8	8	7	6	7	4	2	2	2	2	2	3	3	2	1		1	2		1	1	2	3	7		Sub-Cont
S	1	2	2	1	2	3	3	3	2	2	2	1	2	2		1	1	1	?	1	1	1	1															2	4	2	1	
C	3	3	3	2	3	2	2	2	2	2	2	2	2	2	2	2	3	4	4	4	4	5	5	5	5	2	1	1	1	2	2	3	2	2							Sub-Cont
D1		1	2		1	1	1	1	1				1	1	1																			1	1	2	3	4	2		
W	1	1	1			3	2	2	2	1																							2	3	5	4	3	3	7		
D2																																									
J																																									
G																																					2	3	2		
A																																									
K	3	4	5	2	3	3	2	3	5	5	3	2	2	3	2	3	2	2	1	2	2	1	1	1	1	1	1							1		1	6	9	7	9	
D3																																										

Fig. 13.26 Error map after normalising the data for size and complexity.

If the error levels start to drop below a level where the information displayed is showing where defective areas of code exist (a lack of presence of many 3σ points) then the data is recalculated from historic information. Areas where error levels have fallen to below the 3σ level are excluded from this calculation. This allows continuous re-calibration of the chart with an aim to obtain only 1σ levels at the smallest values in the longer term.

The full chart, Fig. 13.25, demonstrates that several of the modules fall outside the normal capability of the company and when the data has been normalised for complexity and sise this becomes even more apparent. Fig. 13.26 shows the completed chart for the normalised data (see Chapter 8) and demonstrates that module 5 and module 14 are of particular concern. This is even more true when it is noted that these modules are critical to the application. However putting this into context, the modules have not caused any serious reports from customers with only minor defects being reported.

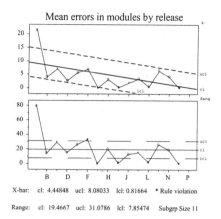

Fig. 13.27 The defectiveness control chart for the release of modules of code.

▨ 13.13.2 Release management using error data Graphical chemical analysis software

This example is from an international company that produces chemical process modelling software, and has been producing update releases of the code for several years. The product is produced by a non-formal process – there are walk-throughs of design and code and the main testing is carried out by the coders. There are no formal testing procedures and no formal inspections.

The data presented shows how the defectiveness declines with time in a process that is not inherently controlled. Data for 15 releases of each of the modules are used to generate a mean defectiveness for the product. This is charted on a control chart with sloping control lines (Fig. 13.27). Note that the rise in the mean for the last two readings is due to major changes being introduced in the new release and the restart of a new cycle of improvement. The control lines would be recalculated after the third such reading and new targets for each release established.

Another point is that the second reading was very low. This is because few changes were made in this code except for corrections. However the low reading is a cause for concern since even after few minor changes in the next release the defectiveness level is back up to the expected levels.

Most researchers consider the graph for this data to be an exponential decay. However the use of sloping control lines based on the variance seen across the whole product indicates that, while there is large step change in the first release, for the rest the step change is closer to a linear decay. For different organisations the shape, level and the slope of the curve will be different because it is dependent on the processes, their capability and the methods being used. Management pressure in some circumstances can benefit the shape of the curve, but remember that it is not wise to request targets, even on the control charts, without providing tools and methods to enable the staff to achieve these targets. For this particular company it would be beneficial to reduce the defectiveness levels generally, but this would mean taking a more formal approach to the development cycle. The company will benefit from the RAD initiative since many of the changes are made in response to customer request and the requirements are changing rapidly as the chemical industry develops new ideas, methods, products and formulas.

To achieve the lower defectiveness levels the error map for the product over time shows which are the modules to be immediately concerned about (Table 13.9). This shows that all modules contribute to defectiveness, but two in particular provide an opportunity for improvement of the overall product.

Table 13.9 The error map for the modules over time.

Release	Modules										
	U	E	G	S	T	A	P	S2	F	E2	S3
1		12	6	5	1	1	16	7			
2	1	2	2	1			3	1			
3		1	5				6	1	2		
4		2					3				
5		2	2	1			5	1	1		
6		4	1	1			7	2	1		
7											
8		1					4	1			
9											
10		1					3				
11		2	1		1		3	1			
12											
13		5	2	1	1		4				
14		2					4	3			
15											

Part IV
Starting to use
Statistical Methods

This part, Chapter 14, provides an outline of **how to get started** using the techniques and helps an organisation to build statistical methods into every part of its structure. The outline of process control, product improvement management and project management, on to process improvement through management information is highlighted, together with the implications for the introduction of such methods.

When implementing change in any organisation the people who are expected to be responsible for, are affected by, or who administer the change, are critical to the success of the project. This chapter provides a few guidelines for selecting the first project, the project team and the success factors. A little success will build more, so the choice and demonstration of success by advertising expectations, can ensure that others see the benefits of the methods and apply them through their projects.

Statistical control is not just measurement – it is about the changing the way people think about the process. This chapter provides background to implementing an SPC system by getting thinking about processes embedded into the organisation.

14 Using Statistical Methods

▇ 14.1 Introduction

The theory and many applications of statistical methods are described throughout this book and the benefits are described through the examples and the descriptions of the methods. To gain these benefits a strategy is required for introduction of the methods. Any measurement and process improvement activity is inevitably seen as an overhead on top of the everyday activities of the organisation. If the three-level model seen at the beginning of this book is followed then the methods become an integral part of the normal process improvement cycle that is used for any quality program.

Statistical methods by themselves can provide benefits. Particularly the benefits obtained from selecting appropriate test cases or pages for inspection, and using these to determine whether the product is ready for a full inspection or testing. The other benefits are less tangible. Repeatability of the process is a difficult idea when every client and product is different. For companies that are maintaining one product it is much easier to see how the process may be repeatable. This is often because the maintenance activity is a case of responding to error reports, corrections, adding functionality and testing. Measurements can be taken for the process involved in each of these stages and for the product. Where the product, the tools and even the staff are different, it is a case of ensuring that the process to be used is well identified. This may be a case of identifying the different processes and defining as the first step the selection of a process suited to the particular circumstances. This is particularly relevant when the level of risk is different both financially and technically from project to project.

▓ 14.2 A Strategy for Introducing the Methods

▓ 14.2.1 The sequence of introducing SPC

Once a company has decided that repeatability and consistency of the processes are the target for their organisation there are several steps before the implementation on a project can start. Fig. 14.1 shows these steps as a series of sequential events that conclude in the implementation project. There are several roles identified in this plan that are important for its success.

The first role identified is for the company's senior management. It is essential that they understand the concepts in overall terms so that they can identify the benefits that are likely to be achievable and set realistic targets for the projects.

The second role is that of facilitator. This is a person with responsibility for understanding the concepts of SPC and for ensuring correct use of charts. The role may be combined with that of quality manager, since it is mainly an audit responsibility. However the person involved must be approachable since the role involves providing advice and generally helping people by engendering enthusiasm.

The third role is that of administrator for the charts. This role involves storing the completed charts and issuing new charts for new projects based on historic data.

Once the people have been appropriately trained and the pilot project chosen the steps are taken for implementing SPC on the project.

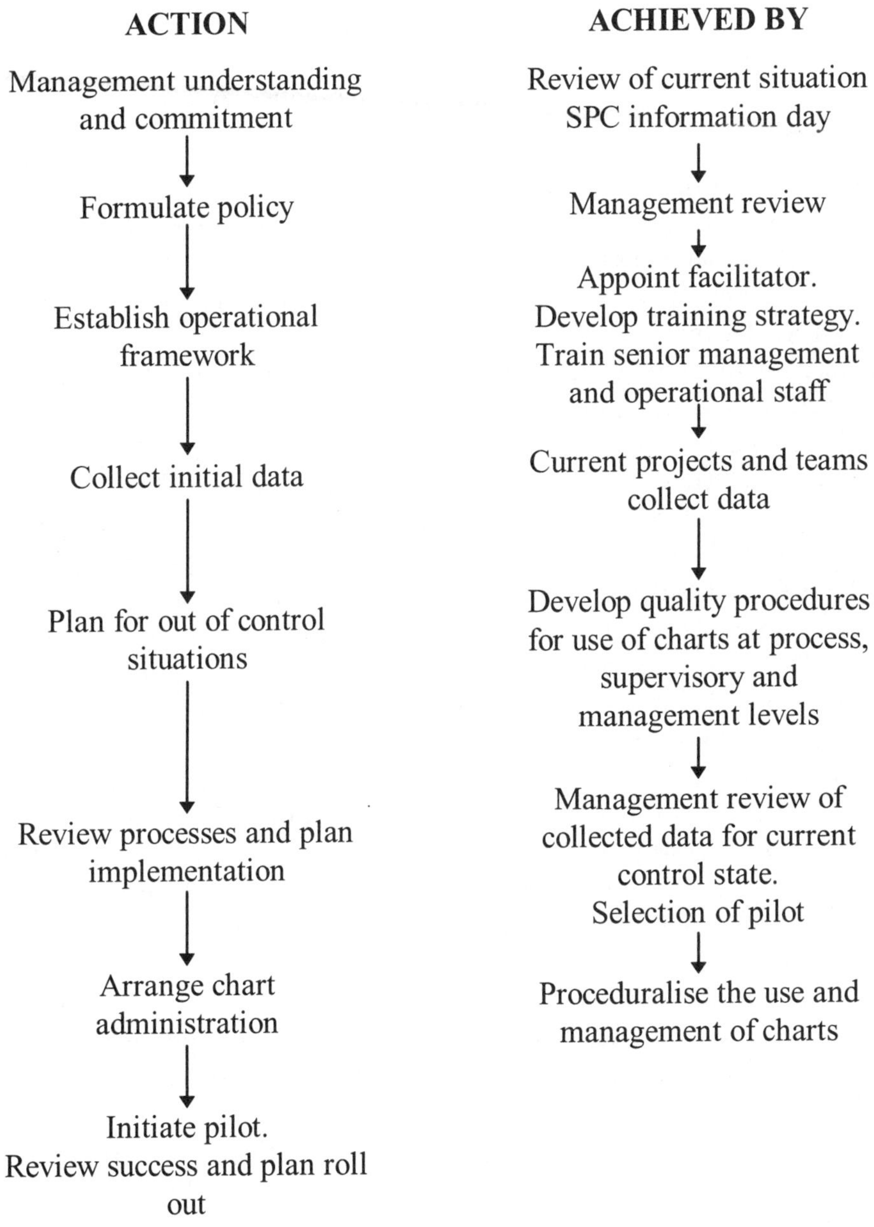

ACTION	ACHIEVED BY
Management understanding and commitment	Review of current situation SPC information day
↓	↓
Formulate policy	Management review
↓	↓
Establish operational framework	Appoint facilitator. Develop training strategy. Train senior management and operational staff
↓	↓
Collect initial data	Current projects and teams collect data
↓	↓
Plan for out of control situations	Develop quality procedures for use of charts at process, supervisory and management levels
↓	↓
Review processes and plan implementation	Management review of collected data for current control state. Selection of pilot
↓	↓
Arrange chart administration	Proceduralise the use and management of charts
↓	
Initiate pilot. Review success and plan roll out	

Fig. 14.1 The sequence for introducing SPC.

■ 14.2.2 The steps for implementing the SPC project

Once it has been decided to implement SPC on a project, there are several simple steps to be taken as shown in Fig. 14.2.

The first of these is to **identify the process**. This should, where possible, be separated from the tools, languages and methods and concentrate on the processes. This stage is attempting to find the overall processes involved and can be generated as a development model such a V, W, X or RAD cycle.

Having identified the overall methods, the second step is to **provide the detail model for each of the separate processes**. We have seen several detailed methods in the previous chapters, in particular the inspection and testing cycles (Chapters 12 and 13). It is this level of detail that is required before the next step can be taken.

The third step is to decide which **metrics to use to control the process.** The process control metrics such as time, effort, efficiency, completeness, effectiveness and defectiveness are used as controls for the process. Equally valid are controls that define the output from the process such as lines of code per module, module complexity and language usage. Some of these measures will become more dependent on the tools, languages and computers to be used, but at this stage they are defined as controls and values are not specified.

The fourth step is to take historical data from the same processes and **find the normal level of operation and the variance for the company**. For a project where this is the first time of using the particular process with a particular tool set or on a particular platform, there will be no historical data. The objective for the fourth step is then to gather this historical data for use in future projects. Note however that there are always activities that are independent from the platforms and tools. Inspections, walkthroughs, acceptance to test, early design activities, and procurement of the requirements are a few examples where the process can be identified independently from the development tools.

If historical data is available then the next step is to **generate the control charts** with statistical control limits for use by the project team. If there is no historical data then the control charts are produced without limits and plotted as the project progresses. The limits are produced from the first 20–25 sets of data recorded.

The next step is to **manage the use of the charts**. This means taking management responsibility for ensuring that charts are properly completed

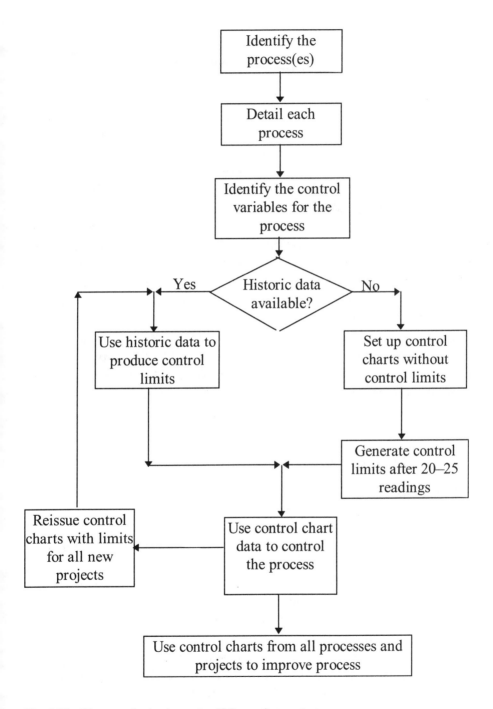

Fig. 14.2 The steps for implementing SPC on a first project.

and are being used as controls for the project. It is not adequate to fill in the charts and then ignore any out-of-control signals that occur. These must either be explained as different and subsequently identified processes, or the actions to correct the situation on the current project must be shown to have been taken.

The final step is to take the data, together with any historical data from previous projects, and identify ways in which control can be improved. This is the process improvement stage which is detailed in Chapter 8.

These steps are the basis of developing an SPC system, but require management support for the effort to be put in place. There is little point in spending time doing all of this work if the company has a short-term goal of making money now. If the company is geared only to reacting to competition and the market place as it becomes obvious that these are impacting the business it can never be the leader of its industry. (Even tracking the effect of competition is a good practical example of the use of SPC – it can help identify real threats and prevent management from reacting to monthly figures.)

For most companies the longer term goal of staying ahead of the competition is vital to the growth of the business. Consequently a strategy for using SPC as a tool to achieve this aim can ensure that the SPC project is controlled for the benefit of the company and does not become an ideological panacea.

▓ 14.2.3 Corporate goals

Any strategy for change will take into account the following factors:
- the long-term goals of the company
- the competition and their strategy
- the ownership of any change by those who are involved in change
- the financial benefits of change.

These factors affect the ability of the company to achieve desirable change and can often lead the company into undesired changes. This is compounded when there is no obvious start point for the changes. Introducing statistical methods has no obvious start point since the financial benefits are all 'up-stream'. There are no simple cost analysis benefits that can be calculated before starting to introduce SPC. This is what has prevented many industries starting on this process.

However management is about taking risks for which there are known fallback conditions. That process improvement is long overdue in the software industry there can be little doubt. The fallback position is that after introducing SPC and then reverting back to old practices, the minimum that can have happened is that the processes are modelled, and some data is available that describes the shortcomings of the process.

Cost justification then is difficult until measurements are started. The easiest measurements are those that are being made all the time, namely costs. If the accountants can be persuaded to understand that many of the production costs are avoidable, then they are more likely to listen to the argument for starting to measure them. This means redefining the project activities in terms of their contribution to quality rather than in terms of the costs of each activity. Fig. 14.3 shows a V cycle with related quality costs for each of the activities. This realisation that many of the activities are contributing to costs rather than profits means a change in emphasis in the organisation away from producing code to producing solutions that customers want and have specified. This is why confidence and completeness play such a large part in this book. They are measures of how well the customer is being satisfied throughout the lifecycle. There are other measures that must be taken into account as well. The cost contributors (rather than profit generators) are opportunities for cost reduction. Most, such as testing, cannot be removed but making them as effective and efficient as possible can only be beneficial.

▓ 14.2.4 Choosing the right place

This immediately provides some starting points for applying statistical control activities. Once a model of the process has been generated and the cost contributors identified, then these are targeted as the areas for statistical control methods.

Examples are: rework at every stage of the process, test selection, testing, test specification, design and detail design, walkthroughs and inspections. In fact the only parts of a project that are revenue generating are the activities associated with:

- establishing customer requirements
- designing a solution
- coding a solution
- providing the documentation to allow the customer to use the system.

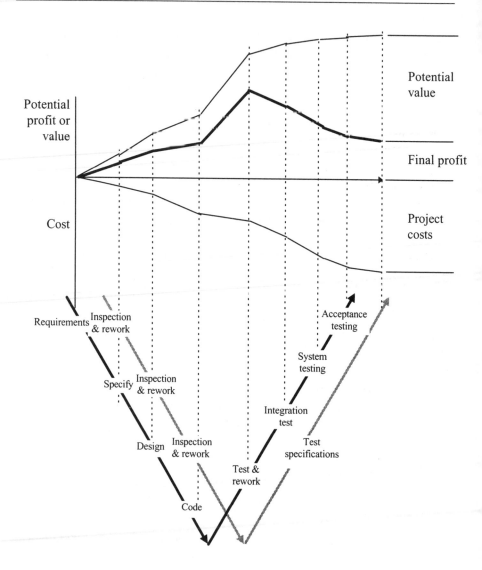

Fig. 14.3 The V cycle in profit and loss terms.

■ 14.2.5 Which project?

It is not practical to implement SPC across a whole organisation in one step. The aim, as with all changes to working practices, is to start with a small trial and demonstrate the significant benefits the techniques. Once this has been achieved new applications can be started. The methods are then slowly moved out to the rest of the projects, each project starting with a small application at first and building its own success.

The size of the project is not significant, just the size of the statistical measurement task that is placed on the team. By using one or two process variables, plus time and management variables, the initial success benefits can be identified. Using confidence as a first metric can be daunting since it is based on experience of interpreting and recording the activities at customer meetings and consequently has significant variance built into the recording process initially.

An ideal project is about 3–6 months duration with three to four development staff. This gives a reasonable time scale for measuring the success and for familiarisation with the process of charting. Commitment to the tasks are essential. This commitment must pervade the whole of the development team and not just those expected to record the data.

▓ 14.2.6 Which people?

Success from this type of project comes from enthusiasm and a willingness to use new techniques. The choice of staff to use the statistical techniques is dependent on the availability of enthusiastic people who can accept the challenge of change. Managers who are committed to using the data generated both for managing the project and for overseeing the use of the charts by the developers for process control are also required. There are no rules for selecting people for this type of project, except for the rule that states that the enthusiasm of a team starts from the top. It is much more difficult to build this enthusiasm from the bottom which means that all management levels must be aware of the project and offer their support to it.

▓ 14.3 Management Statistics

▓ 14.3.1 Success measurement

We have stated several times that statistical methods are expected to bring benefits, and it is measurement of these benefits that can ensure that the project succeeds. Like any other strategic change to a company there are additional costs at the start of the project involving training staff in their understanding of statistical control to remove the fear of complex mathematics (there is nothing complicated about the few formulae in the book). Other costs include obtaining the right tools and setting up the procedures for collection and use of the data.

The software industry, like most others, has metrics about the success of individual projects, hearsay about problems and sometimes documented customer surveys. This information provides the basis for success measurement. We have already seen management charts regarding the process metrics in the form of star charts. These can be used to show continual improvements after a few projects have been completed and this can be set up as one of the success targets. For the first project however the aim should be isolated to the area of influence of the charts being used. If process metrics are used to control lines of code per module, then the project should not be expected to come in earlier. If project time metrics are being used (such as lines of code per hour), then the project can be expected to improve in its consistency of delivery. This is due the removal of areas of difficulty that were identified earlier.

▨ 14.3.2 Quality costs

The cost of quality is made up of several elements as far as software development is concerned. The standard model involves three elements:

- cost of production
- cost of detection
- cost of rework.

It is the balance between the costs of detection and rework, and the cost of prevention, that is the target for statistical control. Each of these costs has an associated software specific activity, shown in Table 14.1. If these are measured then the balance between them can be achieved. The next step is to reduce each of them in order to maximise profit.

Production costs are those elements down the left-hand side of the V model, plus the integration activity. If a RAD cycle is being used, then the cost of production includes the review with the customer to ensure that the product is on target, and this is seen as a prevention cost.

For other quality cycles a different cost structure will be used. The optimisation will be different from the type of curves that might be seen for the V or W cycles shown in Fig. 14.4. For the RAD case it is difficult to get away from a prevention type regime. Statistical measurement, however, will take away the opinion based measurements and provide facts. These

Table 14.1 The quality costs for detection and rework cycles and for prevention cycles.

Quality cost	Software elements
Production costs	Collection of requirements Specification Acceptance specification Design Code Integration Acceptance testing
Cost of failure	
Detection costs	Inspections Walkthroughs Reviews Test specification Testing
Rework costs	Specification rework Design rework Code rework Test specification changes Retest
Cost of prevention	
Prevention costs	Process control preparation Measurement and charting Reaction to out-of-control Modelling and weighting for inspection and testing Reviews and walkthroughs Inspection and acceptance testing

facts are gathered to provide insight into the relationships between the developer and the customer, and the conformance of the product to the changing requirements. It will also provide facts about how many changes the customer is asking for as the project progresses, providing the managers with a valuable input into the risk assessment process for the project.

This model does not take into account the hidden costs of failure once the product is in the customer's hands. These costs are potentially considerably higher than the internal prevention or detection costs. However up to 1993 few companies had obtained redress for failed software projects. There are still a number of projects that fail each year whose customers do not recognise their right to redress. There are even more suppliers who, without facts about the rate of change requirements, could not get redress against customers who stop a project before the completion date because of a failure to meet those requirements. Using preventative

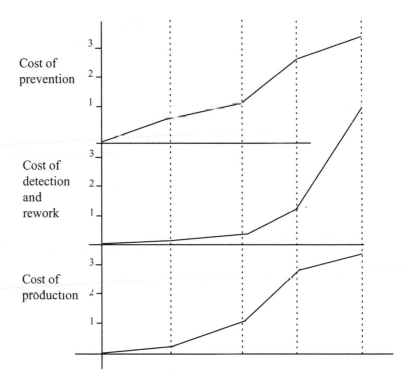

Fig. 14.4 The quality costs for the V or W models.

methods the facts are known and these hidden and often publicly announced quality costs can be prevented.

■ 14.3.3 Benefits analysis

From the quality cost information it is easy to show that preventative methods using statistical control provides cost benefits. However this analysis requires facts about the current cost of quality within an organisation. Few companies actually measure the cost of rework in these terms.

This means that the first project run with statistical methods has to rely on simple benefit analysis through the increased productivity figures and the consistency of delivery. However, on the first project, neither of these benefits are likely to be gained. Training in the new disciplines, the cost of changing procedures and the initial resistance to change is likely to offset any increased productivity.

The benefits from this project should all relate to the reduced defectiveness and the evidence of this, which provides a benchmark for the future projects using the same techniques.

Once the methods are established and quality costs are regularly gathered then the benefits become obvious. Any shift in the mean capability of the company will register either a statistical improvement or as a search into the causes of its reduction. A change in capability over a short period must be greater than 3 standard deviations from the current mean to be detected, so only significant changes will be noted. Small trends may be noted over longer time periods and the target of the process improvement activity will be to achieve this.

One of the secondary benefits from this type of control is that all decisions are based on figures collected and there is usually less discussion about what has happened during the project. While one might suppose this leads to an altogether calmer and more satisfying work environment, that is left for the reader to establish within his or her workplace. The main effect can be greater enthusiasm for the work because of the trust that can be placed in the decisions being made.

▨ 14.4 Project Statistics

Throughout this book we have discussed collecting data from the project. Apart from the benefits previously mentioned there are other reasons for collecting data.

▨ 14.4.1 What can the team get from them?

Most project teams want to produce the most effective results that they can, and often management provide targets for achieving better results to encourage this enthusiasm. However these can never be achieved without the proper tools for improvement. The reason behind many metrication projects is to provide the measurements that improvement projects require to understand the process better. This means that the project team get to use techniques that help them to do the job better. There are also measures that allow them to monitor their own improvement progress such as defectiveness, the lines of code per module, complexity, and the quality costs.

No one expects any of these figures to be minima initially and neither can anyone expect the variance to be small. However with these figures available to the specifiers, developers and coders, the opportunity for measured improvement in the skills of staff is made available.

Secondly the major headache for project managers and developers is the changing specification. The RAD methodology has assisted with this but lacks the measures to keep the situation under control. Statistical confidence, completeness, and defectiveness measures allow the project team to keep their own costs under control. They also have a graph of how the requirements are changing enabling all within the team to understand the implications for the future of the project.

Capability measurement can also be used by teams to understand improvement in terms of benefits to the organisation. Capability measurement as a mean and range figure for first code defectiveness, post-test defectiveness and delivery defectiveness provides a healthy competitive goal for project teams. The second and third measures should be a few defects per million lines of code, but research through the 1980s showed they were was nearer a few defects per 1000 lines of code.

■ 14.4.2 How can the customer benefit?

These same capability figures can also be supplied to the customer. One company (a US statistical software developer) has stated that they consistently achieve a mean of about 30 defects per 100,000 lines of code. They are aiming at 30 defects per million lines. Here a defect is a point at which the code had to be changed to make the software work. This may be the result of one or many errors detected at testing.

With this capability at the first module test point, the company is well placed to compete with customers who have a higher level of defect. However this does require a consistent method of measuring how much testing has been completed and there are several standards being produced in the UK, Germany, USA and Australia to resolve this issue. The British Computer Society standard for module testing has coverage measures for many of the test methods and this is expected to expand as people produce new test methods. However these coverage metrics can be used to provide a standard method of stating the capability of a project team to achieve particular levels of defectiveness at delivery.

The customer can also benefit from knowing the capability of a company to estimate and deliver on time and at cost to this same defectiveness level.

Using confidence and completeness capability at delivery as well as defectiveness and time ratio, actual/estimate, the potential customer can have confidence that the supplier is able to deliver software projects consistently. Of the companies that have been analysed the time ratio would result in many more companies questioning the estimates and the capability of their suppliers.

■ 14.5 Right-first-time Software

Much has been said about 'right first time' as a goal for any process that is based on TQM principles, and this must always be the aim of software developers. However the only way of reducing the error rates to near zero is to measure the current rates and find their causes.

One company has been reporting zero defects produced by right-first-time principles but this has not been proven by data regarding test coverage and defect levels. There is always a suspicion that the product has only been marginally tested, and that customers will find the errors later. Other companies hide behind a facade of an ever improving product and consequently errors are hidden by enhancements and changes.

The second major problem with right first time is that formal specifications are usually stated in non-software terms and so the implementation is left to be interpreted by the designer and the developer. If a package has thousands of users there will always be a probability of a proportion of them reporting faults that are in fact different interpretations of the specified functionality of the product.

For all but the simplest and most tightly specified products produced using V, W or other sequential development processes, right first time will be an unrealisable dream. Hence the need for 'simultaneous engineered' development cycles, or RAD. In this method the products achieve the right solution after several stages of agreement between the developer and the customer of what the specification should be in software solution terms.

■ 14.6 Rolling out to Other Teams and Applications

Once the first project has been completed and the success has been measured then the methods can be rolled out to other projects. Allowing the project team to select a few metrics in each case provides the opportunity for the individuals to make their own contribution to the success of the applications.

To roll the application of statistical charting out to other areas a programme of training is required. This is often best completed in-house once the facilitator and the first team have a real understanding of the meaning and interpretation of the different types of charts.

After a few charting activities have been successful the results can be used to determine the state of control of the company and a process improvement programme can be initiated. This involves deciding which variables and attributes are most effective at controlling the projects and the statistical levels appropriate for the charts. This is likely to be a rolling programme since the different variables become more significant as statistical control of each variable is achieved. It is probable that new causes will be continually identified as new projects and customers are included.

▓ The product support team

For a company or the support group with only one product to update and correct, the rolling out task is continually identifying new variables that contribute to the defectiveness of the product and the effectiveness of support activities. A particular task is measuring and improving the effectiveness of the correction cycle. It is well understood that this cycle provides opportunity both for reducing errors and for introducing new errors and so the ratio of these provides a metric for effectiveness. The rolling out activity usually involves changing the process to discover more effective methods of completing the error removal task and for providing effective error measures using small samples of the whole test suite.

▓ Project management control

Once statistical control is achieved in the development process, project management control systems can be initiated. Because the time scales are in statistical control (due to the control of the process metrics), the project management task is more easily controlled since most of the special causes have already been removed. The use of the charts for project time and costs, and the ratios of actual values to the original estimates, provide mechanisms for reducing the risk of projects.

Once the existing process is well understood, then repeatability is achievable and the same process can be modified to meet the needs of new applications.

The growth of a company into new languages, new types of product and new project formats becomes a much less daunting and risky task because of the new understanding of the process. The company will also have achieved one of the higher levels on the SEI CMM scale. The company is approaching a true TQM capability and is ready for world class competition.

▓ Other applications

Why stop at the software development and project management areas? Statistical control is applicable to all levels and activities of a company. Charts can be drawn for financial control, sales activities, or for the performance of each individual member of a company group. How many companies have been closed on the basis of a downward trend due only to the change in capability of the company rather than a change in its market? These are lost opportunities for jobs and for industry all due to a lack of understanding of variance and its contribution to the quality of an organisation. Table 14.2 shows a few examples of charts in other activities for a company. These examples are drawn from business experience and the book by Mal Owen (71) on the subject of SPC and business improvement.

▓ 14.7 Conclusions

This book has concentrated on variance, with the aim of controlling and reducing it in order to reduce the probability of errors and to control the size, complexity and difficulty of modules.

The applications in software development are designed to help achieve process repeatability by better understanding the process and what controls it. For different companies the metrics, the controls and the capability can be expected to be different. At this stage of the lifecycle of the software development industry clear benchmarks cannot be identified. Once a number of companies have achieved higher levels on the major profiling systems, then the normal capabilities of different types of software developers will become apparent.

As with all quality improvement programmes, there is no end to this process. As improvements in development methods are developed and as

Table 14.2 Business examples of the use of SPC.

Area	Application	Charts	Comment
Accounts	Petty cash	X, Moving R chart	Petty cash has normal flowa and exceptions which become immediately apparent from the charts
	Invoices and account books	X, Moving R chart P chart	Errors on invoices can be tracked and causes investigated. Invoice errors can be tracked as the percentage of errors per invoice
	Profit & loss	X, Moving R chart	This may need seasonal adjustment, or can be run as a chart for each month
Sales	Enquiries	X, Moving R chart	Monthly inquiries – may need seasonal adjustment
	Sales from enquiries	X, Moving R chart Multi-variate charts	How many inquiries per sale
	Customer response questionnaires	Multi-variate charts	Used to find customer hot and cold spots
	Fault reports	Multi-variate charts	Did sales sell what was wanted? Was the product delivered OK?
	Customer losses/gains	X, Moving R chart	The ability to gain customers is the basis of growth, the index ratio of lost/gained customers is plotted
Admin	Document errors	c chart	Errors per page after inspection and on delivery
	Document style	X, Moving R chart	Style metrics including sentence length, ratios such as short/long words, other style ratios
	Filing errors	X, Moving R chart	Equally multi-variate charts can be used to log types of errors in order to find causes more quickly
	Telephone response time	X, Moving R chart	Number of rings (should be < 3). An upper control limit only is used
	Quality audit times & failures	X, Moving R chart	Durations and faults found can provide evidence of gross failure on capability of quality systems
Time and salaries	Time recording	X, Moving R chart	With flexitime and core time schemes a method of recording differences between hours worked and time logged to task is used to find major discrepancies
Quality systems	Changes	X, Moving R chart Multi-variate charts	Changes at one level depict a healthy quality system, but too many causes of one type are a problem
	Improvement	P charts	The percentage of the system improved as a continuing chart
	Quality costs	Multi-variate charts	Quality costs attributed to different categories provides control of the cost capability
Utilities	Gas, water and electricity	X, Moving R chart	Consumption must be seasonally adjusted or charted for each season
	Telephone costs	X, Moving R chart	Find exceptions quickly and the causes
Training	Scores	X, Moving R chart $\overline{X}$, R chart	Scores for particular courses are charted depending on the number of people on the course. Individuals are charted on X, Moving R charts
	Skill levels	$\overline{X}$, R chart	The skill levels are charted to provide a skill profile

new technologies emerge so the benchmarks will change both in level and composition. This means that the variables and attributes that are statistically charted must also change with them. The result will be an industry where the difference between software will be reduced, the selection being on the product performance and fitness for purpose and not on the quality of the product. We first have an education problem – few purchasers of software insist on the same quality metrics that they currently insist on for other purchases. However this is changing slowly, particularly since companies are now aiming to achieve ISO 9000 registration.

There are still a few companies insisting on 100% coverage during final system testing. Since many of these tests rely on test software and compilers, the probability that this type of testing will achieve zero defects is small. In fact many of these tests require manual observation of defects and this results in the problem of the effectiveness of manual inspections.

For all the documented evidence of document and product inspections the best manual inspection effectiveness that can be achieved is only about 80%. 100% coverage or not, the effectiveness ratios are going to prevent zero defects being achieved. Using statistical selection, multiple coverage and defect estimating, the problems can be overcome. These techniques provide greater coverage and effectiveness than the 100% inspection activities and consequently improve the product and reduce the time taken to test the product.

Statistical control is not about populations – we do not know what a population of errors, or even of modules, will look like before we start a development process. The control of the process is the task in hand – a process that is repeated every time a requirement is considered and a developer starts down the long road to producing the final code. Several of these processes have been identified, but they are as individual as each of the companies producing the code and consequently cannot be directly compared.

The tools for developing your own particular style, your own metrics with particular levels and limits, have been explained in this book. Whether you agree with all the ideas or find them alien to your process, the central theme of controlling and minimising variance must be recognised as the only route to repeatable and controllable processes.

Start charting simple metrics and discover for yourself what these powerful techniques, provided over 50 years ago and long before the software industry was born, can do for you. If software metrics are too difficult initially, start on something simpler. There are numbers all around and they can nearly all be charted to provide some benefit.

▓ 14.8 summary

- Using statistical methods is like any other major change within an organisation. It requires change management.
- Statistical methods provide the tools for understanding the processes better and for improving the efficiency of processes.
- A model of the process, coupled with an understanding of which are the cost generators and which are the profit generators, provides a picture of which of the processes can best be targeted for statistical improvement.
- Using the right project and the right people at a time when the company is ready and management are committed is important to the success of statistical methods.
- No amount of training can replace experience. However no amount of experience without basic training can provide benefits.
- Start small – a project that generates a success can easily be rolled out to the rest of the company. A project that starts big and fails kills the methods dead for a long time to come.
- There is little to do with formal population statistics in the use of statistical control theory. Statisticians are not necessarily the best qualified staff to apply these techniques.
- Shewhart and Deming started in 1930 and it has taken manufacturing 50 years to get to grips with the methods. Don't be put off by the first few failures and the limited successes. As the process is better understood so the benefits will start to appear and the rewards accrue.
- Charts can be applied to almost any sets of figures. Start by looking at a few other areas to convince yourself and others that reducing process variation will be of real benefit to your organisation.

Appendices

Appendix A
Nomenclature

Symbol	Definition
USL	Upper Specification Limit
LSL	Lower Specification Limit
X	Observed value of some item, which may be either a variable or an attribute. Specific values of X may be designated X1, X2, X3, etc.
f	Frequency. Generally a number of observed values
$\overline{X}$	Arithmetic mean of a set of numbers
Σ	Sum of
n	Number of items or observed values in a sample or subgroup
$\overline{n}$	Mean sample size
σ (Sigma)	Standard deviation of the population, i.e. the larger group from which the sample came
σ	An estimated value for the standard deviation of the population based on the sample values
SE	An alternative for σ, an estimated value for the standard deviation of the population based on the sample values
R	The range of a set of numbers (highest value minus the lowest value)
$\overline{R}$	The mean range
$\overline{\overline{X}}$ (X double bar)	The mean of a series of $\overline{X}$ values
UCL	Upper Control Limit
LCL	Lower Control Limit

A_2	Constant, dependant on sample size, used in determining the lower control limits on a $\overline{X}$ chart
D_3	Constant, dependant on sample size, used in determining the lower control limit on a R chart
D_4	Constant, dependant on sample size, used in determining the upper control limit on a R chart
d_2	Constant, dependant on sample size, used in calculating σ or SE from $\overline{R}$. Used particularly for calculating control limits on a X chart
p	Proportion of non-conforming units in sample
$\overline{p}$	Mean proportion of non-conforming units in a series of samples
np	Number of non-conforming units in a sample of constant size n
$\overline{np}$	Mean number of non-conforming units in a sample of constant size n
u	Proportion of non-conformities in a sample
$\overline{u}$	Mean proportion of non-conformities in a sample
c	Number of non-conformities in a sample of constant size n
$\overline{c}$	Mean of number of non-conformities in a sample of constant size n
C_p	A capability index. A measure of the spread of the process in terms of the specification
C_{pk}	A capability index. A measure of both the spread of the process and its position in relation to a specified target
FRC	First run capability
DHU	Defects per hundred units
C_{is}	Confidence Index derived from single readings
C_{ig}	Confidence index derived from readings in groups of size n

Appendix B

Tables of Constants and Formulae

▨ Tables of Constants

	Xbar and R charts				X and s charts			
	Chart for Means (Xbar)	Chart for Ranges (R)			Chart for Means (Xbar)	Chart for Standard Deviation (s)		
Sample Size	Factors for Control Limits	Divisors for Estimate of Standard Deviation	Factors for Control Limits		Factors for Control Limits	Divisors for Estimate of Standard deviation	Factors for Control Limits	
n	A2	d2	D3	D4	A3	c4	B3	B4
2	1.880	1.128	-	3.267	2.659	0.7979	-	3.267
3	1.023	1.693	-	2.574	1.954	0.8862	-	2.568
4	0.729	2.059	-	2.282	1.628	0.9213	-	2.266
5	0.577	2.326	-	2.114	1.427	0.9400	-	2.089
6	0.483	2.534	-	2.004	1.287	0.9515	0.030	1.970
7	0.419	2.704	0.076	1.924	1.182	0.9594	0.118	1.882
8	0.373	2.847	0.136	1.864	1.099	0.9650	0.185	1.815
9	0.337	2.970	0.184	1.816	1.032	0.9693	0.239	1.761
10	0.308	3.078	0.223	1.777	0.975	0.9727	0.284	1.716
11	0.285	3.173	0.256	1.744	0.927	0.9754	0.321	1.679
12	0.266	3.258	0.283	1.717	0.886	0.9776	0.354	1.646
13	0.249	3.336	0.307	1.693	0.850	0.9794	0.382	1.618
14	0.235	3.407	0.328	1.672	0.817	0.9810	0.406	1.594
15	0.223	3.472	0.347	1.653	0.789	0.9823	0.428	1.572
16	0.212	3.532	0.363	1.637	0.763	0.9835	0.448	1.552
17	0.203	3.588	0.378	1.622	0.739	0.9845	0.466	1.534
18	0.194	3.640	0.391	1.608	0.718	0.9854	0.482	1.518
19	0.187	3.689	0.403	1.597	0.698	0.9862	0.497	1.503
20	0.180	3.735	0.415	1.585	0.680	0.9869	0.510	1.490
21	0.173	3.778	0.425	1.575	0.663	0.9876	0.523	1.477
22	0.167	3.819	0.434	1.566	0.647	0.9882	0.534	1.466
23	0.162	3.858	0.443	1.557	0.633	0.9887	0.545	1.455
24	0.157	3.895	0.451	1.548	0.619	0.9892	0.555	1.445
25	0.153	3.931	0.459	1.541	0.606	0.9896	0.565	1.435

* Reprinted with permission from STP ISD – Manual on the Presentation of Data and Control Chart Analysis. Copyright American Society for Texting and Materials.

■ Formulae for variable charts

X bar and R charts

$$UCL_{\bar{X}} = \bar{\bar{X}} + A_2\bar{R}$$
$$LCL_{\bar{X}} - \bar{\bar{X}} - A_2\bar{R}$$
$$UCL_R = D_4\bar{R}$$
$$UCL_R = D_3\bar{R}$$
$$\sigma = \frac{\bar{R}}{d_2}$$

X and s charts

$$UCL_{\bar{X}} = \bar{\bar{X}} + A_3\bar{s}$$
$$LCL_{\bar{X}} = \bar{\bar{X}} - A_3\bar{s}$$
$$UCL_s = B_4\bar{s}$$
$$UCL_s = B_3 s$$
$$\sigma = \frac{\bar{s}}{c_4}$$

■ Formulae for Attribute charts

	TYPE OF CHART	CONTROL LIMITS
p	Used where there is a *proportion* of items which are unacceptable, or non-conforming, and the sample size is *varying*	$UCL_p = \bar{p} + 3\sqrt{\dfrac{\bar{p}(1-\bar{p})}{n}}$ $LCL_p = \bar{p} - 3\sqrt{\dfrac{\bar{p}(1-\bar{p})}{n}}$
np	Used when analysing the *number* of items which are unacceptable, or non-conforming, and the sample size is *constant*	$UCL_{np} = \overline{np} + 3\sqrt{\overline{np}\left(1 - \dfrac{\overline{np}}{n}\right)}$ $LCL_{np} = \overline{np} - 3\sqrt{\overline{np}\left(1 - \dfrac{\overline{np}}{n}\right)}$
u	Used where there is a *proportion* of errors or non-conformities, and the sample size is *varying*	$UCL_u = \bar{u} + 3\sqrt{\dfrac{\bar{u}}{n}}$ $LCL_u = \bar{u} - 3\sqrt{\dfrac{\bar{u}}{n}}$
c	Used when analysing the *number* of errors, or non-conformities, and the sample size is *constant (or not known)*	$UCL_c = \bar{c} + 3\sqrt{\bar{c}}$ $LCL_c = \bar{c} - 3\sqrt{\bar{c}}$

	Nonconforming units	Nonconformities
Proportion	**p**	**u**
Number	**np**	**c**

Appendix C

Proof of formula for A$_2$

For the X section of the $(\overline{X}, R)$ chart, the upper limit $\text{UCL}_{\overline{X}}$ is given by

$$\text{UCL}_{\overline{X}} = X + 3 \text{ standard deviations}$$

For the distribution of sample means, the standard deviations i given by $\dfrac{\sigma}{\sqrt{n}}$

where n is the sample size.

In addition, we know that σ can be obtained from $\dfrac{\overline{R}}{d_2}$. Hence

$$\text{UCL}_{\overline{X}} = \overline{\overline{X}} + \frac{3}{\sqrt{n}} \frac{\overline{R}}{d_2}$$

$\dfrac{3}{\sqrt{n}\, d}$ is known as A_2, giving

$$\text{UCL}_{\overline{X}} = \overline{\overline{X}} + A_2 \overline{R}$$

With n=5, for example

$$A_2 = \frac{3}{\sqrt{5}} \frac{1}{2.326} = 0.577$$

which corresponds to the values in the table

Appendix D

Further Reading

Quality and total quality

Aune, A., *Teams and Total Quality*, Bedford, UK: IFS, 1995

Atkinson, Philip E., *Creating Culture Change, the Key to Successful Total Quality Management*, Bedford, UK: IFS, 1990

Bicking, C.A., The Application of Quality Control to Administrative Problems, *Industrial Quality Control*, 1950

Burr, A., *Quality Management*, London: Cambridge Market Intelligence, 1995

Gitlow, H. and, Gitlow S., *The Deming Guide to Quality and Competitive Position*, Englewood Cliffs, N: Prentice-Hall, 1987

Joiner, B.L., *The Team Handbook*, Madison WI: Joiner Associates

Kilian, C.S., *The World of W. Edwards Deming*, Washington, D.C.:, Cee Press Books, 1988

Mann, N.R., *The Keys to Excellence*, Los Angeles, CA: Prestwick Books, 1985

Morton, A.Q., *Proper Words in Proper Places*, Glasgow, UK: Department of Computing Science, University of Glasgow, 1991

Neave, H., *The Deming Dimension*, Knoxville, TN: SPC Press, 1990

Nolan, T.W., and Provost, L.P, Understanding Variation. *Quality Progress*, May 1990

Ott, E.R., *Process Quality Control: Troubleshooting and Interpretation of Data*, New York: McGraw-Hill, 1975

Price, F., *Right Every Time: Using the Deming Kpproach*, Aldershot, UK: Gower Press 1990

Rosander, A.C., *Applications of Quality Control in the Service Industries*, New York: Marcel Dekker, 1985

Rummler, G., and Brache, A., *Improving Performance: How to Manage the White Space on the Organisation Chart*, San Francisco: Jossey-Bass, 1991

Scherkenbach, W.W., *Deming's Road to Continual Improvement*, Knoxville, TN: SPC Press, 1991

Scherkenbach, W.W., *The Deming Route to Quality and Productivity, Road Maps and Road Blocks*, Washington, DC: Cee Press Books, 1986 and 1988

Schonberger, R.J., *Building a Chain of Customers*, London: Hutchinson, 1990

Tribus, M., The Germ Theory of Management, Paper presented at the British Deming Association National Forum, UK, 1989

Using Quality Tools and Techniques Successfully, Frodsham, Cheshire, UK: TQM International, 1995

Walton, M., *The Deming Management Method,* London: Mercury Business Books, 1989

■ Statistical methods

Amsden, R. T., Butler, H. E. and Amsden, D. M., *SPC for Simplified Services: Practical Tools for Continuous Quality Improvement,* London: Chapman & Hall 1991

Bender, Barry and Stair Jr., Ralph M., *Quantitative Analysis for Management,* Massachusetts, Ally and Bacon, 4th edition 1991

Campbell, S., *Flaws and Fallacies in Statistical Thinking,* Englewood Cliffs, NJ: Prentice Hall 1974

Owen, M. H., *SPC for Business Improvement,* Bedford, UK: IFS, 1993

Wheeler, D. J. and Chambers, D. S., *Understanding Statistical Process Control,* New York: Addison Wesley, 1990

Wheeler, D. J., *Charts Done Right,* Knoxville, TN: Don Wheeler, 1989

Wheeler, D.J., *Shewhart's Charts: Myths, Facts and Competitors',* ASQC Annual Congress, 1991

■ Software development

Beizer, Boris, *Software Testing Techniques,* New York: Van Nostrand, Reinhold, 2nd edition 1990

Gilb, T. and Graham, D. R., *Software Inspections,* London: Addison Wesley, 1993

Gillies, Alan C., *Software Quality, Theory and Management,* London: Chapman & Hall, 1992

Hutchinson, M.L., *The Most Important Tests (MITs) Method* in Proceedings for EuroSTAR'94 Conference, Brussels, October 1994, London: EuroSTAR

McCabe, Thomas J., and Schulmeyer, G. Gordon, The Pareto Principle Applied to Quality Assurance, in *Handbook of Quality Assurance,* 1992

McCabe, Thomas, *Structured System Testing,* USA: McCabe & Associates, 1985

Eds. Schulmeyer, G. Gordon and McManus, James I., *Handbook of Software Quality Assurance,* New York: Van Nostrand Reinhold, 1992

Strauss, S.H., Ebenan, R.G., *Software Inspection Process,* New York: McGraw-Hill

Schulmeyer, G. Gordon, *Zero Defect Software,* New York: McGraw-Hill, 1990

Whitty, .*Managing the Testing Process: the COSMOS Approach,* London: BCS Specialist Interest Group in Software Testing, July 1993

■ Statistical methods in software development

Ann Marie Neufelder, *Methods of improving System Software Testing Efficiency,* Hebron, USA: NK Consultants, 1993

Burr, A., *A Statistical Conformance Index,* in Proceedings EuroSTAR 93, Software Testing Conference, Heathrow, London 1993

Duran, J. W. and Ntafos, S. C., *An Evaluation of Random Testing*, IEEE Transactions on Software Engineering, SE-10, 4, 1984

Frazer, M.I., *Retail Systems Department: Measuring Software Development for Continuous Improvement using SPC*, Training report, Birmingham: GEC Avery, 1995

Frankl, P. G. and Weynker, E. J., *Assessing Fault Detecting Ability of Testing Methods*, ACM Software Engineering Notes, 16, 5, 1991

Hamlet, R., *Theoretical Comparison of Testing Methods*, Proceedings 3rd IEEE Symposium on Software Testing, Analysis and Verification (TAV-3), KeyWest, USA, 1989

Marshall, R., *Statistical Process Control in SWF/IT*, in Statistical Methods Specialist Interest Sub-Group Newsletter, issue 1, Haverhill, UK: BCS SIGMA, 1994

Mills, H. and Poore, J.H., Bringing Software under Statistical Quality Control in *Quality Progress*, Milwaukee, WI: ASQC, pp. 52—55, November 1988

Mills, H., Cleanroom Engineering: Engineering Software under Statistical Control, *American Programmer*, 4, 5, May 1991 pp. 31–37

Runeson, P., *Statistical Usage Testing for Software Reliability, Certification, and Control*, in Proceedings EuroSTAR 93, Software Testing Conference: Heathrow, London 1993

Thevenod-Fosse, P. and Waeselynck, H., *An investigation of Statistical Software Testing*, in Proceedings of EuroSTAR 1994 Brussels, London: EuroSTAR, 1994

█ General magazines

Software Quality Management – British Computer Society Quality Group News Magazine

UK: Tesseract Publishing, Tilford Reeds House, Farnham, Surrey GU10 2DJ, UK

Americas: 3617 Belcher, Tampa, Fl 33629, USA

Australia: Information Systems Department,School of Computing Science, PO Box 123, Broadway, NSW 2007, Australia

SIGMA News – British Computer Society Statistical Methods Sub-group of the Specialist Interest Group in Software Testing

13 Helions Road, Steeple Bumpstead, Haverhill, Suffolk CB9 7DU,UK

Software Testing, Verification and Reliability

Centre for Systems and Software Engineering, South Bank University, London, UK

Quality Progress

American Society of Quality Control, PO Box 3005, MilwaukeeWI 53201-9402, USA

Quality World
Institute of Quality Assurance, 10 Grosvenor Gardens, London SW1W 0DQ, UK

European Foundation for Quality Management News
EFQM, Avenue des Pleiades 19, B-1200 Brussels, Belgium

The British Deming Association
The Old George Brewery, Rollestone Street, Salisbury, Wilts SP1 1BB,UK

TQM News
IFS Ltd, Wolseley Business Park, Kempston, Bedford, MK42 7PW, UK

■ SPC Charting Materials for Software and Service Industries

Manual chart masters, Software for Microsoft Excel to generate charts, and Management Software plus training and lectures available from:

Mal Owen	Adrian Burr
Training for Excellence	tMSc
Longwalls	13 Helions Road
1 The Manor Close	Steeple Bumpstead
Abbotts Ford	Haverhill
Bristol	Suffolk
BS8 3RW	CB9 7DU
UK	UK

References

1   Neil, M. D., *Statistical Modelling of Software Metrics*, London: South Bank University PhD Thesis, 1992

2   Davey, S., Huxford, D., et al., *Metrics Collection in Code and Test as part of Continuous Quality Improvement*, London: Proceedings of 1st EuroSTAR Conference, October 1993

3   *SystemsCRAFT Development Method, A Quality Guide*, Italy: Ing C. Olivetti & C. SpA., Version 1, June 1995

4   Quentin, G., *Testing Handbook*, Shoeburyness, UK: QCC Training, 1993

5   Myers, G. J.,   *Software Reliability: Principles and Practice*, New York: Wiley, 1976

6   Cho, C. K, *An Introduction to Software Quality Control*, New York: Wiley, 1980
A Summary of the method appears in: Schulmeyer, G. G. and McManus J. I., *Handbook of Software Quality Assurance*, New York: Van Nostrand Reinhold, 1992. Other references to SIAD Methods and their application appear in: Eagles, S..L., *SIAD Tree Experiments*, Control Data Corporation, November 1993 and in: Miller, C.R., SIAD Tree Report, Control Data Corporation, November 1993

7   Carter, E.B., Hancock, A.E., Morin, J.-M., and Robins, M.J., *Introducing RISKMAN*, Oxford: NCC Blackwell, 1994

8   Welzel, D., Hausen, H.-L., *Metric based Software Evaluation Method*, in Proceedings of EuroSTAR 93, London: EuroSTAR, 1993

9   Deming, W. E., *Out of the Crisis*, Cambridge MA: Cambridge University Press, 1986, 1988

10 Juran, J.M., *Quality Control Handbook*, 3rd Edition, New York: McGraw-Hill, 1979

11 Crosby, Philip B., *Quality is Free*, New York: McGraw-Hill, 1979

12 Kennedy, C., *Guide to the Management Gurus*, London: Random House, 1993

13 Morley, D.J., *Handbook of MIS Application Testing*

14 Yacoob, S., *Software Testing a Process View*, in Proceedings of EuroSTAR 94, Brussels 1994, London: EuroSTAR, 1994

15 Hausen, H.-L., Welzel, D., *Guides to Software Evaluation*, Germany: Gesellschaft fur Mathematik und Datenverarbeitung mbH, 1993

16 Crawford, J. and Reno, M., *Risk based Software Testing*, in Proceedings of 10th International Conference & exposition on Testing Computer Software, Washington, DC: 1993

17 Mellor, P., *Software Reliability Data Collection: Problems and Standards*, London: City University, 1985

18 McClave, J.T., and Benson, P.G., *Statistics for business and Economics*, 5th Edition,

San Francisco: Dellen Publishing, 1991

19 Wall, W. *Stansted Project Fieldwalking A Report on Techniques*, Chelmsford, UK: Essex County Council, Planning Department, Archeology Section, 1987

20 Fenton, Norman E., *Software Metrics, Theory, Tools and Validation*, IEEE Software Engineering Journal, Jan 1990
Fenton, Norman E., *Software Metrics A Rigorous Approach*, London: Chapman & Hall, 1991

21 Ince, D.C., *System Complexity, Information Technology Briefings*, Open University, 1988

22 McCabe, T.J., *A Complexity Measure*, IEEE Trans. Software Engineering, SE-2, pp. 308–320

23 Halstead, M.H., *Elements of Software Science*, New York: Elsevier, 1977

24 Graham, D. and , Herzlich, P., *Computer Aided Software Testing*, London, Cambridge Market Intelligence, 1995

25 Mair, P., *Computer Aided Software Engineering*, London: Cambridge Market Intelligence, 1995

26 *ISO 9000, Quality Management Systems Standard*, Geneva: International Standards Organisation, 1994

27 *A Guide to Software Quality Management Systems Construction and Certification using EN 29001*, London: TickIT Project Office, 1992

28 *ISO 9000-3, Guidelines for the Application of ISO 9001 to the Development Supply and Maintenance of Software*, Geneva: International Standards Organisation, 1992

29 Brown, Mark Graham, *Baldridge Award Winning Quality: How to interpret the Malcolm Baldridge Award criteria*, 4th Edition, Milwaukee, WI: ASQC, 1994

30 *Determining Business Excellence: A Questionnaire Approach*, Brussels: EFQM, 1994.
1996 Guide to Self Assessment, London: The British Quality Foundation, 1995.
Russell, J.P., *Quality Management Benchmark Assessment*, Milwaukee, WI: ASQC, 1995 (based on criteria from ISO 90004-1, ISO 9001, and Malcolm Baldrige Award)

31 *Capability Maturity Model for Software*, Technical report CMW/SEI-91-TR-24, Carnegie-Mellon University, 1991

32 Primatesta, F., *Software Maturity Assessment, Using the BOOTSTRAP Method on the Testing Process*, in Proceedings of EuroSTAR 94 Conference, Brussels, October 1994, London: EuroSTAR, 1994

33 Robinson, Richard, *The Lattice Methodology*, Proceedings of a Seminar at the London Quality Centre, 1994

34 Shewhart, W.A., *Economic Control of Quality of Manufactured Product*, New York: Van Nostrand, 1931

35 Tribus, Myron, *Prize winning Japanese firms, Quality Management Program for inspection*, AMA Forum, Management Review, Feb. 1984

36 Stamatis, D.H., *Failure Mode and Effects Analysis: FMEA form Theory to Execution*, Milwaukee, WI: ASQC, 1995

37 Harrington, *Business Process Improvement*, Milwaukee, WI: ASQC, 1991

38 *Investors in People*, London: UK Department of Trade & Industry, 1992

39 Zultner, R.E., *Software Quality Deployment: Applying QFD to Software*, in Transactions from the 2nd Symposium on QFD, Novi, MI: ASQC. Zultner, R.E., *Software TQM*, Princeton, NJ: Zultner & Company

40 Taguchi, Genichi, Elsayed, A. Elsayed and Hsiang, Thomas, *Quality Engineering in Production Systems*, New York: McGraw Hill, 1989

41 Shingo, Shingeo, *Zero Quality Control: Source Inspection and the Poka-yoke System*, Japan Management Association, 1985

42 Iami, M., *Kaizen: The Key to Japan's Competitive Success*, New York: Random House, 1986

43 Sayle, A.J., *Management Audits – The Assessment of Quality Management Systems*, Hampshire, UK: Allan J. Sayle, 1988

44 Dale, B. G. and Pluckett, J.J., *Quality Costing*, London: Chapman & Hall, 1991

45 Thevenod-Fosse, P. and Waeselynck, H., *STATEMATE applied to Statistical Software Testing*, in Proceedings of the 1993 International Symposium on Software Testing and Analysis (ISSTA 93), Toulouse, France, 1993

46 *Standard for Software Component Testing, Issue 3*, London: British Computer Society Specialist Group in Software Testing, 1995
   Glossary of terms used in Software Testing, London: British Computer Society Specialist Group in Software Testing, 1995

47 *SPICE Report*, London: City University, 1996

48 *Software Solution: Executive Software 5-up Chart, Managers guide*, Blackrock, Ireland: Motorola, 1993

49 Ishikawa, Kaoru, *Guide to Quality Control*, Tokyo: Asian Productivity Association, 1976

50 Gerald, C.F., *Applied Numerical Analysis*, Reading, MA: Addison-Wesley, 1970

51 Burr, A., *Efficiency of Inspection, A Study at Dowty Malta*, GST Report, 1986

52 *BS 6001, Sampling Methods Standard*, London: British Standards Institute, 1987

53 Fagan, M.E.*Design and Code Inspections to Reduce Errors in Program Development*, IBM Systems Journal, 15(3), pp.182–211

54 BS 5703, *Guide to Data Analysis and Quality Control using Cusum Techniques*, London: British Standards Institute, 1981

55 *AMI: A Quantitive Approach to Software Management*, London: South Bank University, for ESPRIT project 5494, 1992

56 Burr, A., *Cutting through the Paperwork – A review of Quality Management Support Software*, Haverhill, UK: tMSc, 2nd Edition 1995

57 Burr, A., *Quality Tools – A Review of Software for Quality Control*, Haverhill, UK: tMSc, 1995

58 *Software Development Methodology, PRINCE*, Norwich, UK: CCTA

59 Barrentine, L.B., *Concepts for R&R studies*, Milwaukee, WI: ASQC, 1991

60 Montgomery, D.C., *Design and Analysis of Experiments*, Milwaukee,WI: ASQC, 1991

61 Primavera, *Monte Carlo, Project Risk Analysis & Simulation Software*, Bala Cynwyd, PA: Primavera, 1993

62 Myers, G., *The Art of Software Testing*, New York: Wiley Interscience, 1979

63 Hetzel, W., *The Complete Guide to Software Testing*, OED Information Sciences, 1984

64 Heil, J.H., Practical Applications of Software Quality Assurance to Mission Critical Embedded Software, *Handbook for Software Quality Assurance*, ed. Schulmayer, G.G. and McManus, J..I, New York: Van Nostrand Reinhold, 1992, pp. 343–396

65 Hall A., *Seven Myths of Formal Methods*, IEEE Software, 11-19, 1990

66 Dreger, B.J., *Function Point Analysis*, Englewood Cliffs, NJ: Prentice-Hall Advanced Reference Series, Computer Science, 1987

67 Layden, J., Developing statistical systems using statistical methods, in *Issue 1, Newsletter of BCS Specialist Interest Sub-group of Testing Group (SIGIST) on Statistical Methods*, Haverhill, UK: BCS SIGMA, 1993

68 Mays, R.G., Jones, C.L., Holloway, G.J., Studinski, D.P., Experiences with Defect Prevention, *IBM Systems Journal* 29 (1), pp. 4-32

69 Mays, R.G., Defect Prevention and Total Quality Management, *Total Quality Management for Software*, ed. Schulmeyer G. and McManus, J. New York: Van Nostrand Reinhold, pp. 389-402

70 Gilb, T., Graham, D. I., *Software Inspection*, London: Addison-Wesley, 1993

71 Owen, M. H., *SPC and Continuous Improvement*, IFS, Bedford, UK: 1989

Index